Revd Dr Mark Griffiths is married to Rhian and they have three children, Nia, Owen and Elliot. He has developed outreach children's clubs, children's discipleship groups, after-school clubs, Sunday schools, holiday clubs, schools ministry and summer camps and passionately believes that successful children's ministry is a major key to church growth. He is author of *Fusion, Impact,* and *Detonate,* and *Don't Tell Cute Stories – Change Lives.* He is a Church of England minister.

ONE GENERATION FROM EXTINCTION

How the church connects with the unchurched child

Mark Griffiths

MONARCH
BOOKS
Oxford, UK & Grand Rapids, Michigan, USA

First published in the UK in 2009 by Monarch Books
(a publishing imprint of Lion Hudson plc),
Wilkinson House, Jordan Hill Road, Oxford OX2 8DR.
Tel: +44 (0)1865 302750 Fax: +44 (0)1865 302757
Email: monarch@lionhudson.com
www.lionhudson.com

ISBN: 978-1-85424-929-6

Distributed by:
Marston Book Services Ltd, PO Box 269, Abingdon, Oxon OX14 4YN

Unless otherwise stated, Scripture quotations are taken from the Holy Bible, New International Version, © 1973, 1978, 1984 by the International Bible Society. Used by permission of Hodder & Stoughton Ltd. All rights reserved.

This book has been printed on paper and board independently certified as having come from sustainable forests.

British Library Cataloguing Data
A catalogue record for this book is available from the British Library.

Printed and bound in England by MPG Books.

IF YOU WANTED TO CHANGE
TOMORROW, WHERE WOULD YOU
BEGIN?

For my wife Rhian and for my children Nia, Owen and Elliot

A WORD FROM THE AUTHOR

This book looks at child evangelism. Specifically, it considers the work of Robert Raikes and the formation of Sunday Schools in 1780, the development of those Sunday Schools through history, and the church-based projects that have been developed in the latter part of the twentieth century and early part of the twenty-first century.

It is a comparative study. It asks what comparisons can be made between the original Raikes model of child evangelism and the examples identified in the twentieth and twenty-first centuries. The word *evangelism* is deliberately used because these projects exist primarily to communicate a Christian message to children from homes where parents / guardians are not churchgoers.

It looks at issues of theology, sociology and practice. It uses historical research, primarily biographical and autobiographical. It involves survey, case study, interview, participant observation and ethnography. Some of the issues are complex, some of them are controversial, and, of course, not everyone will agree with my conclusion. That is not important; what *is* important is that others are stimulated to join the conversation about how the church better connects with the unchurched child.

It will stand up to academic scrutiny;[1] but I have set out to produce more than a scholarly work. I have endeavoured to uncover the tools and mechanisms that lay at the heart of the very first child evangelism movement and to re-present them for today. I have studied the books written on child evangelism and those books from associated disciplines, I have analyzed many child evangelism projects up and down the UK and across the world, and I have sat at the table with some of the best minds and deepest thinkers in this field; I have listened and learned and recorded. Nevertheless, I am not primarily a theorist. I started my first child evangelism project in 1990 in a small Welsh valley; the project soon grew to over 100 children. I later launched *Frantic* for the Christian Centre, Milton Keynes, a project that peaked in 1998 when over 750 children attended the Christmas special. I then went on to launch *Dream Factory*[2] for St Mary's, Bletchley, a project that would teach me the benefit of focusing on a fixed geographical area, in this case the local parish. It was during this time, while firmly at the coalface, that I wrote *Fusion, Impact* and *Detonate* as curriculum materials to reach unchurched children and *Don't Tell Cute Stories – Change Lives* to inspire a new generation of children's workers. All these projects continue to run. And although I spend most of my time leading churches, speaking in theological colleges and training children's workers, I suspect I have a few more child evangelism projects in me yet!

It is against this background that I dare to believe the insights of this book can be advanced as a model of child evangelism for the twenty-first century. It is written to inform and to educate, but primarily it is written to make us better equipped to communicate the compelling Jesus story to a new generation of boys and girls and to help them to respond appropriately to that story.

NOTES

1. It was initially written for the Doctor of Philosophy degree with Nottingham University.

2. Probably still my favourite name for a Children's Outreach Project.

CONTENTS

PART 2
CONNECTING WITH THE UNCHURCHED CHILD

ACKNOWLEDGMENTS

Special thanks:

To all those who completed the initial survey, but particular thanks to the following project leaders and workers who allowed me the time to observe their various projects in action: Chris Beveridge, Paul and Julie Bristow, Natalie Campbell, Gavin and Louise Chittick, Bernie Fell, Sarah Turner, Laura France-Hodgkinson, Jon McCowen, Ceri Neil, Miriam Patterson, Luke Plumley, Wes Richards, David and Elizabeth Ritchie, David Sharples, Dominic and Sarah Smith, Frankie Theobald.

Also to my Southern Hemisphere friends who distributed the questionnaires there: Rob Bradbury, David Goodwin, Peter Lusk and Andrew Shepherd.

To Claire Johnson, Rick Otto, Ruth Radley and Helen Shannon for pilot-testing the original questionnaires. Also to Jonathan Brook, Simon Neill and Peter Wyatt who debated the issues of children's spirituality with me so that I could earth my thoughts and write the theology chapter. (And thank you to the Nottingham establishments that hosted us, sometimes until very late into the night!)

To the Birmingham University Special Collections, the British Library, Gloucester Library Archives, Manchester University Archives, Nottingham University Library and St John's College Library, Nottingham, for the use of their facilities and research materials.

To the Bayne Benefaction, Culham Institute and Ministry Division of the Church of England for their financial support.

To Ruth Oxley who proofread the final draft.

A special thank you to Revd Dr Howard Worsley who gave many hours of input over five years. His input shaped me so that I could shape this research.

But, of course, my greatest thank you goes to my wife Rhian without whom this research could never have happened. And to my children Nia, Owen and Elliot who have sacrificed time with Dad as I typed, visited and read – they are significant children who will lead this rising generation.

And to Starbucks where I spent many hours reading and typing and, of course, drinking lots of coffee!

ISSUES OF ETHICS

Issues of selection and ethics were considered and the Revised Ethical Guidelines for Educational Research[1] were consulted. This was particularly important with regard to children's paintings, drawings and writings used in Chapter 6. Attention has also been given to Article 12 of the United Nations Convention on the Rights of the Child, so that each child has been allowed to give permission or withhold permission for their picture/words to be included in the research. However, this has been handled directly by the schools that agreed to be involved. Pictures/words have been included only where appropriate permission has been given. The child's name is not displayed, although the age of the child is shown as this was deemed necessary. The identity of children was also protected when receiving feedback from the children at Outreach Projects.

The data stored was registered in accordance with the 1998 Data Protection Act. Further to the terms of the act, consent forms were requested from those involved at the interview stage in the form of a contract that outlined what was expected of both researcher and informants.

Mirvis and Seashore[2] comment that 'Naivety itself is unethical'. This is an astute observation, and although all participants gave informed consent, it is acknowledged that, despite extensive explanation, some of the respondents had not completely grasped what they were getting into or the extent to which the findings would be made available to others. For that reason, it was necessary to ensure that people were not exploited by my innocent questions.[3]

In the relatively small field of Children's Outreach Projects, it is impossible to keep the names of the informants anonymous – the initiated will have no difficulty guessing which projects are being described and who leads them. For that reason, it was necessary to ask, even though they had given express permission, whether their recognition of themselves or being recognized by others would cause harm to these leaders. It was concluded that it would not.

All necessary acknowledgments are made with regard to centres for local studies at Gloucester and Manchester Libraries, to Birmingham University Library Special Collections, and to the British Library for locating and reprinting various London newspapers, particularly *The Gentleman's Magazine* of 1800.

NOTES

1. 2004.
2. 1982, p. 100.
3. See comments by Huberman and Miles (1994, p. 288).

FOREWORD

I was fourteen when I first encountered the church. We lived in Dagenham in Essex, on a huge council estate where most of the men worked at the Ford Motor Co. My younger brother Bob had started to act peculiarly – it showed first in his behaviour and later in the things he said. He was only ten and our large family of seven was impressed. We found out that he was attending Sunday School at Dagenham Parish church. It was through Bob that I too started to go to church and found a living faith for myself. It was a wonderful, serendipitous moment that changed my life, as well as six of our family, and gave us a purpose for living that has shaped our lives ever since.

I have sometimes wondered if I would be a Christian had I started my journey into adulthood at a time such as today, where there are so few connections between the church and children, and I doubt very much that I would have.

I use my personal story as an introduction to Mark Griffiths' latest book to illustrate the importance of his argument and the serious challenge facing the church in the United Kingdom. Let us make no bones about it; it is not merely declining, it is disappearing from the face of the nation faster than the ice flows are melting in the Antarctic.

However, what is crazy about our situation is that the trend is reversible. Though there would be considerable agreement that only a major shift in attitude and strategy can stop the drift, the action needed is so colossal and overwhelming, that it is doubtful the church would consider it. It is no less shameful that more than half of our Anglican churches have no ministry to children and young people at all.

This is why Mark Griffiths' book so relevant. He shows that Robert Raikes, the founder of the Sunday School movement, was also working against the grain of church life and faced formidable social challenges. While the success of Raikes' work can in part be attributed to his personality and drive, Griffiths' study shows how others were swept along with it and how teamwork was essential to the entire enterprise. This is far from a sociological and historical study however. The book examines contemporary work among children and young people that give considerable hope to the future of Christianity in this land.

But have we the courage to listen to the story? It is my hope that this book will galvanise us to action so that we include children as part of our mission. In *Mission-Shaped Church* (SCM Press, 2004), it is said: 'Start with the church and the mission will probably get lost, start with the mission and it is likely that the church will be found'. That is my testimony also. The church did not 'find' me, the Sunday School did – through my brother, and only then did I find the 'church'. Unless we do something about it, very few youngsters will find their ways into the arms of a loving God.

George Carey
Archbishop of Canterbury (1991-2002)

INTRODUCTION

Philip B. Cliff[1] concludes his PhD thesis and subsequent book on the Sunday School movement with these words: 'Sunday School teachers cannot do for parents what they must do themselves. The classroom is no substitute for the family.' It is a common view, drawing together teaching from the Old and New Testament to demonstrate that the rightful place for the communication of a system of belief from adult to child is within the context of the family.[2]

Christianity has historically focused its evangelistic efforts on adults. It was taken for granted, as a matter of common understanding, that, in a change of religion, the children went with their parents; if the parents became Christians, then their children would become Christians.[3] Children were born into the Christian home and nurtured in that belief system, or they would be deemed Christians because their parents had converted to Christianity. This twofold pattern of community nurture for those who were already believers and household conversions for those who were not has been the prevalent position throughout church history. The obvious drawback to this system is that children whose parents are not part of the faith community have no mechanism for becoming Christians. The first systematic and structured attempt to evangelize children who were from homes where the parents did not attend church took place in the 1700s with the formation of the Sunday School movement by Robert Raikes.

Initial responses to the words 'Sunday School' are often negative, and my intention is to look at the original model of Sunday School that Raikes developed, and to present a useful and effective model for child evangelism based on significant twenty-first-century examples. This is a comparative study, the methodology for which is as follows:

1. *Establish the cultural norms embedded within the early Sunday Schools.*
2. *Gain an overview of existing church-based child evangelism projects – referred to as Children's Outreach Projects throughout this book.*
3. *Look at five twenty-first-century Children's Outreach Projects in detail.*

As a result of the historical and biographical research (Chapter 1), a model of child evangelism emerged that was both dynamic and effective. At the same time, I discovered in Raikes a man of remarkable character, a tenacious entrepreneur with unwavering self-belief, who developed and propagated a model for child evangelism that was to reach 300,000 children within its first decade. By the 1800s, the model of child evangelism that Raikes developed was soon changed, and in some ways corrupted, as essential components of the original model were removed, or lost to history. History itself was often rewritten to present a more spiritual Raikes, but also a more sterile, two-dimensional Raikes, bearing very little resemblance to the dynamic founder of the movement. Nevertheless, in those first decades Raikes presented a model of child evangelism that was to revitalize the eighteenth-century church and cause a sharp increase in church attendance for over a century to follow, before it eventually lost momentum in the middle of the twentieth century.

Further to this, I discovered in my exploration of the twenty-first-century projects in Chapter 4 and Chapter 5 that many of the components of the original Raikes model were present in these modern child evangelism projects. These projects were chosen for evaluation as a result of the survey of UK Children's Outreach Projects outlined in Chapter 3.

Chapters 6 to 8 draw the threads together and make the comparisons between the early Raikes model and some of the most significant twenty-first-century examples. Chapter 6 looks at the theology embedded within the projects and specifically their understanding of conversion. Chapter 7 focuses on the present sociological context that influences the children attending these projects, and Chapter 8 then identifies the elements of the Raikes Sunday Schools that are still present today, the form in which they exist and the practices that have been added.

Having formed the portrait of Raikes and the cultural portrait of the Children's Outreach Projects, it is then possible to begin to answer the question: Are the emerging child evangelism projects of the early twenty-first century providing an effective method for child evangelism today?

I address this by asking two sub-questions:

1. *Are there similar patterns and 'cultural norms' embedded within the projects?*
2. *If so, have they independently and exclusively developed similar patterns of practice?[4] And have these groups learned from each other or from a common outside source, possibly Raikes?[5]*

In many ways I have written to put the record straight, to re-present the enigmatic Robert Raikes and his effective model of child evangelism, with the principles embedded in it that are just as potent today and are therefore advanced as a model of child evangelism into the twenty-first century.

NOTES

1. 1986, p. 322.

2. They are right to draw on the biblical examples, of course, but with a slight caveat. It is true that the word 'bah'-ith' is used occasionally within the Old Testament and is rightly translated *family*, most notably in the instructions for the Passover meal (Exodus 12:21–28). It is also true that bah'-ith communicates the concept of parents and children, what may now be termed the immediate family. Nevertheless, the word most commonly translated *family* in the Old Testament is 'mish-paw-khaw'. This word carries within it the sense of clan or community. It is the word translated as family in Deuteronomy 6:5–7 and again in Deuteronomy 11:18–19, when instructions are given for the passing on of the belief system from one generation to the next. That which constitutes a *family* in the Old Testament is the bond of kinship that unites its members; the *family* includes all those to whom that kinship extends (Pridmore, 1967, p. 26). The word most commonly translated *family* in the Bible therefore has more in common with a church community than it does with the *nuclear* family.

3. Bushnell (1847, p. 15). The New Testament examples of this are numerous: the household of Stephanas (1 Corinthians 1:16), Cornelius and his household (Acts 11), Lydia and her household (Acts 16:15), the jailer and his entire household (Acts 16:33) and Crispus and his household (Acts 11:8). The stories of Lydia, the Roman jailer, and Crispus represent rich variations of a theme that begins in the household of Cornelius, the first Gentile convert in the Book of Acts. Despite these variations, the general contours of the pattern remain visible: proclamation leading to initiation of an entire household (Matson, 1996, p. 182).

4. Outworking the hypothesis of the ethnologist Lewis Henry Morgan (1818–1881) that similarities mean that different groups had passed through the same stages of cultural evolution.

5. Ethnologist Grafton Elliot Smith (1871–1937) argued that different groups with similar cultural norms must somehow have learned from one another or from a common source, however indirectly.

PART 1

THE HISTORY AND PRACTICE OF CHILDREN'S OUTREACH

This section looks at Robert Raikes and the pattern of child evangelism that he developed, and then goes on to develop an overview of child evangelism in the twenty-first century and a detailed examination of five key projects.

Chapter 1
ROBERT RAIKES AND THE SUNDAY SCHOOL MOVEMENT

By careful analysis of the Sunday School movement's formation, it is possible to identify the practice of the earliest Sunday Schools with their regular repeated pattern and built-in norms and sanctions.[1] No timeline can be exact in this respect, but by identifying the pattern of working for the first decades, it is possible to use it to evaluate the development of child evangelism that emerged into the twenty-first century.

ROBERT RAIKES

Raikes was the product of a family that loved him, and Raikes in turn would prove to be a loving father and husband and one who could turn this compassion further afield. The material written about Raikes suggests a man of good character.[2] In many ways he was the epitome of the eighteenth-century Gloucester gentleman. Raikes' ancestry, rich with clergy influence, may have attuned his conscience to the needs of the poor and to the suffering of those around them. It is likely that the love he enjoyed in his own home as a little boy and its influence upon his own personality is attributable to his

Fig 1.1 Robert Raikes

mother,[3] but it was the skills he learned from his father, and the character modelled by his father, that would enable him to make the Sunday School movement so influential. It is for this reason that some observations on Raikes' father are necessary. (Both Robert Raikes and his father share the forename Robert; for that reason, Robert Raikes' father will be referred to as Raikes Senior.)

At the age of sixteen, Raikes Senior was bound apprentice to printer John Lambeth. He was to hold various positions within the printing trade over the next fourteen years until, in 1718, he had learned his trade well enough to set up his own press in St Ives and produce his own newspaper, the *St Ives Post Boy* which he sold for three halfpence a copy. Raikes Senior was to begin many newspapers in the same way as the *St Ives Post*. After the *Post* came the *Northampton Mercury*, but it was *The Gloucester Journal* that was his most successful publication and the main vehicle for presenting his views.

Fig 1.2 The Gloucester Journal 1783

Raikes Senior printed whatever was necessary while at the same time using *The Gloucester Journal* as the means to advocate his personal propaganda. For example, on 12 March 1728 Raikes Senior included in *The Gloucester Journal* thirty lines he had written on the subject of the national debt. The article was critical of the government's policy. Parliament was indignant and Raikes Senior was forced to apologize in person and fined £40.[4] This was the first of two occasions on which he had to apologize to Parliament. Raikes Senior was to express many opinions on subjects as diverse as waste of grain foods, the inhuman treatment of debtors and criminals, and cock fighting.[5]

It is clear that his friction with Parliament did not do any permanent damage to his community standing. In the same year that he was forced to apologize to Parliament for a second time, Booth[6] notes that he was appointed overseer of St Mary de Crypt, a position of great respect and influence within the community.[7]

Raikes Senior married Sarah Niblett in 1722. They had a daughter, but Sarah died shortly afterwards. Raikes Senior had been a widower for less than a year when he married Anne Mond. She gave birth to Robert, Elizabeth and Martha. All but Elizabeth died in infancy. In 1734 Anne died, leaving Raikes Senior a widower for the second time. A year later Raikes Senior married again, this time to Mary Drew, twenty-five years younger than Raikes, who by this time was forty-six. The following year Robert, the eldest of four sons born to Mary, was baptized in the church where his father was now the overseer.

Raikes Senior's entrepreneurial skills were not just evident in his dealing with *The Gloucester Journal*. Booth[8] talks of the episode in which one Henry Wagstaff, county sheriff, died in 1725, leaving large debts that his widow could not settle. Raikes Senior, seeing a business opportunity, took over the mortgage of Wagstaff's considerable house. In 1732 Raikes foreclosed and took up the tenancy of Ladybellegate House, and later, in 1735, he took over the complete and extensive Wagstaff property portfolio. The picture of a shrewd businessperson is developing. The Raikes family knew how to make money; their wills and other deeds show clearly that each generation was wealthier than the one before it.[9]

Raikes Senior showed tenacity and fortitude in the face of the deaths of his wives and children. He showed entrepreneurial prowess in his financial dealings. He is a man of clear influence and, despite his shrewdness, lived his life with integrity and favourable reputation. He often stood against injustice, had a well-developed social conscience, and knew what it was to work hard and to persevere. These are the character attributes and skills that Robert inherited.[10] Raikes Senior had nurtured and moulded his son in his own image and it was no surprise that in 1757, when Raikes Senior died, Robert Raikes inherited the business. In reports that are otherwise exceptionally positive regarding the character and integrity of both Robert Raikes and his father, it may be surprising to note the comments of Harris that both were also described as 'vain and conceited'.[11] This statement is not easily reconciled with the comments that have gone before, but it is not unique. Kendall,[12] citing the diaries of Madame D'Arblay, records her description of Raikes as 'somewhat too flourishing and forward'. It is also not as simple as suggesting that these comments came from enemies of the Raikes family as this is clearly not the case. Madame D'Arblay goes on to say that Raikes is worthy, benevolent, good-natured and good-hearted, and that therefore the overflowing of successful spirits and delighted vanity must meet with some allowance.

In reading about Raikes Senior and Robert Raikes it is clear that both men possessed large quantities of self-belief. In Raikes Senior, this is seen clearly in his ability to persevere despite experiencing personal sorrow, and not only to persevere but to excel in his chosen field; and in Robert Raikes, his self-belief is shown in the way he continues in his philanthropic endeavours, despite his early attempts at social reform, by his own admission, being failures.

It is possible that the unwavering self-belief exhibited by father and son would be misinterpreted by many as vanity and conceit. Nevertheless, it must also be conceded that the very fact that writers such as Harris and Kendall mention these indiscretions at all indicates that there were at least tendencies for the Raikeses to be proud of their achievements, even on occasion to the point of arrogance.

ROBERT RAIKES' ENGLAND

Raikes' paradigm of child evangelism did not operate in a vacuum; there are external factors that both shaped it and influenced its outworking. To understand these factors fully, it is necessary to understand the cultural context in which it was birthed. To draw the necessary comparisons involves looking at four significant factors of eighteenth-century life that were to influence this development: the social environment, the prevailing world view, the state of the church and the influences on the child.

Robert Raikes was born in September 1736 into an age of major contrasts. The French Revolution, with the ripples it would cause in Britain, was half a century away. The Reverend Gilbert White[13] described it as 'a golden age', and for some it was. Where employment, food and other necessities were freely available, life could be enjoyable. This was achieved in the places where landowners cared for their workers and their children. These were the communities to which White[14] referred:

> We abound with poor, many of whom are sober and industrious, and live comfortably, in good stone or brick cottages, which are glazed, and have chambers above stairs... Beside the employment from husbandry, the men work in the hop gardens, of which we have many; and fell and bark timber. In the spring and summer, the women weed the corn; and enjoy a second harvest in September by hop picking... The inhabitants enjoy a share of health and longevity; and the parish swarms with children.

Stratford,[15] writing of the period around 1780, paints a very different picture:

> Great outbreaks as the mobs of London and Birmingham burnt houses, flung open prisons, and sacked and pillaged at will... they[16] were ignorant and brutal to a degree which is hard to conceive. The rural peasantry, who were fast being reduced to pauperism by the abuse of the poor laws, were left without moral or religious training of any sort.

However, a warning is necessary. The historiography of the eighteenth-century church is profoundly ideological. Victorian historians defended their class, professional and intellectual interests, and diverted attention from the need to change by consciously depicting their predecessors as incapable of reaching Victorian standards. The Victorians were writing a history that would defend their own ideology and the construction of their own religious establishment.[17]

Virgin[18] further states, 'Self-confident and self-assertive, they developed a mythology about their Georgian predecessors, and this mythology has held sway since then.' It is for this reason the realities of the eighteenth century are difficult to ascertain. Stratford is an excellent example: other than his book, there are no other historical documents that mention the city riots he describes! Virgin suggests that piecing together the real history of the Georgian age may be more difficult than either side suggests. It is probable that eighteenth-century life was not as bleak as Stratford and other nineteenth-century writers suggest; however, there is enough evidence to suggest that the situation described by White was far from universal. According to Kent,[19] half of the poor lived in 'shattered hovels'. His further comments are insightful:

> Those who condescend to visit those miserable tenements, can testify, that neither health nor decency, can be preserved in them. The weather frequently visits the children of cottagers earlier than any others, and early shakes their constitutions. And it is shocking that a man, his wife, and half a dozen children should obliged to live all in one room together... Great towns are destructive both to the morals, and to health.

The industrial revolution had changed where people lived and how people lived. The exodus of people from villages and cottage industries to the towns and cities with their machinery and efficient production systems was well under way. Thousands of families whose traditional skills and occupations in agriculture no longer afforded them a livelihood sought employment in new industries.[20]

The cautions of Virgin and Gibson must be heeded, nevertheless; there are elements that are not in debate. By twenty-first-century standards, the political system of the day was unfair. The House of Commons was not representative of the people. Many large towns were not entitled to send any members to Parliament; other so-called rotten boroughs, with only a handful of residents, would return one and sometimes even two members to Parliament. Votes could be bought, and where a conscientious person refused to accept the bribe, the next step was often intimidation. The working classes had no vote and therefore no power to institute change.

Parliament took little interest in the workings of the country as a whole. Local communities were controlled and administrated by the landowners. Where the landowners were just and fair, the idealistic communities described by White could become a reality; where the reverse was true, the conditions of life could be horrific. Accounts of the poor starving to death were common. To ensure balance, however, it is important to say that although this was clearly not democracy in the twenty-first-century usage of the word, and, in the main, Parliament represented property rather than people, in most parts of England government was at least functional.

There was no police force; justice was in the hands of the magistrates who had taken a judicial oath to 'Do right to all manner of people after the laws and usages of this realm, without fear or favour, affection or ill will'.[21] In reality, the magistrate was chosen because of his social class and tended to show favour to those of a similar class. The law was designed to protect the landowners, and greater punishment was handed out for theft or damage to property than for assault or manslaughter.

What is clear is that the eighteenth century was a time of great change; the fabric of society itself was changing. In addition, the role of children within that society was changing. It was quite usual to employ children from the age of seven in factories, often conveying them to distant towns for the purpose. Working conditions were unhealthy and squalid. Employers sought ways to pay lower wages and the obvious solution was to employ women and children. Not only were the working conditions inhumane, but the way the children were treated was barbaric. One account speaks of a supervisor 'pinching a child's ear until his nails met through the flesh'.[22]

The world view of the eighteenth century was also to play a subtle yet important role in the development of Sunday Schools. The intent of the reformers, in the view of Collins and Price,[23] was 'To rescue the church from the malaise they perceived had plagued it. Their ultimate goal, regardless of theological persuasion, was to draw people closer to God'. It is unlikely that the reformers would have anticipated that less than 150 years later, in a period called the Enlightenment (c. 1650–1790),[24] so many eminent thinkers would deny the claims of religion completely and begin instead to advocate more humanistic world views. These beliefs first presented themselves in the form of Deism.[25] Prominent thinkers such as René Descartes,[26] John Locke[27] and Immanuel Kant[28] were Deism's strongest advocates. Isaac Newton also embraced a form of Deism but tried to reconcile this with his belief that Jesus was the redeemer sent by God for human salvation. However, Voltaire[29] was to take Deism to its furthest extremes in denouncing all forms of Christianity and denying the existence of a good and all-powerful God. The effects of the Enlightenment were to become synonymous with the period that sociologists would refer to as modernity[30] – although it has been suggested by many that modernity probably started in the mid 1400s with the invention of moveable type.[31]

Toulmin[32] suggests that there are four primary movements caused by the Enlightenment (figure 1.3), and therefore four primary characteristics of modernity. The first of these is the move from oral to written communication. After the 1630s, the tradition of modern philosophy in Western Europe concentrated on formal analysis of chains of written statements, rather than on the circumstantial merits and defects of persuasive utterances.[33] What was considered reliable and credible became that which was written down. Printed materials became more and more important. In relation to this study, it gives greater significance to the fact that Raikes owned his own newspaper; in the context of modernity, the owner of *The Gloucester Journal* was in a position of great influence. It is possible that the written words of the newspaper were beginning to carry more weight than the preached words of the pulpit. This formal presentation of words with its deductive style of presentation would epitomize the form of teaching materials published by firstly Raikes and later the Sunday School Union. Teaching materials reflected the stage of modernity into which they were released; they were concerned with the presentation of fact in formal and logical ways – formal logic was in, rhetoric was out. Alongside this emerged two related effects: a move from the particular to the universal, and a move from the local to the general. Aristotle is credited with having said that 'The good has no universal form, regardless of the subject matter of situation: sound moral judgement always respects the detailed circumstances of specific kinds of cases'.[34] Modernity rejected this and instead became concerned with 'the comprehensive general principles of ethical theory'.[35] Further to this, these general principles were not only held as true in every *time*, but also true in every *place*. What was truth in one situation was truth in every situation and in every place. The final strand of this area is introduced by Descartes' view that philosophy's aim was to bring to light permanent structures underlying all the changeable phenomena of nature, and, once discovered, these structures would not be time-related, but would be constant throughout time. Toulmin notes that:

> These changes of mind... were distinct, but taken in an historical context they had much in common, and in their joint outcome exceeded what any of them would have produced by itself.[36]

Modernity had introduced the philosophy of moral absolutes: absolute in that they were universal, general and timeless.

Movement	Effect
from oral to written	what is reliable is what is written
from the particular to the universal	real truth is what is true everywhere
from the local to the general	real truth had to be the same from locale to locale
from the timely to the timeless	the real is the unchanging

Fig 1.3 Movement and effect Table

Ariès suggests that the eighteenth century was the time when Europe's attitude to the child and the concept of childhood were being revolutionized. He states that the sixteenth- and early-seventeenth-century idea was that children should be kept out of sight and be cared for by mothers and nannies until they were ready to take their place in adult company. However, this has become a strongly debated viewpoint. In Ariès' most simplistic analysis of the development of childhood, the sixteenth-century child had little contact with parents until adulthood. The seventeenth-century child began to develop some prominence, and children are coddled and treated as objects of entertainment. By the eighteenth century Ariès[37] concludes that 'The child has taken a central place in the family' – a position that still exists on the whole today. There is a tension in the eighteenth century, but it is not between the classes as one might expect. It is between the parents and the moralists, the former group still involved in coddling and the latter concerned with the nurture of the child.

However, Ariès' view is not without challenge. Strauss, Ozment and Pitkin, although disagreeing over points of pedagogy, agree that adults in Reformation times were far from indifferent, and were instead profoundly interested in their children and often deeply affectionate towards them. Traina[38] points out that 'Philippe Ariès' complaint about the absence of a medieval perception of the "particular nature which distinguishes the child from the adult" finds no support in the writings of Thomas Aquinas'.[39] Ariès suggests that the reason for parents' dispassion towards their children in the medieval era was to do with the high mortality rates amongst children that caused parents to detach themselves to avoid hurt.[40] It is suggested that this level of dispassion has never been part of human nature and to suggest otherwise is to make an assumption without basis. There are no signs of dispassion in the moving account of the death of Martin Luther's[41] daughter Magdalena:

> I believe the report has reached you that Magdalena, my dearest
> daughter, has been reborn into the everlasting kingdom of Christ,
> and although I and my wife ought to do nothing but joyfully give
> thanks for such a felicitous passage and blessed end, by which
> she has escaped the power of the flesh, the world and the devil,
> nevertheless, so great is the force of our love that we are unable to
> go on without sobs and groaning of heart, indeed without bearing
> in ourselves a mortal wound.

Three years later Luther writes, 'It is astonishing how much the death of my Magdalena torments me. I have not been able to forget.'[42]

Working-class children in the eighteenth century may have been active members of the workforce and as such contributors to the economic sustainability of their families. They may have been exposed to desperate living conditions and experienced great social deprivation. Nevertheless, this should not lead to the conclusion that the children of the working classes were not loved or were treated with dispassion.[43] What can be concluded is that there were far fewer opportunities available to working-class children and a much greater need for them to contribute to the family income as soon as they were physically able.

Nevertheless, while this three-stage development model depicted by Ariès is rejected, it is accepted that the seventeenth and eighteenth centuries were a time when childhood itself was under review. Hendrick[44] writes:

> In the 1680s, the Cambridge neo-Platonist philosophers asserted
> the innate goodness of the child and in 1683 Locke published
> *Some Thoughts Concerning Education*, which included an attack
> on the idea of infant depravity, and portrayed children as *tabula
> rasa*.[45]

In 1762, Rousseau[46] published *Émile* and in so doing reaffirmed the natural and innate goodness of the child.[47] He proposed that all humanity was intrinsically good. The profile of children and childhood had taken on a new significance and their innate spiritual state would be debated for centuries to come.

The characteristics of modernism were embraced by the church. The written word, with its formal, logical format would become embedded within Protestant[48] liturgy and the church would campaign for moral absolutes with very little recognition that the concept was birthed in, and through, the Enlightenment. The eighteenth-century church was in difficulty, although again some caveats are needed. One group suggests that the church was completely incompetent – this was the prevailing view of the Victorians and the majority of scholarship through the earlier parts of the twentieth century; the other group suggests a much more united and healthy church – writers such as Sykes and Gibson fall into this category. Virgin[49] explains the difficulty:

> The diocesan archive of the eighteenth century is vast, unwieldy, and often poor in condition; nor, to make matters worse, did parliament show any interest in publishing nationwide data regarding the state of the church until after 1800.

There are some facts that can be established. The rise in population from 5.5 million in 1701 to 9 million a century later,[50] and the subsequent movement of the population from rural areas to new centres of industrial expansion, caused the Church of England organizational difficulties. The Church of England, like that of France, had relied heavily on the parish for the Christianization of successive generations. In the new circumstances, it was inevitable that increasing numbers would slip through the traditional network of pastoral oversight.[51]

When you weigh the overly negative projections of the Victorian writers against the more objective research of Gibson, it is probable that parish attendance had been a static figure for quite some time, giving churches a false sense of well-being: their attendance figures were constant but the population was rapidly increasing. The Church of England was structured around an England such as the one described by Gay,[52] commenting on the year 1701:

> The picture emerging suggests that between 70 and 80% of the total occupied population was primarily engaged in agriculture. The strictly rural population, that is those who lived in hamlets and villages, was equal to about 75% of the total, while a further 10% was to be found in London and its suburbs.

The England that was emerging towards the end of the eighteenth century was unrecognizable compared to the one described in 1701. The Church of England, with its basis in English law, did not have the ability to respond to the vast movements of people, and the result was that large groups of people in the newly industrialized areas were without a church. Leeds was a single parish until 1840, but by 1801 it had a population of 30,669 and by 1881 it had reached 309,126 (figure 1.4).

For this reason, even considering the comments of Gibson, the Church of England in this period can be described as dysfunctional.

	1685 [53]	**1760** [54]	**1881** [55]
Liverpool	4,000	40,000	552,425
Manchester	6,000	30,000	393,676
Birmingham	4,000	28,000	400,757
Leeds	2,000	n/a	309,126
Sheffield	4,000	30,000	284,410
Bristol	29,000	100,000	206,503
Nottingham	8,000	17,000	111,631
Norwich	28,000	40,000	87,845
Hull	n/a	24,000	161,519
York	10,000	n/a	59,596
Exeter	10,000	n/a	47,098
Worcester	8,000	12,000	40,422

Figure 1.4 Population estimates in twelve provincial towns

Gay[53] writes:

> The Church of England almost completely failed to take any positive action until well into the 19th century. There were virtually no new churches built from the beginning of the 18th century to the time of the Million Act in 1818. During this period the population of the country doubled... At the beginning of the 19th century one-third of the English population was living in urban areas; by the end of the century this proportion had increased to four-fifths. Furthermore, the greatest growth was in the largest towns and cities. The percentage living in cities of over 100,000 grew from 11% in 1801 to 43.6% in 1901.

The problem was further compounded; by 1700, derelict churches were a common sight. An 1812 parliamentary enquiry found 4,813 incumbents who were non-resident. Again too much should not be attached to the parliamentary enquiry, the fact that incumbents were not in residence does not of itself imply a neglected parish, for many parishes may well have been administrated by 'over pressed and underpaid curates'.[54] Parishes at this time were bought and sold as livings on the open market. Having secured a living, it was possible to pay an unqualified curate to look after it.

The church at the start of the eighteenth century, according to Booth,[55] was 'if not wantonly heartless, so damnably caught up in its own corruption as to neglect its holy trust'. The eighteenth-century bishops were at their most aristocratic, as was the clergy in general. Ordained ministry was the domain of the younger sons of nobility; clergymen, while being paid to look after certain parishes, rarely if ever visited those parishes.

Other religious orders such as the Jesuits grew up to fill some of the vacuum in Europe. These were primarily teaching orders and Ariès[56] notes that their teaching was primarily aimed at children and young people. Their *propaganda* taught parents that they were guardians of their children's souls and bodies before God. However, these orders did not officially begin their work in England until much later.

Before the picture becomes too bleak, it should be stated that there were devoted clergy at this time who worked energetically and diligently. Many of these would become common names in the development of the Sunday School movement. Raikes himself was an office holder within the Church of England. In addition, this was the time when tens of thousands would hear the preaching of John Wesley and George Whitefield. These men travelled thousands of miles proclaiming a message of salvation and redemption for the common person.

There were clearly glimpses of hope emerging in the eighteenth-century church, but, on balance, although it was not technically declining, it was dysfunctional. Population movements that created vast urban people centres had further damaged an already crumbling parish structure. When the established church eventually saw the need, it was not flexible enough to respond to the extreme cultural and demographic changes that were affecting society.[57]

Despite the difficulties the church was experiencing, the social sciences were developing quickly. The dawn of the nineteenth century promised to take the development of childhood further. Children's rights were asserted. Hendrick[58] writes:

> During the course of the debates between, say, 1780–1840s, a
> new constriction of childhood was put together by participants,
> so that at the end of the period the wage-earning child was no

longer considered the norm. Instead, childhood was now seen as constituting a separate and distinct set of characteristics requiring protection and fostering through school education.

Social reform had placed children in a far more protected environment; however, the advances of Locke and Rousseau were soon to be undermined by the Evangelicals and their strong agenda to reassert the Augustinian[59] doctrine of original sin; so much so that the advancements made 'became sentimentalised and static in the hands of Victorian literature'.[60]

An interesting side effect of Rousseau's assertion that all humanity was intrinsically good was the establishment of the concept of the individual. The concept of the individual would provoke ongoing contention. Rousseau's followers considered the individual naturally good and therefore endowed with political rights that come straight from God, whereas the Evangelicals saw the individual as depraved and in need of a personal conversion experience.

Eighteenth-century children's life expectancy was low and they may well have lived in conditions of extreme social degradation. Cases of depravity abounded, and children as young as seven were employed to work as many as sixteen hours each day. Nevertheless, the child born into an economically poor family was still the centre of family life; this is asserted in contradiction to the view presented by Ariès. The main influence on the child in the eighteenth century was undoubtedly parental, as it had been throughout history.

It was within this cultural backdrop that the Sunday School movement emerged.

RAIKES' MODEL OF CHILD EVANGELISM (1780–1800)

The events that led to the establishment of Robert Raikes' first Sunday School are often commented upon, but rarely without an underlying agenda, such as Cliff's[61] assertion that the early Sunday Schools were primarily 'an attempt at the popular education of the masses'.[62] It is a view shared by many others. Orchard[63] suggests that the Sunday Schools only turned to religious instruction when they no longer had a role as 'educators in skilful knowledge'.

To understand what Raikes intended will involve looking at some of the documents written at the time. An account of that formation in Raikes' own words can be found in a letter to Richard Townley.[64] This letter will prove particularly useful in adding clarity to the purpose of Sunday Schools and the process of their establishment.

There is no doubt that the nineteenth-century writers believed that the formation of Sunday Schools was an act of God. However, with Raikes himself claiming the event to be an 'accident' and 'a harmless attempt, if it were productive of no good', it is likely that they believed God was involved in the formation rather than being the instigator of that formation – although theologically it would be difficult to draw a line between the two definitions. What is clear from the letter to Richard Townley is that Sunday Schools were formed, at least in part, to be a Bible-teaching institution. The women that Raikes employed are 'to instruct in reading and in the church catechism'.[65] There is further evidence in the articles of *The Gloucester Journal*. Raikes records the letter of a clergyman[66] who writes:

> Our children are now restrained from spending the Sabbath both in idleness and vice, their late constant practice; and where they have been more accustomed to frequent the service of the church, and are taught to behave with becoming reverence there; where they are taught to spend the rest of the day in learning the general principles of Christianity.

When other Sunday Schools were formed within this early period, Bible-teaching can be seen as a clear priority. The rules for the Birmingham Sunday School set up in 1783 stated 'That the Scholars be catechised in the school or Church some part of the day'. There is only mild debate here. Cliff himself acknowledges that there are Bible-teaching elements in the early Sunday Schools but refutes that this was their primary objective; what he arduously denies is their *evangelical* nature. Booth[67] clarifies:

> Raikes cannot be classified as an *Evangelical*, in the 18th-century interpretation of the word. He was a religious man, but for him there was not the same conviction as Wesley and Whitefield 'that nothing except religion mattered'.

If by *Evangelical* it is meant that each child would undergo a personal conversion experience, then Booth and Cliff are correct and Raikes does not fall within this definition. However, if it is meant that Raikes had no intention to see these children become part of the Christian faith, then the evidence seems contrary. This area seems to cause Cliff difficulty. It is possible that his Congregational background predisposes him to look for this attempt at conversion, the lack of which leads him to conclude that Sunday Schools at inception were an attempt at 'the popular education of the masses'. Nevertheless, it is suggested that his definition of evangelism is too narrow. It is clear that Raikes is involved in child evangelism, if child evangelism is defined in terms of a combination of Christian education and facilitated encounter.[68] What is also clear is that Raikes did not set out to use this methodology of evangelism in his Sunday Schools. This is something Raikes stumbled into experientially, not through design.[69] Raikes lived in an era when the predominant assumptions with regard to belonging to the church were very different. Whereas the evangelical model suggests that people have to *opt in* – by whatever mechanism[70] – to be part of the church, this would have been foreign to Raikes and to the Church of England at this point in history. He would have been firmly of the opinion that all were part of the church unless they chose to leave it.

Cliff[71] returns to this idea of Raikes not being *Evangelical* in his concluding remarks on the first twenty years of Sunday Schools:

> If one examines the hours of attendance and the amount of time to be given to devotions, teaching and catechism learning, it can be seen that there was little time for a teacher to try any kind of indoctrinating, pressurizing or similar activity.

What Cliff consistently fails to recognize is that Raikes is not drawing the distinction that emerged at the end of the eighteenth century, and is prevalent today, between what is religious and what is social.[72] Raikes would not define his understanding of religion as involving pressurizing or indoctrinating, whether children or adults are the object. For Raikes, there was not the emphasis on making personal decisions to follow Christ or any such thing that Cliff[73] would term 'indoctrinating'.

Evidence of the strong Bible-teaching dimension can be gleaned from the materials that Raikes provided for the Sunday Schools. Raikes was not only a publisher but also an importer and distributor of literature. Cliff[74] lists 'Spelling books, catechisms and copies of the scriptures' as items that Raikes provided for his initial Sunday Schools and sold wider afield when the Sunday School idea began to spread. Furthermore, it is clear that Raikes was about more than teaching people to read; his philanthropic endeavours were fuelled by a belief that 'Vice is preventable'.[75] Harris[76] records, 'He eventually concluded, vice is preventable, begin with the child.' His aim was to prevent vice rather than cure sin. In his editorial in *The Gloucester Journal* of 17 May 1784 Raikes writes, 'The promoters of the design seem to concur that prevention is better than punishment.' Harris represents a nineteenth-century interpretation and is not free from the degree of bias that Cliff is keen to expose. However, placed alongside the evidence of the last paragraph, and the zeal that characterized Raikes' work in the prisons, it leads to a conclusion that although literary skills are important, they are only a part of Raikes' wider campaign of Christian education.

When Harris[77] interviewed those who had attended Raikes' first Sunday Schools, with regard to their use of materials they commented on 'A Book which explained the meaning of the fast days, collects, etc., a reading book and texts and Psalter'. Another interviewee commented, 'We used to learn from a reading book, the collects, Bible and Testament.' Although the interviewee explains that this was only for those who could read, those who could not would learn their 'A, B, C's',[78] although he added, 'No one was exempt from catechism.'

There is very little information on Robert Raikes' own teaching of Sunday School, but what there is, is insightful. Harris[79] recounts an example of Raikes making an Old Testament story relevant to his audience:

> The subject of my conversation with them was the history of Joseph... I brought it down to a level with their conditions, with Joseph as a poor boy like one of them. You would have been agreeably struck with the fixed attention of their little minds. I dare say many went home and told the story to their parents.

Harris[80] continues with an example of a Raikes' object lesson:

> I have lately had a flock of children come about me from a singular circumstance. I was shewing my Sunday scholars a little time ago how possible it is for an invisible power to exist in bodies which shall act upon other bodies without being able to perceive in what matter they act. This I prove to them by the powers of the magnet. They see the magnet draws the needle without touching it. Thus, I tell them, I wish to draw them to the paths of duty and thus lead them to Heaven and happiness; and as they saw the needle, when it had touched the magnet, then capable of drawing another needle, thus when they became good they would be made the instrument in the hands of God of making other boys good.

In *The Gloucester Journal* editorial of 17 May 1784, one of the early advocates of Raikes writes that 'The children are engaged in learning the general principles of Christianity'. Raikes goes on to explain how his strategy of children helping to make others good saw impressive results with large numbers of them gathering with Raikes every morning at 7 a.m. for prayers at the Cathedral.[81]

Raikes' produced teaching materials for his Sunday Schools and sold them further afield through *The Gloucester Journal*. Kendall[82] cites a copy of the *Sunday Scholar's Companion* which further reveals the religious nature of the teaching with a range of sentences explaining various passages; at the back of the publication is a new catechism which Raikes developed to run alongside the authorized catechism. Although it appears complex for children, Raikes' catechism is one of the clearest insights into his theology.[83] It runs as follows:

Q. Did the world make itself?
A. No, if that clock had a maker, much more the whole world had a maker.

Q. Why must you believe in God?
A. Because if we do not believe in him, I should deny and forget my Maker, and be without God in the world, like those who spend their money in the public houses while their wives and children are without bread.

Q. How do you prove there is a God?
A. 1st by common sense; 2nd by our conscience; 3rd by tradition; 4th by the Sabbath; 5th by the Scriptures.

Q. How do you prove the truth of the gospel or that Jesus Christ was the Son of God?
A. By the miracles that he wrought and the prophecies that were fulfilled.

Q. Have you any additional proof of the truth of Christianity?
A. It was spread and established in the earth by a few poor men, in opposition to the prejudices and passions of mankind. The first preachers of Christianity therefore must have been assisted by the power of God.

Q. Can you bring any evidence of the truth of the Gospel from the substance of religion itself?
A. No other religion has proposed a plan of morality so just and perfect as that of Christianity, or enforced that plan by such powerful motives.

Having shown what was taught, it is now necessary to establish *who* taught. There are clues in the letter to Townley:

> I then enquired of the woman if there were any decent, well
> disposed women in the neighbourhood who kept schools for
> teaching to read. I presently was directed to four.

The letter continues to show the nature of the employment: 'To remedy
this evil, persons duly qualified are employed to instruct those that cannot
read; and those that may have learnt to read are taught the catechism and
conducted to church.'[84] This would not always be the way, and financial
restrictions would be a key motivator in encouraging volunteer workers
to take the place of the paid professional. Certainly, at inception teachers
were recruited for their various skills. Jones[85] points out that:

> The official minimum requirements were to be a communicant of
> the Church of England, of good temper and behaviour, one who
> keeps his own family in order, and to be approved by the parish
> clergyman.

They needed to be able to instruct in reading and in catechism and,
importantly, to maintain order. Booth[86] refers to the recruitment of Mrs
Critchley who had been 'prevailed upon by Raikes to open a Sunday
School' because 'Mrs Critchley [was] previously a regular school mistress
and known for her ability to cope with rough boys'. What is interesting is
that Mrs Critchley ran a 'mixed school'. Sunday Schools from inception
were for both sexes. The practice of paying teachers is further emphasized
by Orchard[87] who comments, 'By 1796 the Methodists were still paying
teachers on the grounds that a purely voluntary system was not reliable.'
    Cliff[88] also gives insight into other formational aspects of the Sunday
Schools and observes:

> He seems to have taken his share of visiting the homes of the
> scholars, of hearing them read, of taking them to church, and of
> providing encouragement by the giving of prizes or trinkets.

This reference to taking them to church and to the giving of prizes is also
evidenced in Raikes' letter to Townley:

> These little ragamuffins have taken it into their heads to frequent
> the early morning prayers which are held at the Cathedral at seven
> o'clock. I believe there were nearly fifty there this morning. They
> assemble at the house of one of their mistresses and walk before

her to church, two and two... the Society for Promoting Christian Knowledge sometimes make me a present of a parcel of Bibles which I distribute as rewards for the deserving.

This is shown again in his letter to Mrs Harris (1787) in which he talks of 'rewards to the deserving'. The Bishop of Rochester was clearly not an advocate of this particular practice and commented in *The Gentleman's Magazine*: 'The poor are even bribed by pecuniary gifts to send their children to these schools.'[89]

The practice of home visits is also illustrated in the Townley letter. Raikes writes:

I went around to remonstrate with them on the melancholy consequences that must ensue from so fatal a neglect of their children's morals. They alleged their poverty rendered them incapable of cleaning and clothing their children fit to appear either at school or at church. But this objection was obviated by a remark that if they were clad in garb fit to appear in the streets I should not think it improper for a school calculated to admit the poorest and most neglected. All that I required were clean faces, clean hands, and hair combed. In other respects they were to come as their circumstances would admit.

There are standards in the first Sunday School, but the standards are such that the poorest can attain them. Cliff[90] further emphasizes the practice and highlights its wider affiliation:

Raikes also used a technique which became the constant idea held out to those who would really serve the cause. He visited the homes of all his scholars, talking with the parents about their children's welfare, and helping the parents understand what he was trying to do, and explaining how they could help.

What is evident here is not only Raikes' practice of visiting the homes of the children within his area but the degree to which he interacts with his wider community. Harris[91] was able to observe of Raikes, 'He knew the parents of these children, and the habits of their class.' There is no detachment here; Raikes is active within the Sunday School – 'Hearing them read', active in 'Taking them to church and providing encouragement by the giving of prizes' and 'Visiting the homes'.[92] It must not be overlooked that these are not children who usually attend church. In his letter to Townley, Raikes comments, 'Upon the Sunday afternoon, the mistress takes the scholars to church, a place into which neither they nor their ancestors had ever entered.' The children that Raikes is working with at the start of the Sunday School movement are primarily unchurched.[93] At the inauguration of Sunday Schools, Raikes made the link between church, Sunday School and community. The Sunday School Society, in attempting to replicate Raikes' practice, issued a rule that 'All scholars shall attend places of public worship every Sunday; but such as their parents may respectively approve (Rule XVI)'.[94]

There is one more account of the formation of Sunday Schools that should be considered as it raises a question that cannot be overlooked. It is cited in Stratford,[95] Gregory[96] and Booth[97]. It is the letter of the Reverend Thomas Stock written in 1788:

> The undertaking originated in the parish of St John's, in this city, of which I was curate. The facts are as follows: Mr Raikes, meeting me one day by accident at my door, and in due course of conversation, lamenting the deplorable state of the lower classes of mankind, took particular notice of the situation of the poorer children. I had made, I replied, the same observation, and told him, if he would accompany me into my own parish, we would make some attempt to remedy the evil. We immediately proceeded to the business, and procuring the names of about ninety children, placed them under the care of four persons, for a stated number of hours on the Sunday. As minister of the parish, I took upon me the principal superintendence of the schools, and one third of the expense.

This raises the question of whether or not Raikes was the actual founder of Sunday Schools. The answer is undoubtedly not: the first Raikes Sunday School was in 1780 and there are many reports of experiments of this nature before this point. The letter of the Reverend Stock would at best suggest that Raikes was only a joint partner. Kendall[98] cites the examples of Hannah Ball opening a Sunday School in High Wycombe and Sophia Cooke opening a Sunday School in Gloucester before 1780 (unfortunately Kendall does not provide accurate dates); Harris[99] comments on the work of the Reverend Moffatt who opened a Sunday School in Nailsworth in 1774. There are many other examples of Sunday Schools before 1780. Some were clearly attempts at education whereas others were more church-based projects with an emphasis on catechesis. Harris[100] strives to prove that Raikes' first Sunday School was not indebted to them: 'If they preceded him he was unaware of them in every way.' It is unlikely that Harris is correct. Raikes' grandfather was vicar of Nailsworth and his mother had grown up there. In light of this, it is unlikely that Raikes had no knowledge of the activities taking place there, and running *The Gloucester Journal* would have allowed him a comprehensive overview of the activities of that city. However, it is unclear why Harris is so keen to prove his point. The aforementioned letter makes it clear that Raikes knew of the Reverend Stock's work. It is not important that Raikes knew or did not know of existing Sunday School provision; what Raikes did was formalize the Sunday School concept and after a period of three years, in which he would observe what he would term his 'little experiment' grow and develop, he began to promote the concept more widely through his newspaper. Stock acknowledges:

> The progress of this institution through the kingdom is justly to be attributed to the constant representations, which Mr Raikes made in his own paper, of the benefits which he perceived would probably arise through it.

In his letter to Townley, Raikes comments on just this practice: 'And it was in order to excite others to follow the example, that I inserted in my paper the paragraphs which I suppose you saw copied in the London papers.' Like his father before him, Raikes had learned to use his newspaper as his pulpit.[101] To this extent Cliff[102] rightly concludes:

> The evidence from across the country from the late 18th century would appear to be that there were forms of Sunday School before Raikes, that his great contribution was to give publicity to the effects of the schools, to keep alive the growth, extent and progress of them. In this sense he was the founder of the Movement.

By 1784, Wesley recorded in his Journals that Sunday Schools were 'springing up everywhere'. They were not restricted to the Church of England. Before 1800, a group of Bristol Baptists experimented with canvassing an area of the city and very soon had 300 children attending.[103]

In his letter to Mrs Harris of 1787, Raikes comments that the Sunday Schools had expanded so quickly that attendance now numbered 250,000.

By 1788, the Sunday School Society quoted 300,000 attendance in their annual report.

By the end of the century, according to Bamford,[104] hymn-singing and prayer were also part of the programme:

> Every Sunday morning at half past eight was this old Methodist school open for instruction of whatever child crossed its threshold. A hymn was first led out and sung by the scholars... At 12 o'clock singing and prayer again took place, and the scholars were dismissed.

Young and Ashton[105] record this practice of singing and other professional aspects of the teaching programme in the Sunday School established by the More sisters in Cheddar in 1789:

> Hannah and Martha More attempted to make school sessions entertaining and varied... Programmes had to be planned and suited to the level of the students; there needed to be variety; and classes had to be as entertaining as possible (she advised using singing when energy and attention was waning). She also argued that it was possible to get the best out of children if their affections 'were engaged by kindness'.

The comparisons between this high standard of engagement and entertaining teaching here and the more ad hoc teaching encountered in some of the nineteenth century should not be overlooked. It is also noteworthy that the sisters opened their Sunday School in a dedicated building (this became more common through the spread of Methodism). They had a barn for instructing the children and a house where the school's mistress would live. Prize-giving can also be seen as a key characteristic:

> I encourage them [she said] by little bribes of a penny a Section to get by heart certain fundamental parts of Scripture. Those who attend four Sundays without intermission receive a penny. Once in every six to eight weeks I give a little gingerbread. Once a year I distribute little books according to merit. Those who deserve most get a Bible. Second-rate merit gets a prayer book – the rest, cheap repository tracts.[106]

However, although in practice the More sisters' Sunday School contained the same form as Raikes' earliest Sunday Schools, there is a significant difference that will be returned to in more detail later. The More sisters, with their links to the Clapham Sect,[107] could most definitely be considered 'Evangelical' in the eighteenth-century use of the word. Hannah More stated:

> Is it not a fundamental error to consider children as innocent beings, whose little weakness may, perhaps, want some correction, rather than beings who bring into the world a corrupt nature and evil disposition, which it should be the great end of education to rectify.[108]

Hannah and Martha More were very much in the business of *converting* boys and girls.

Although it is not possible to be too dogmatic, a clear form of Sunday School had emerged within the first twenty years. Its key components were professional teachers, reinforcement of positive behaviour through prizes, clear connections between Sunday School, church and community (the community link being made primarily through home visits), hymn-singing, prayer, and Christian education through Bible-based material. In addition, it must not be overlooked that the teaching of literary skills is an important part of Raikes' initial experiment. For some reason there seems to be a tension between meeting a social need and meeting a spiritual need. There is almost a sense in which some of Raikes' biographers (particularly Harris and Stratford) would feel the spiritual agenda being compromised if a social need were being met, but as Marshall[109] points out:

> Christianity at its best has always been suspicious of a purely spiritual view of the Church which seeks to keep it clinically antiseptic and uninvolved with the institutional forms and packaging of the age and environment in which it seeks to witness and minister.

The evidence shows that both religious education and social action were key components of the initial Sunday Schools; rather than being conflicting, they are complimentary.

The nineteenth-century writers looked back on Raikes' work and embellished it, the emphasis being that the development of Sunday Schools was a divine act and Raikes was the object of that action. From what has been previously seen, it is likely that Raikes' motivation was mixed. There can be little doubt from his previous philanthropic endeavours that Raikes was intent on doing good, and his community roles show his willingness to work for the well-being of others. There are also enough indications to suggest that part of his motivation was for public recognition, and he was clearly not immune to drawing attention to himself in promoting the Sunday School work nationally. To balance this, Raikes did not set out to establish the Sunday School movement, but, as part of his Christian duty, he was responding to the need he perceived in his own locality – in his own words, 'a harmless attempt... to check this deplorable profanation of the Sabbath'.[110]

From 1800 onwards, the Sunday schools had developed a life apart from Raikes. Cliff[111] writes:

> It would seem that in the first twenty years of the Sunday Schools, they prepared the population, in an indirect way, for recruitment to the membership of the various churches. Several people have noted that the number of children recruited directly into church membership has always been disappointingly small. What they have not taken into account is that, at least among the non-Anglican churches, membership did not usually take place until the candidates were of legal age. If one allows for the passage of say ten years, between a child's leaving Sunday School and his becoming a church member, one can begin to see some reason for the rapid growth in church membership.[112]

Working on this basis, the effects of the period up until 1800 will not be seen statistically until several decades later. The figures speak for themselves. Currie, Gilbert and Horsley[113] record that in 1800 there were 1,230,000 adults in church; by 1830 there were 1,958,000. The church population increased significantly in the thirty-year period. Other factors contributed to this growth, including the rise in population[114] and the formation of many nonconformist churches, in particular Methodism. However, the part played by the Sunday School is significant (figure 1.5).

Raikes' work was as the founder and propagator. Once the Sunday School movement had gained enough momentum he stepped back, and by 1802 he had retired from public life (he died eleven years later, aged 76). Nevertheless, the momentum was considerable. Sashkin, drawing on the work of Max Webber,[115] observes the instability of charismatic authority. In Raikes' case, the instability is due to the short period of time he controlled the movement; when Raikes stepped down, there arose a need to *routinize*

SUNDAY SCHOOL ATTENDANCE BY DENOMINATIONAL AFFILIATION		
1904	The congregational union schools	734,986
1905	The Presbyterian Church of England	89,558
	The Bible Christian Church	47,242
1906	The Baptist Union	586,601
	The Methodist New Connexion	88,042
	The Primitive Methodist Church	477,114
	The United Methodist Church	194,826
	The Wesleyan Methodist Church	1,013,391
1910	The Church of England	2,437,000
	TOTAL	5,668,760

Fig 1.5 Sunday School attendance by denomination, based on figures from Currie, Gilbert and Horsley

the movement into a more structured form of authority.[116] Not only are elements of the original pattern lost in this routinization, but often the absence of the energy, enthusiasm and entrepreneurship that the charismatic leader brought to the project makes the project difficult to maintain.

Raikes had used his newspaper as his pulpit and propagated a message with all the passion of a Wesley or Whitefield. He formulated a pattern of Sunday School that he observed for three years and then began converting the world to his paradigm. His paradigm had no conversion element; he believed that all children were part of the church of God and therefore conversion was unnecessary. The attendance of Sunday Schools in England is widely debated,[117] but all are agreed that by 1830 Sunday School attendance had exceeded a million, by 1850 it had exceeded two million, and by 1880 was fast approaching four million. By 1910 Currie, Gilbert and Horsley[118] estimate that there were approximately six million children in Sunday School (the population in the 1900 census was 38 million.[119]) Croft[120] comments, 'It is estimated that at the turn of the century something like 85% of the child population was in contact with a church or Sunday School.'

There is one other significant effect of the establishment of Sunday Schools that should not be overlooked. This is the number of international missionaries who attribute their call to overseas missions endeavour to the influence of Sunday Schools. In her exhaustive study of the missionary vocation at the start of the twentieth century, Rouse[121] concluded:

Decisions in childhood are very numerous. In the biographies examined, one-third of the missionaries distinctly attribute their first interest in missions to impressions received as children. In almost half of these cases, the impressions seem to amount to a distinct call.

She continues, 'Many and various are the means by which the missionary call comes home to children. Many responded to a direct appeal made by a Sunday School teacher to his class.'

By 1900 many of the elements of the Raikes paradigm had been lost. In their place, a model of conversion that was foreign to the original paradigm had emerged and become dominant. Attendance was at its highest, but the seeds of destruction had been sown. The Birmingham Sunday School Union record of 1903[122] reports the advice of the Lord Mayor (who was a Sunday School teacher) that it might be time to 'alter our methods'. It is the main argument of this book that the need then, and now, is not to find new methods of doing Sunday School, but instead to recapture the methods and practices that characterized Raikes' initial Sunday School model.

It is important to see that what Raikes developed was a pattern and not a rigid structure. It is the ability of the paradigm to develop and evolve that allows it to be sustainable. However, when elements of the paradigm are lost or inactive, the model is not as effective.

Notes

1. Cliff (1986, p. 51).

2. Certainly this is the case in the writings of Kendall (1939), Stratford (1880) and Harris (1885, 1890).

3. Booth (1980, p. 43).

4. Booth (1989, p. 33).

5. Compare Kendall (1939, p. 39).

6. 1989, p. 35.

7. Harold Smith in 'The Welfare Parish in the 18th century' comments, 'The Poor Law Act of 1601 laid down a system which lasted for the next two hundred years based on the principle that the parish of one's birth was responsible for looking after one's welfare. Under the act parishioners were appointed by Justices of the Peace to serve as Overseers of the Poor for one year. The costs of administration were paid for by taxes raised in the parish by levies on every inhabitant.'

8. 1980, p. 35.

9. Harris (1890, p. 23).

10. Raikes Senior's ability to nurture and mould his sons is not just evident in Robert. His other children were to show the values of integrity, determination and a willingness to work hard that their father had instilled in them; Richard became a clergyman, William a rich merchant and Thomas would become the Governor of the Bank of England (Harris, 1890, p. 30). Charles, who would have been only an infant when his father died, married his wealthy cousin and became a private gentleman in Cambridgeshire. There is almost a sense in which Charles was not touched or affected by his father's character and drive to the degree of his brothers, and so chose to live out his life in comfort and wealth without the philanthropic drives that his brothers so clearly possessed.

11. 1890, p. 41.

12. 1939, p. 15.

13. 1787, p. 17.

14. 1787, p. 18.

15. 1880, pp. 26–27.

16. 'They' being a reference to the poor.

17. Gibson (2001, p. 4).

18. 1989, p. iv.

19. 1775, pp. 229–231.

20. Booth (1989, p. 26).

21. The same magistrate's oath is still used today.

22. Cited in both Kendall (1939, p. 11) and Mantoux (1961, p. 72).

23. 1999, p. 156.

24. McGrath (1999, p. 15) suggests that the true effects of the Enlightenment were felt around 1750.

25. A belief that although there was a creator, he only created and set in motion the natural laws that would govern the universe. After he had created, he stepped back from his creation and had no more to do with it.

26. René Descartes (1596–1650).

27. John Locke (1632–1704).

28. Immanuel Kant (1724–1804).

29. François-Marie Arouet (1694–1778) – Voltaire was his pen name.

30. Toulmin (1990) would refer to this period as the first stage of modernism.

31. No attempt will be made here to pinpoint the start of modernism, or to explore its cause; the area of investigation is the effect of modernism on the thinking of the late eighteenth century.

32. 1990, pp. 31–35.

33. Toulmin (1990, p. 31).

34. Cited from Toulmin (1990, p. 32).

35. Toulmin (1990, p.32)

36. 1990, p. 34.

37. 1962, p. 133.

38. 2001, p. 110.

39. Thomas Aquinas (1224–1274).

40. Infant mortality figures were significantly high (House of Commons Journal 1767, cited in Booth, 1989).

41. Martin Luther (1483–1546).

42. Strohl (2001, p. 157).

43. History, both modern and ancient, demonstrates that economics often force the vulnerable members of the family into difficult situations. Shemilt's (2004) recollection of an event in Afghanistan highlights the point being made:

> A little girl sits huddled against the winter cold. She is modestly dressed but she is unaccompanied and begging – her reputation and hope of marrying well are in tatters. Where is her father? How can he be so uncaring as to allow his daughter to place herself in this position?
>
> Eventually, after several days of seeing the young girl in such a vulnerable position, one beggar among many, her father appears. He is a broken man, visibly incapable of earning money through physical labour. He gently takes off her worn out shoes and rubs her feet, to warm them and restore circulation. She catches his hands in her own and covers them with kisses.
>
> This is not an uncaring father; this is a father who has run out of options. How else can they eat? Where else could the money come from?

44. 1997, p. 36.

45. The empiricist doctrine was first expounded by the English philosopher and political leader Francis Bacon early in the seventeenth century, but John Locke gave it systematic expression in his essay *Concerning Human Understanding* (1690). He believed the mind of a person at birth was a *tabula rasa* – a blank slate – upon which experience imprinted knowledge, and did not believe in intuition or theories of innate conceptions. Locke also held that all persons are born good, independent, and equal.

46. Jean-Jacques Rousseau (1712–1778).

47. This assertion caused Rousseau problems with the Church in France. In many places, his book was burned and eventually he was forced to flee the country.

48. The term 'Anglican' was not used; 'Protestant' was the word used to describe the Church of England.

49. 1989, p. iv.

50. Cited by Cliff (1986, p. 17).

51. Ward, 1972, p. 7.

52. 1971, p. 69.

53. 1971, pp. 72–73.

54. 1971, pp. 72–73.

55. 1979, p. 23.

56. 1962, p. 412.

57. When the Church of England did respond, it responded dramatically. Colin Withers (1998) summarizes:

> The CBS lobbied Parliament to provide funding for a radical church building programme, and were successful in 1818 when Parliament passed the Church Building Act, and voted £1,000,000 to the building of new churches, to be administered by appointed Commissioners. This Act then became popularly known as the 'Million Act'. In 1824, Austria unexpectedly repaid a £2,000,000 war loan, which the government had already written off. This windfall resulted in a further £500,000 being voted to the coffers of the Church Building Commission. The Commissioners were also empowered to raise further sums by accumulating common interest and loan interest on the sums they administered, and by the reclamation of duty paid on materials used in the building of the churches.
>
> In parallel with Parliament's efforts, the Church Building Society also raised funds, by voluntary subscriptions, towards the same purpose. During the 1820s the CBS had given its aid, for the most part, to those parishes which the commission was legally inhibited from assisting. The CBS was, in reality, the Commission in the guise of the Church, as distinct from the State. The leading Commissioners usually sat also on the Society's committee....
>
> It was calculated that 2,029 new churches had been built between 1831 and 1851, based on a study of the 1851 Ecclesiastical Census.
>
> This was further bolstered by the 1840 Ecclesiastical Commissioners Act which stated: 'Additional provision shall be made for the cure of souls in

parishes where such assistance is most required, in such manner as shall be deemed most conducive to the efficiency of the established church'. It may also be noteworthy that this Act has never been repealed.

58. 1997, p. 39.

59. Augustine (AD 354–430).

60. Hendrick (1997, p. 36).

61. 1996, p. 2.

62. To illustrate how an agenda can prevent objectivity it is only necessary to look at Cliff's (1986) account of the formation of the Sunday School Movement. Cliff (1986, p. 2) cites Stratford (1880) as writing:

> When they reached a certain place the elder of the two said 'pause here,' and so saying he uncovered his brow, closed his eyes, and stood for a moment in silent prayer. The place was the site of the first Sabbath school, and the elder man was Robert Raikes, its founder. He paused on the spot and his prayer ascended to the ears of the crucified Christ, and the tears rolled down his cheeks as he said to his friend, 'This is the spot on which I stood and saw the destitution of the children, and the desecration of the Sabbath by the inhabitants of the town;' and I asked, 'Can nothing be done?' and a voice answered, 'Try,' and I did try, and see what God hath wrought.

As Cliff (p. 2) points out, it is 'a kind of Isaiahnic vision' used to bolster the position that Sunday Schools were a God-ordained tool for evangelistic enterprise. Cliff goes on to show that this is not how the formation of Sunday Schools came about, and in so doing undermines the view of Sunday Schools as an evangelical institution. Unfortunately, it would appear that Cliff has actually edited Stratford's (1880, p. 105) account to reinforce his view. Firstly, Stratford makes it very clear that his account is the recording of Dr Kennedy of Connecticut's address to Sunday School teachers, and Dr Kennedy clearly employs an apocryphal story to aid his preaching, and to ensure there are no misunderstandings precedes the paragraph above with the words:

> Many years ago in one of the oldest cities of England, two men might have been seen walking together, the one older than the other leaning on the arm of younger friend…

Although, it must be stated that Cliff's unfortunate editing of Stratford's work does not in itself show that Cliff's view is wrong, what it does illustrate is the difficulty in allowing the facts to speak for themselves, rather than projecting a preconception on to them.

63. 2007, p. i.

64. The letter appeared in *The Manchester Mercury* of 6 January 1784. Richard Townley was a Rochdale magistrate, indicated in his *Manchester Mercury* letter of 27 January 1784. Raikes' letter and Townley's response advocating the Sunday School appear in Appendix 4.

65. Catechism was (and is) a basic presentation of the principles of Christianity, in the form of questions and answers. In past generations, people were required to memorize a specific catechism before they could be confirmed into the Church of England. Other denominations had similar practice.

66. Cited from *The Gloucester Journal*, 24 November 1784 (copy in Appendix 4). For no apparent reason, the clergyman's name is kept anonymous, as is the location of his parish.

67. 1980, p. 42.

68. The polemic for this is explored more fully in Chapter 6.

69. What must be avoided is the suggestion that Raikes' work is any less valuable due to its accidental discovery. The method of discovery does not in any way increase or decrease the value of that discovered.

70. Usually by means of a set prayer asking for forgiveness and stating repentance. And usually accompanied by some public acknowledgement that the prayer has been prayed.

71. 1986, p. 67.

72. It is also important to understand the significance of the particular social need that Raikes was meeting. He was teaching children to read and write at a time when the Enlightenment was at its strongest and society was immersed in modernism, with the modernistic shift from the oral to the written. Children who could read and write could move out of their social situation. Raikes was not only meeting a social need; he was empowering children with the currency of the age, literacy.

73. 1986, p. 67.

74. 1986, p. 26.

75. The first area where Raikes exercised his philanthropy was within the prisons of Gloucester. Harris (1885, p. 52) comments, 'He arrived early at the conclusion that vice is preventable. If we follow him closely, we shall find him obstinately clinging to this idea through numerous failures.' He helped at Bridewell Prison and Castle Gaol. He read with the prisoners and fought for prison reform, using his newspaper as his main weapon. He wrote of those at Castle Gaol who were 'naked and covered with prison mould' (Harris, 1885, p. 56). When the prisoners left the prisons, Raikes worked to find them employment. He visited the prisons over the course of thirty years but often commented that those he helped would return to prison in a worse state than when they left, to the extent that Raikes was forced to conclude that his work with prisoners proved to be a failure (Harris, 1885, p. 59). It was at the age of forty-four that Raikes turned from prison reformer and began his great Sunday School experiment. Interestingly, it would be through Sunday Schools that Raikes would make his most positive contribution to law and order. Briggs (1981, p. 18) illustrates the point:

> The Salford magistrates passed a long resolution at their August Quarter Sessions in 1786 very specifically relating the growth of Sunday Schools to crime control, noting how 'idle, disorderly and dangerous persons of all descriptions' were wandering around and that 'where Sunday Schools have been opened, their good effects have been plainly perceived in the orderly and decent compartment of the youth who are instructed therein'. 'If these institutions had been established throughout the Kingdom,' the magistrates went on, 'there is good reason to hope that they will produce a happy change in the general morals of the people, and thereby render the severities of justice less frequently necessary.'

76. 1885, p. 52.

77. 1890, p. 32.

78. Harris (1890, p. 40).

79. 1899, p. 82.

80. 1899, p. 82.

81. Kendall (1937, p. 83). Also recorded in Raikes' letter to Townley.

82. 1937, pp. 85–86.

83. His discourse with Townley into the basis of the Sabbath (in the letter of Appendix 4) and his conclusion that Sunday Schools were certainly something that should be encouraged on the Sabbath (because the Sabbath was created for people, not people for the Sabbath) shows his ability to think through some of the implications of Sunday School theologically.

84. At inception, Raikes paid the teachers himself. Raikes' family were people of substance and Raikes had the financial backing to accomplish the various philanthropic endeavours he undertook, and this combined with the entrepreneurial expertise that his business background gave him ensured that all his projects were well managed and resourced.

85. 1938, p. 98.

86. 1980, p. 80.

87. 2007, p. 11.

88. 1986, p. 26.

89. *The Gentleman's Magazine* (1800, pp. 1076–8). To place this in context, the Bishop includes these comments in a section of his letter criticising those ministers who are gathering congregations but who are not accredited by the Anglican Church, and, within this, criticizes the Sunday Schools they run, and the practices they use to ensure attendance. The letter is written in open condemnation of dissenters, and should not be taken as a criticism of Sunday Schools per se. The letter from the bishop is included in Appendix 4.

90. 1986, p. 67.

91. 1890, p. 62.

92. Although it cannot be overlooked that Raikes continues to act as the benefactor to the ragamuffins.

93. This term will be used to describe children whose families are not regular church attendees.

94. Much has been made of Sunday Schools being places not just for children. By the mid-1800s this may well have been the case in some churches, but from this rule alone it can be seen that this was not the case at inception. One of the rules of the Sunday School Union formed in 1803 was 'Members were united: 1st – To stimulate and encourage each other in the religious instruction of children and youth'. In addition, Raikes' letter to Townley of 25 November 1783 mentions that 'These children are from age 6 to 12 or 14'.

95. 1880, p. 108.

96. 1880, p. 42.

97. 1980, p. 78.

98. 1937, p. 59.

99. 1885, p. 138.

100. 1885, p. 140.

101. Raikes' father was the founder of *The Gloucester Journal* and often used his newspaper to present his strong political and social views. On two separate occasions he was forced to apologize to Parliament for the statements he printed (Harris, 1890, p. 28).

102. 1986, p. 5.

103. Cliff, 1986, p. 84.

104. 1843, p. 111.

105. 1956, p. 239.

106. Young and Ashton, 1956, p. 240.

107. The Clapham Sect was a group of English social reformers, so named because their activities centred on the home in Clapham, London, of Henry Thornton and William Wilberforce. Most of the members were Evangelical Anglicans and members of Parliament. They included Zachary Macaulay, Thomas Babington, John Venn, James Stephen and Hannah More. They worked for the abolition of the slave trade and slavery, improvement of prison conditions, and other humane legislation. Shenk (1977, p. 3) speaks of the work of the Sect including helping the poor, teaching children to read, writing and publishing literature, combating the slave trade and sending missionaries to other lands. Henry Venn believed, as did the members of the Clapham Sect that he came to be affiliated with, that his mandate was evangelization of the world.

108. Robertson (1976, p. 421).

109. 1984, p. 165.

110. In recent years, this way of working – recognising the need first – has become more central to the churches thinking on evangelism. The Anglican report *Mission-Shaped Church* (2004, p. 124) stated, 'Start with the church and the mission will probably get lost. Start with the mission and it is likely that the church will be found.' This is what Raikes is doing; he is quite naturally recognising a need. Moltmann (1977, p. 64) commented, 'It is not the church that has a mission of salvation to fulfil in the world; it is the mission of the Son and the Spirit through the Father that includes the church.' Bosch (2004, p. 391) highlights this when he writes:

> Our missionary activities are only authentic insofar as they reflect the mission of God. The primary purpose of the *missiones ecclesiae* can therefore not simply be the planting of churches or the saving of souls; rather, it has to be service to the *mission dei*, representing God in and over against the world, pointing to God, holding up the God-child before the eyes of the world in a ceaseless celebration of the Feast of Epiphany. In its mission, the church

witnesses to the fullness of the promise of God's reign and participates in the ongoing struggle between that reign and the powers of darkness and evil.

111. 1986, p. 322.

112. Cliff (1986, p. 124).

113. 1977, p. 25.

114. Although the population had been rising considerably since 1701 (cf. John Gay, 1971).

115. Max Webber (1864–1920).

116. Sashkin (2003, p. 55).

117. By 1803 Kay and Francis (1997, p. 11) record there were 7,125 Sunday Schools with 88,860 teachers and 844,728 pupils. By 1830 Laqueur (1976, p. 44) concluded that Sunday School attendance was just over a million. There is often huge discrepancy in the figures. The parliamentary returns of 1818 record 5,463 schools with 477,225 scholars. The 1833 return records 16,828 schools with 1.5 million scholars. The Educational Census of 1851 records 23,514 schools with 2.4 million scholars. Parliamentary Returns and Educational Census cited in Cliff (1981, p. 124).

118. 1977, p. 25.

119. Research Paper 99/111 – House of Commons Library.

120. 1999, p. 118.

121. Rouse (1917, p. 244) drew her research from interviews with missionaries active in various countries and from the missionary application forms and references made available to her by several missionary organizations.

122. Information taken from Birmingham University Library – Special Collection.

Chapter 2

CHILD EVANGELISM AT THE END OF THE TWENTIETH CENTURY

An Anglican Report in 1945[1] noted:

> The figures for the past are not very encouraging: 67% of the children of our country are baptised at our fonts, 34% attend our Sunday instructions, 26% are confirmed, 9% receive communion at Easter, and a far smaller percentage become regular communicants.

The twentieth century saw Sunday School attendance drop from 6 million in 1903 to less than 500,000 by 1998[2] – this was despite an overall increase in the population. The period contained two world wars, and the demands of war necessitated women working in factories for long hours, including Sundays. Worship was no longer possible for many, and when it was possible, many found that they no longer felt the need. Those who survived the wars found their theological position shaken. Questions of innocent suffering undermined the beliefs of many.

The social imperative of the initial Sunday Schools – the teaching of literacy – was now confined to history. The almost universal role of the Sunday School in the twentieth century was summed up by the Reverend J. Williams Butcher:[3]

> We shall not improve our schools simply by adopting new methods. A method is of value just in proportion as it secures the end aimed at. The mere fact that our methods are old or new says little about their utility; the determining factor is: are they helping to bring our scholars to Jesus Christ as Lord and master?

Before looking at this era further, it is important to note again that in the Sunday School world there is a lag of approximately thirty years between the words of the change-agent and its acceptance at grass roots level.[4] The negative or positive impact of decisions taken may not be felt on a national level until some thirty years after the decision.

The vast majority of discussion in the latter part of the twentieth century follows one subject: what is going wrong? Montgomery[5] writes:

Loss of interest means that there must be something wrong in either the lesson material, or in its presentation; where teachers are lacking in vision or enthusiasm, and their teaching is dull and unimaginative, with outdated teaching methods, they may be doing more harm than good.

'FIFTIES FREEFALL'?

The Church of England commissioned further reports,[6] but the emphasis was on the progress of the child through its church from baptism to confirmation. Several authors wrote on the reasons for the huge decline of Sunday School attendance during the twentieth century. Some of these pointed to specific changes that took place in the 1950s as the main contributing factor to the decline. One example of this is Coupe's 2004 article where she writes:

> A study of the 'Fifties Freefall' demonstrates that the huge loss of children from the church is attributable, not just to social changes, but also to church policy... The 'Fifties Freefall' refers to the sudden dip in the Sunday School Scholars graph between 1955 and 1960. In the last century, the church has been losing children on Sundays at a faster and faster rate. Superimposed on this general trend are two dips caused by the world wars. There is also a big block of losses, lasting about 25 years between 1955 and 1980.

The statistical information is a matter of fact: the church is losing children. The debate revolves around why. Coupe comments that:

> There was a policy change in the late fifties. In 1957 two reports, one by the British Council of Churches and the other by the Free Church Federal Council, recommended that afternoon Sunday Schools should meet at the same time as the morning service.

The reports were taken seriously and, by 1970, 82 per cent of churches had Sunday School at the same time as morning worship. Alongside this, the overall attendance reduced radically. Coupe observes:

> It seems possible that the biggest single cause of church decline (which is particularly bad in Britain) was the moving of the old-style Sunday Schools to the morning service. It is possible that this change in policy caused the church to lose half its children

over one generation. The change did not stop the loss of children coming to church. In the long run, it made things worse.

It would be easy to conclude that Coupe's 'fifties freefall' was indeed the reason for the huge loss in Sunday School membership and to follow her to the logical conclusion: 'If church policy can do so much damage, then the reverse ought also to be true. Policy is easier to change than culture.' However, before that conclusion is adopted it is important to identify the factors that led to the British Council of Churches and the Free Church Federal Council making their initial recommendation. Part of it was stated by Coupe herself when she notes:

> Teachers who remember making the change say that action had been necessary. Recruiting teachers had been increasingly difficult once families had cars. The change provided welcome relief to overworked leaders. Soon ministers introduced rotas so teachers could themselves attend worship. Now they were on duty less often and for a shorter period of time.

The other contributing factor was the way Sunday School attendance had been dropping up to that point. The writers of the reports could be forgiven for resorting to crisis measures in an attempt to stop the exodus of children from the church. A related issue may have been the strong impression the Parish Communion Movement[7] had made since its formation in the 1950s. A strong emphasis was placed not only on the eucharistic service but also on the need to share the eucharistic service as a family. When consideration is given to Cliff's thirty-year time lag, it becomes clear that the policy decisions of the 1950s did not cause the huge decline that followed but instead were an attempt to try to salvage an already sinking ship.

The tragedy of the 1950s decision is that it turned many children from non-churchgoing homes away from the church. Whatever the reason for the policy change, the change had taken place. By 1977, 80 per cent of the Sunday morning children's groups were made up of children from church families.[8]

Nevertheless, against this backdrop of serious decline, some enterprising Sunday School practitioners had begun to experiment with the concept of the mid-week children's club (some even before the start of the Second World War). Cliff[9] comments:

> Those churches and Sunday Schools who began weeknight activities, play hours for beginners and primary children, adventure clubs for juniors found themselves winning a hearing

for the gospel. This was especially true of the new estates, where
a million new homes were built between the wars.

These were, at the same time, the forerunners of the Children's Outreach
Project, and the re-emergence of Raikes' Sunday Schools, in that they had
embedded within them many of the principles that characterized Raikes'
early model, including the definitive feature that they existed primarily for
the communication of Christian values to non-church children.[10]

ALL-AGE WORSHIP

During the mid-1970s and into the 1980s, new champions arose to take up
the call for families to worship together. Children's workers such as Ian
Smale (Ishmael, figure 2.1)[11] began advocating the family praise party, a
church service designed for the whole family. Through the 1980s, Ishmael
became associated with Spring Harvest[12] children's groups and as such

had a significant impact on the way churches from
primarily Evangelical Anglican, Baptist and New
Churches conducted their children's work. Many
churches were already experimenting with all-age
worship services, and the methods modelled by
Ishmael allowed churches to improve the quality
of those services. He worked hard to encourage
churches to run all their services with all ages
together. The result was that many churches adopted
a compromise policy of running one Sunday a month
as an all-age worship service. This is a practice that
many churches, particularly Anglican churches,
have continued to implement into the twenty-first
century. Nevertheless, there is a difficulty with this.

Fig 2.1 Ian Smale

Where there are charismatic figures to lead such all-age worship events,
the events are generally a positive experience, but those who can run all-
age worship services to the satisfaction of all who attend are rare. In many
churches, parents, children and members without children find this the
least beneficial service they attend. Many churches are unclear as to their
reasons for running all-age services at all, and others comment that it gives
their Sunday School teachers a week off.[13]

The Church of England's report *Children in the Way* (1988) promoted
a new way of thinking about the church's children, based on what it termed
'the pilgrim church model'. In essence, it suggested that children were on

the same journey of faith as adults. Alongside this, it recommended losing the educational image of Sunday Schools. Groups became Sunday Club, Junior Church or some other name designed to avoid the word 'school', and they had leaders rather than teachers. However, this was little more than an exercise in relabelling and the product itself remained unchanged. Of more significance, the report suggested that the training of leaders and teachers should become a priority. It acknowledged that this area had been neglected for some time and backed this up with the recommendation that parishes provide realistic finance for resourcing and training children's leaders.[14]

The final Church of England report on children in the twentieth century, *All God's Children* (1991), was subtitled *Children's Evangelism in Crisis*. Its most useful contribution was to address the issue of whether Sunday was the best day to reach children and to affirm the important role of schools – in many ways paving the way for the 2001 Dearing Report. Nevertheless, the report contributed little and went widely unnoticed, possibly because it had no scheme for implementation.[15]

BILL WILSON AND THE METRO SUNDAY SCHOOL

Before moving on, there is one more champion of church-based children's work whose name may be compared with that of Raikes himself. His name is Bill Wilson (figure 2.2). Bill Wilson arrived in New York City from Davenport, Iowa, in 1979. His plan was to form a children's outreach club in Brooklyn. Wilson[16] writes:

> On the first Saturday, in June 1979, we had no idea what to expect. But that Saturday, there was a total of 1,010 kids. We did have a slight problem. The church[17] only seated three hundred. So we kept the other seven hundred outside and brought them inside in shifts. It was one of the happiest nightmares of my life.

Over the following decade, the children's club spawned a youth programme and an adult church. By the end of the twentieth century, Metro Sunday School (as the programme was named, although Sunday is the only day they do not run their children's programme!) had an average weekly attendance of over 20,000 children.[18] The programme consists of games, songs, stories and Bible lessons. All those who attend are given a prize of some description, usually confectionary of some sort, but often other prizes such as books are given. Wilson comments, 'The way we conduct Sunday School sessions is the result of thousands of errors. But without question, what we do today works.'[19]

Fig 2.2 Bill Wilson – Metro Ministries

There are other features of the Metro Sunday School that should be noted. The first is their programme to visit all the children who attend. Wilson[20] writes:

> If there is one key to the long-term success of our Sunday School it is the thousands of home visits that take place all week long – from the time the students return home from school until the sun goes down.

The second factor is the sponsorship programme that they run under the heading of 'This child is mine'. People from all over the world send gifts and cash to sponsor the children who live in some of the poorest conditions in New York City.

Finally, the teachers of the Metro Sunday School are drawn from all over the world. Many come to develop their teaching skills in some of the most difficult circumstances. Wilson writes of his staff, 'They must be people who are committed to give their lives to such a ministry. That may mean five or ten or twenty years; or maybe a lifetime.'[21]

This North American pattern is cited here because the survey findings illustrate clearly that a large percentage of the Children's Outreach Projects in the UK owe their existence, at least in part, to the influence of Bill Wilson and the Metro Sunday School pattern. In the latter part of the twentieth century and early part of the twenty-first century, the Metro programme had become the most used pattern for child evangelism in the UK. This has been due to the work of Bill Wilson[22] at conferences throughout the UK and to the visits of many UK children's workers to the New York programme. David, the leader of the Fraserburgh project, stated:

Because I was in charge of the Sunday School they sent me to a children's workers conference in Weston-Super-Mare and that's where I heard Bill Wilson and my heart really started to go towards unchurched kids.

Bernie, the leader of the Leeds project, referring to the formation of the project, stated:

At the same time as we were thinking that there was a visit to the city by Bill Wilson from Metro Ministries New York. After his visit, we put a sheet of paper at the back and said if anyone is interested in doing what Bill is suggesting with unchurched kids put your name here. We got a few churches out of that and started working with those churches.

MIDWEEK ATTENDANCE

Many of the largest Children's Outreach Projects have adopted the format and adhere to the visitation programme that accompanies it. Midweek projects throughout the UK have clubs based on the Metro programme.

Nevertheless, the emergence of the Children's Outreach Projects does not yet appear to be making significant impact on church attendance numbers (figure 2.3); the statistics for the last decade of the twentieth century appear bleak. Jackson[23] writes:

The decline shown by the Usual Sunday Attendance[24] figures in the number of children (defined as under 16s) attending church in the 1990s was double that of adults. Between one in three and one in four children disappeared from Sunday Church between 1990 and 2000. This decline has been going on for so long that there are now also far fewer young adults in church life. For every 100 children in Church of England churches in 1930 today there are nine.

In the paragraph before this, Jackson[25] sounds a warning against drawing optimism from midweek figures:

It is sometimes suggested that the actual decline in church attendance is not as steep as the Sunday figures suggest because there has been an increase in churchgoing on other days of the week. There is a much talk of changing patterns rather than declining totals. However, there is little evidence at the moment to support this.

However, two points need to be made. Firstly, there is clearly much confusion concerning the way the figures are collated. The definition of midweek attendance is 'those attending a church activity where there is a worship element'.[26] On this basis the large number of midweek children's clubs running a Metro Sunday School style programme should record weekly attendance for the church return, and the parents and toddlers group that has a Bible study over coffee while the children play should do likewise. It is probable that this is not happening in every case.

Secondly, despite concerns that the returns are not completely understood by members of the parish completing the forms, the midweek attendance figure is significant. Jackson[27] observes that in October 2000 the Sunday figure for children's attendance at Church of England churches was 300,000 and the midweek figure for Church of England churches was 155,000. There is no cause for excitement with the return also showing 23 per cent of Church of England churches have no children or young people at all, but it may be that midweek children's clubs are beginning to make their presence felt – even in statistical terms.[28]

The twentieth century closed with many parts of the church in the UK beginning to make the distinction between children from households with Christian parents and children from households without. Nevertheless, it is the twenty-first century that will show whether Children's Outreach Projects are able to exert influence over the figures.

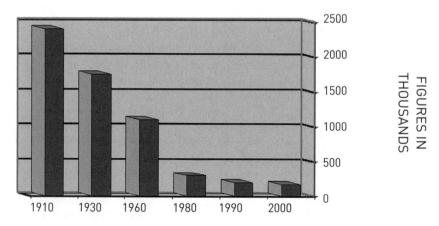

Fig 2.3 Decline in children's attendance on Sundays (Jackson 2002)

NOTES

1. *Towards the Conversion of England*.

2. The figures quoted from the 1998 church attendance survey only take into account Sunday attendance.

3. *British Weekly*, 25 September 1913

4. See Cliff (1986, p. 235).

5. 1965, p. 14.

6. *Children Adrift* (1949), *Children in the Way* (1988), *All God's Children* (1991).

7. The Parish Communion Movement of the 1950s was an attempt to gather church congregations together around the Eucharist. The motto of the movement became 'The Lord's Service on the Lord's day for the Lord's people'. It was an attempt to encourage all ages in all churches to celebrate a Eucharistic service on a weekly basis.

8. Compare Cliff (1986, p. 246).

9. 1986, p. 235.

10. Unfortunately, no statistics were collated for midweek children's activities for most of the twentieth century so there is no mechanism for evaluating just how successful these clubs really were.

11. Further information on the work of Ian Smale is contained within his books *The History of Ishmael* (1988) and *Angels with Dirty Faces* (1989) – republished as *Reclaiming a Generation* (2001).

12. According to its own website, 'Spring Harvest is an inter-denominational Christian organisation best known for its residential Christian conferences'.

13. This, of course, is a perfectly valid reason.

14. 1988, pp. 84–91.

15. Withers (2006, p. 23).

16. 1992, p. 44.

17. Bill Wilson had hired a Brooklyn-based Spanish church for use on Saturdays.

18. When I visited in Easter 1995 the weekly attendance total was just over 23,000. This is not the largest 'Sunday School' in the world – that honour goes to a similar programme in Mexico City where well over 30,000 children attend each week. Interestingly, the Mexico City programme was launched by a man who trained with Bill Wilson in New York City.

19. 1992, p. 66.

20. 1992, p. 67.

21. 1992, p. 70.

22. Bill Wilson seems to be one of those characters who are constantly surrounded by controversy. Nevertheless, there can be no denying the significant impact that he has had on child evangelism in the UK and throughout the world.

23. 2002, pp. 10–11.

24. Usual Sunday attendance figures are collated by Church of England churches to show average attendance on a given Sunday when there are no festivals or baptisms. An attempt to rationalize the process began from 2000 when churches were asked to record the average of attendance throughout October. The return showed an increase of 10 per cent from the figures presented in 1999. Either there are clear difficulties in collating the figures or remarkable church growth took place between 1999 and 2000; it is likely to be the former rather than the latter.

25. 2002, p. 10.

26. Definition given by Lynda Barley (Head of Research and Statistics for the Church of England).

27. 2002, p. 8.

28. Although Jackson suggests that the large number may be due to Harvest services in October, he acknowledges that this is guesswork. The weekly attendance figures being produced in the early twenty-first century would suggest that Jackson's guess was wrong!

Chapter 3

CHILD EVANGELISM IN THE TWENTY-FIRST CENTURY

Having looked at the historical model of child evangelism, this chapter develops an overview of child evangelism in the twenty-first century using a self-completion questionnaire (Appendix 2). From the findings of this questionnaire, it will be possible to identify child evangelism projects for further study.

THE QUESTIONNAIRE

The following children's advisors and organizations were asked to distribute the questionnaires to their respective networks:

- Anglican National Children's Advisor
- The Methodist Children's Advisor
- Pentecostal National Children's Directors (Elim and Assemblies of God)
- Baptist National Children's Director
- Scripture Union
- New Wine

The Anglican national children's advisor sent the questionnaire to the diocesan children's advisors and invited them to send the questionnaire on to the Children's Outreach Projects that they were aware of within their diocese; this had varying degrees of success and was dependent on how well the diocesan advisor knew the churches within their diocese. The Methodist advisor held a directory of Methodist children's workers and sent a blanket e-mail to them, with a good response. New Wine and Scripture Union followed similar patterns. The Baptist children's director distributed a small number to those to whom he felt the questionnaire particularly applied; the result was a good return on those he distributed. The Pentecostal children's directors (Assemblies of God and Elim) had no formal e-mail distribution lists for their networks, so distributed informally.[1] All but three of the respondents answered by e-mail; of the three, one did not run a Children's Outreach Project, and the other two included e-mail contact information for future contact.

Several projects were listed as ecumenical in the return. These projects were picked up because one or more of the ecumenical partnership received the questionnaire through their denomination or network – for example, the ecumenical project in Leeds received the questionnaire because the project is based in the Elim Pentecostal Church.

ANALYSIS

Approximately 1,600 questionnaires were distributed, of which 127 were returned. Of those returned, 97.6 per cent were involved in running Children's Outreach Projects.[2] This 97.6 per cent represented over 2,000 children's workers, who had contact with 19,548 boys and girls primarily from unchurched homes.

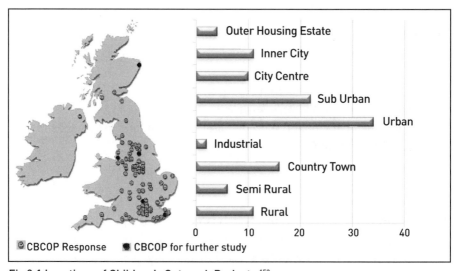

Fig 3.1 Locations of Children's Outreach Projects [152]

The Children's Outreach Projects were from a wide geographical area and there was no statistical distinction in their location. It is appropriate to conclude that Children's Outreach Projects are found in all parts of the country[4] and all localities (figure 3.1).

In general, the more densely populated areas have the largest Children's Outreach Projects, with the largest projects being in Liverpool, Leeds and Slough/Windsor. However, there is an exception that ensures that this is not a firm rule: Fraserburgh in north-east Scotland has a child population of 1,200; the Children's Outreach Project based there, run by the Elim church under the name Powerhouse, is one of the largest projects in the UK with more than 200 children. The point is reinforced by the fact that the Elim project is one of two projects of similar size within this town.[5]

On a typical Friday evening, over a third of the population of Fraserburgh is attending Children's Outreach Projects![6]

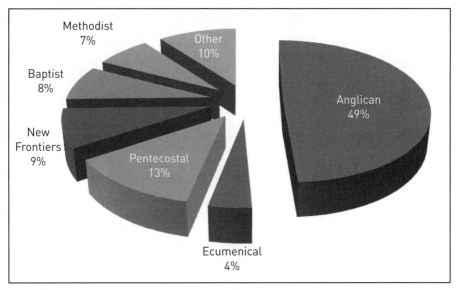

Fig 3.2 Denominations of respondents

The projects analysed were primarily weekly children's clubs, but there were also special events and holiday play schemes represented. Of the respondent Children's Outreach Projects 49 per cent were Anglican,[7] 13 per cent were Pentecostal (Elim or Assemblies of God), 9 per cent were Newfrontiers,[8] 8 per cent were Baptists and 7 per cent were Methodist. The 'others' included those who described themselves as Free Church, G12,[9] Independent or Community Church (figure 3.2).

Nevertheless, when the attendance figures at the Children's Outreach Projects are considered, a different picture begins to emerge (figure 3.3): 30 per cent of those who attend a Children's Outreach Project attend a Newfrontiers Children's Outreach Project. Four of the top ten most-attended Children's Outreach Projects are projects of Newfrontiers churches. Although the mainline denominations do not record high attendance figures in their own right, ecumenical projects, in which they are partners, do record high attendance. The Leeds ecumenical project in particular, which is partnered by eighteen churches, records regular attendance of 400 children.

Admission fees are charged by 42 per cent of the Children's Outreach Projects, with £3 being the largest fee. However, there is no discernable pattern as to which projects charge: some inner city projects charge, others

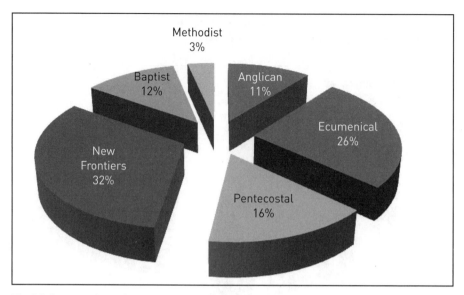

Fig 3.3 Average Attendance at Children's Outreach Projects

do not; some rural projects charge, others do not. The decision to charge also has no correlation with the number of full- or part-time leaders, whether or not the children are brought on buses to the project, or the church's denomination. The decision to charge and the amount to charge appears to be completely random.

Leaders of 19 per cent of the projects attended training courses organized by their denomination (figure 3.4). Of those who attended training organized by non-denominational organizations, 16 per cent attended the New Wine Children's Conference and 14 per cent attended the Children' Ministry Conference organized by Kingsway. The events organized jointly by Kidz Klub Slough and Kidz Klub Liverpool, which are specifically designed for Children's Outreach Projects, were also attended by 14 per cent. Scripture Union training events were attended by 7 per cent of the Children's Outreach Projects, possibly suggesting that Scripture Union is still seen to be more focused on ministry to churched children. Interestingly, 9 per cent of respondents attended courses organized by secular agencies; this form of training was primarily concerned with health and safety and first aid. However, leaders of 8 per cent of the Children's Outreach Projects had not attended any form of training in the last twelve months.

Although there was some significant flexibility in the overall programmes – with such diverse elements as sports of various kinds, drama/theatre skills, face-painting, table tennis, pool/snooker, café-style

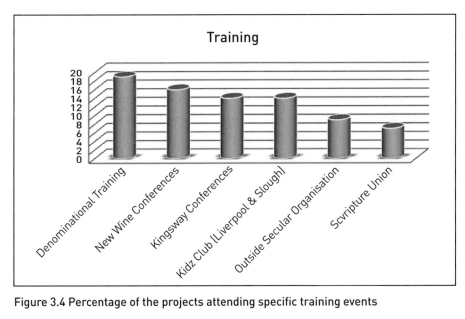

Figure 3.4 Percentage of the projects attending specific training events

events and craft activities – there were some consistencies (figure 3.5): 96 per cent of the projects featured prayer and Christian teaching, and 90 per cent of the projects included singing – although the Children's Outreach Projects tended to refer to singing as 'praise and worship'.

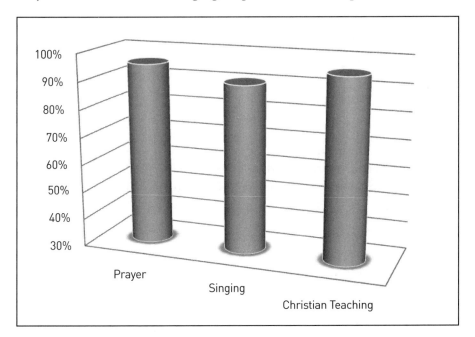

Fig 3.5 Programme content

Over half the projects surveyed (56 per cent) write their own curriculum material at some point, but they tend to subsidize this with purchased materials (figure 3.6). Of the materials purchased, 29 per cent purchased Scripture Union materials, although these were split between several Scripture Union products including, Supa Clubs, Eye Level, Jaffa and modified versions of holiday club materials such as *Seaside Rock*; 26 per cent use the *Fusion/Impact/Detonate* series produced by Monarch; and 23 per cent use the Metro Ministries material produced by Bill Wilson or the Anglicized version produced by Kidz Klub Liverpool.

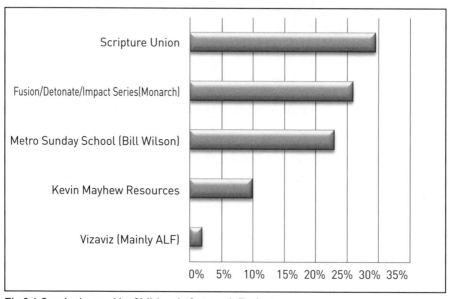

Fig 3.6 Curricula used by Children's Outreach Projects

The response to the question 'Do you run any social action projects alongside, or as part of, the Children's Outreach Project?' was exceptionally positive. The following gives an overview of the diversity and creativity in the answers:

- Parents and Toddlers
- Advice Centres
- Family Drop ins
- Events for Parents
- Breakfast Club and After School Clubs
- Drama or Dance Clubs
- Coffee Shops
- Play based activities
- Community Clean Up projects
- Charity Shops
- Family social events, including Easter egg hunts and Christmas parties.

Among the wide range of social action projects, several projects were clearly of the empowerment type modelled by Raikes. A leader of a free church project on the south coast, as well as listing coffee bars run during the Children's Outreach Project, and a parent and toddler group, also listed a range of projects that cover a variety of classes in practical skills such as 'parenting, knitting, computing, etc.'. The various advice centres and homework clubs listed were also a clear indication that the Children's Outreach Projects were involved in empowerment projects.

The survey question that asked the groups to identify areas of uniqueness also produced interesting responses. A leader of an inner-city project commented on a project he runs alongside the children's club for young families:

> It is not just a parent and toddler group, but aims to instil Christian values and the gospel into children (and secondarily their parents) from birth. The group uses Christian songs and teaches Bible lessons using puppets. It has become very popular and now has three groups at two bases with up to 50 children coming to each session (primarily unchurched families).

The leader of another inner city project commented:

> Ours is a very long-standing project which encompasses the whole family. At the same time as our kids' club, the parents are next door having a cooked breakfast and making friends with other workers.

A leader in Buckinghamshire commented on 'The Coffee Boys', a team that erects a gazebo outside the Children's Outreach Project, serving coffee and biscuits to the parents as they come and pick up their children (she comments that parents are now petitioning for bacon and egg rolls!).

The Children's Outreach Projects ranged in size from average weekly attendance of six to average weekly attendance of 500. The largest percentage of Children's Outreach Projects average attendance of 20–49 children (figure 3.7).

There were some interesting responses to the question that asked how long the project had been running. Westminster Chapel, London, commented that they had been running Children's Outreach Projects since 1840! However, they then went on to state that their Children's Outreach Project had been running in its present form for only three years. Over half

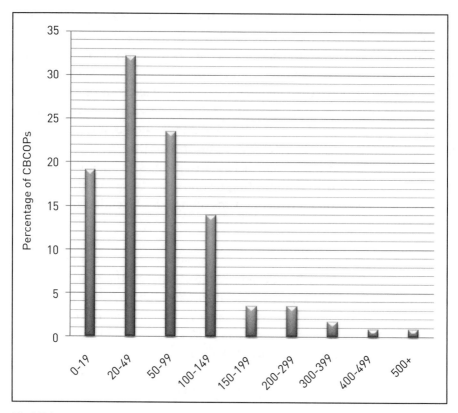

Fig 3.7 Average Attendance at Children's Outreach Projects

the projects surveyed (52 per cent) have been running for less than five years, 35 per cent for between five and ten years, and 13 per cent for over ten years.

Of the top ten most attended projects, 80 per cent are between five and ten years old. There are two tentative observations that can be made regarding this fact. Firstly, the length of time a project has been running may have no bearing on the size of that project. Secondly, since the majority of the largest projects have only been in existence for up to a decade, it is very difficult to assess the long-term impact on the local church. The large project in Fraserburgh has been running for more than a decade, so some assumptions were made based on this project.

On first inspection the number of buses used to pick up children in relation to the size of project does not produce any surprises (figure 3.8). All of the Children's Outreach Projects with attendance over 200 use buses to transport the children to their projects. Liverpool, Leeds and Slough all use six buses each to transport the children to their projects and collect children from a wide geographical area. Interestingly, over half the projects with 150–200 children do not use buses to achieve their attendance figures. The figures suggest that it is possible to build projects of up to 200 children without the need to provide transport, although the actuality is undoubtedly more complex than this. To gather 200 children in a rural setting may seem impossible without transport; however, it is likely that those who live in rural situations are used to transporting their children to various events, and the Children's Outreach Project is simply another of those events. By the same consideration, 200 children may live within easy walking distance of the Children's Outreach Project in an inner city, but safety considerations may make parents reluctant to allow their children to walk.

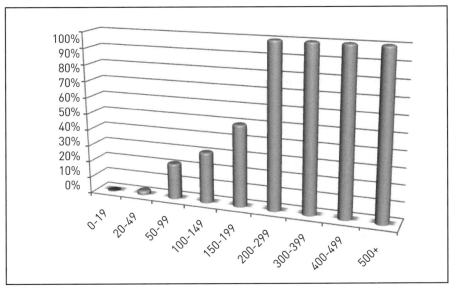

Fig 3.8 Percentage of projects using buses by size of project

Just over a third of the Children's Outreach Projects acknowledged an outside influence that had a part in the establishment of the Children's Outreach Project (figure 3.9). Of this third, 39 per cent pointed to Bill Wilson of Metro Sunday School as a direct influence, 34 per cent to Frontline Church Liverpool,[10] 21 per cent to Scripture Union and 7 per cent to New Wine. The fact that the Children's Outreach Project at Frontline Liverpool itself exists primarily because of the influence of Bill Wilson suggests that a large percentage of the Children's Outreach Projects in the UK owe their existence, at least in part, to the influence of Bill Wilson and the Metro Sunday School pattern.

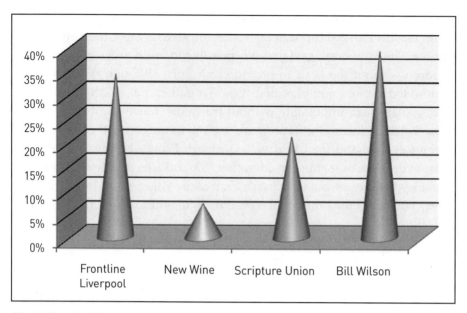

Fig 3.9 Outside influences that played a part in the establishment of the Children's Outreach Project

Contact outside the Children's Outreach Project fell into the categories of small groups, e-mail, home visits, postal contact and school visits (figure 3.10). It is noteworthy that of these forms of contact, the highest is contact through school visit; 69 per cent of the Children's Outreach Projects are taking the time to engage with their local schools. This is primarily through school assemblies, although one project had taken this a stage further; commenting on their work in local schools (both church schools and non-church schools), they wrote:

> We operate *cell* groups, which include welcome, worship, study of the word, witness and prayer. We also do *Holy Loitering* – generally being available to pupils, mentoring, pastoral support, sharing God's love whenever and wherever.

Just over a third of the Children's Outreach Projects used conventional mailing (as opposed to e-mail, which was only used by 7 per cent of the projects) and home visits to keep in contact with the children outside the Children's Outreach Project environment. However, what was interesting to see was how these forms of contact were used by the larger projects.

The larger the project, the less likely they were to use any form of contact other than school assemblies and home visits (figure 3.11). Of

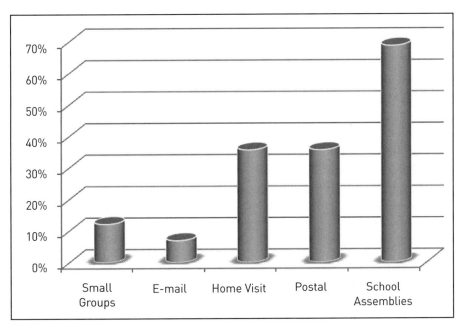

Fig 3.10 Contact outside of Children's Outreach Project

projects with over 150 children, 80 per cent were involved in home visits, and 100 per cent of the projects with over 200 children had made home visits a priority.

The staffing of the projects was also considered in the survey. Firstly,

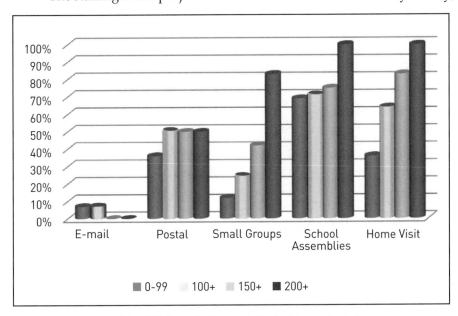

Fig 3.11 Contact outside of Children's Outreach Project by project size

the survey revealed that 48 per cent of the churches running a Children's Outreach Project employed a full-time worker to run it; 23 per cent of the remaining projects employed a part-time worker.[11] The projects between them accounted for 1,950 volunteers. All the projects with over 150 children employed a full-time worker. What cannot be assumed is that employing a full-time staff member guarantees high attendance. Several projects recorded a full-time member of staff alongside low attendance at the Children's Outreach Project.

More than half (57 per cent) said that children had moved from the Children's Outreach Project to the youth service in the last year and 56 per cent said that people had joined the adult church in the last year as a direct result of the Children's Outreach Project. When this question is put to the projects with over 150 children in attendance, 81 per cent reported that people had joined the main adult congregation because of the Children's Outreach Project, and 100 per cent reported children moving on to a Christian youth service from the Children's Outreach Project.

CONCLUSION

One of the objectives of the survey was to identify projects for further study, some as intense contacts and one for prolonged ethnographic study. After giving due consideration to the responses, it became clear that there were a significant minority (five) that had extraordinary weekly attendance and also had high indicators for all other areas – for example, number of leaders, social involvement, contact outside Children's Outreach Project, families joining the church. These projects recorded the following attendance figures on their survey returns:[12]

Fraserburgh project:	Fraserburgh, Scotland (Elim)	200
Slough and Windsor project:	Slough & Windsor (Kings Church International)	300
Leeds project:	Leeds (Ecumenical Project)	400
Hastings project:	Hastings (New Frontiers)	190
Liverpool project:	Liverpool (Frontline Church)	500

It was evident that these projects should form the basis of the third research phase. The survey also generated additional data of interest – for example, the way the larger projects use buses to transport the children to the projects, and the seemingly disproportionate high attendance clubs that certain denominations have. These factors and others highlighted by the survey are considered further in Part 2.

Notes

1. Elim have since appointed a National Children's Director who has in mind to build a network of children's workers. Assemblies of God have a distribution list for mail, but not electronic mail.

2. The high number of respondents running Children's Outreach Projects is explained by the fact that those not running Children's Outreach Projects chose not to respond.

3. Approximate location of respondent Children's Outreach Project – the primary aim of this chart is to show the spread of Children's Outreach Projects throughout the UK.

4. There were no returns from Wales. It is uncertain what can be deduced from this; it is probable that the questionnaires did not find their way to Welsh projects.

5. The other project is an Assemblies of God project that meets two streets away!

6. The study of Fraserburgh and the effects of these two children's clubs would make an interesting ethnography in its own right.

7. Since Anglican churches outnumber all other denominations in the UK, both in number of buildings and in attendance, this figure should not come as a surprise.

8. Newfrontiers describes itself as 'A worldwide family of 500 churches with a passionate commitment to building the church according to New Testament principles'.

9. Strictly speaking, G12 is a way of structuring church around small groups (cells) rather than a particular denomination.

10. A leader running a children's club in West Yorkshire went as far as to comment, 'I love the Frontline guys – I owe my own ministry, vision and equipping to them more than almost anyone else.'

11. This figure represented the curate in many Anglican churches who had been given the oversight of the Children's Outreach Project as part of their responsibilities.

12. The figures recorded are those stated on the questionnaire. The majority of the projects had similar attendance figures when I visited to the figures they recorded on the questionnaire. The Slough and Windsor project was the only project to record lower attendance on the questionnaire than I saw on my visit. The attendance on my initial visits was as follows:

Fraserburgh project: 190 (5 May 2007)

Slough and Windsor project: 315 (14 July 2007) rising to 450 (8 December 2007)

Leeds project: 350 (23 June 2007)

Hastings project: 150 (13 October 2007)

Liverpool project: 270 (24 June 2007)

Chapter 4

FOUR KEY PROJECTS

Having gained an overview of child evangelism in the twenty-first century, this chapter will now look at four key projects in detail.

INTRODUCTION

An initial visit to the five projects in the third research phase suggested that each of them would make for an interesting ethnography. Nevertheless, the next phase of research was to interview the leaders[1] and conduct visits (intense contacts) with only four of these projects (Phase 3a), setting aside the fifth project for the more detailed ethnography (Phase 3b). For that reason, a decision was needed on which project should form the ethnography of Phase 3b. The Fraserburgh project had the highest ratio of children involved in the Children's Outreach Project to size of population, and an effective practice for incorporating the graduates of the Children's Outreach Project into the youth programme, Sunday church and back into the leadership programme of the Children's Outreach Project itself. The Leeds project provided a well-presented and organized programme in an ecumenical setting, with large numbers of children from diverse backgrounds. The Hastings project had a unique emphasis on reaching parents as well as children, and many parents accompanied their children to the project on Saturday mornings. The Liverpool project appeared to show the largest attendance figures on the survey, although an initial visit showed that actual numbers were lower; however, it was led by a multitalented, charismatic leader whose communication to the children was exceptional. This alone would make the Liverpool project worthy of study. The Liverpool project is also the most influential of the Children's Outreach Projects,[2] with a strategy to promote Children's Outreach Projects throughout the UK. Its leader's ability to promote was shown graphically at the 2007 Conservative Party Conference where he stood in front of a full auditorium and explained the needs of the inner city.

Nevertheless, the Slough and Windsor project was selected as the setting for the detailed ethnography. The Slough and Windsor project had elements of all the above incorporated within its programmes, in terms of leadership development, schools impact, development of the youth programme from the Children's Outreach Project and the overall impact of the project on the church and the community, and its increasing influence and training of other Children's Outreach Projects. Alongside this, it also had a small-group programme for discipleship and development.

Field notes were collected over one to three visits (primarily in the setting of the main programme, but also including the journey on the bus to and from the Children's Outreach Project, where appropriate) and written up as a single event. It was these notes and the interviews with the project leaders that form the basis of the analysis.

The field notes for the Slough and Windsor project were gathered over multiple visits; however, as in Phase 3a, they were compiled and written up as one event but with footnotes to show the weekly changes. Because Phase 3b also looked at the complementary activities to the main children's programme – school assemblies, home visits and small groups – multiple locations and contexts were recorded. To this was added other data – material such as interviews with several leaders of the project and with the leader of the church of which the Slough and Windsor project is a part. Alongside this, field notes collated by others[3] were also incorporated.

The in-depth analysis of the projects was kept for the interpretation section of Chapters 6 to 9, allowing Chapters 4 and 5 to deal with those elements of the projects that were unique to them, more basic analysis of the projects, and cross-case analysis. Chapter 4 explores this by way of intense contacts and Chapter 5 by a more prolonged ethnography.

THE FRASERBURGH PROJECT

Project name: Powerhouse
Location: Fraserburgh, Scotland
Denomination affiliation: Elim Pentecostal Churches
Leader: David Ritchie

Fig 4.1 Fishing Port at Fraserburgh

The Fraserburgh project meets in a town in the extreme north-east corner of Scotland. It is forty miles north of Aberdeen and has a population of 12,216 (2007), making it the second largest population centre in Aberdeenshire.

It has the largest shellfish port in Europe; it is also a major whitefish port and a busy commercial harbour. Unemployment is below the national average. Fishing is the town's main industry with many of the subsidiary industries being linked to this – for example, it has several large fish-processing plants and one of Europe's most modern ship-repair facilities for fishing vessels.

Although the town has many commendable attributes, it has received adverse publicity in recent years due to the size of the drug problem in the area, with some reports suggesting that it is the drugs capital of Scotland and the heroin capital of Europe.[4]

There are approximately 1,200 children of primary school age in the area and there are two Children's Outreach Projects, each with an average attendance of 200 children. They are run by two separate free churches that are two streets apart. Both projects take place on Friday evenings. On a typical Friday evening over 30 per cent of the primary school aged children in the town are in Children's Outreach Projects.

One of the Children's Outreach Projects was started by David in 1996. Writing of its beginnings David commented:

> I heard Bill Wilson speak at a conference and my heart really started to go towards unchurched kids. I came home from that conference and God started to put things on my heart. I looked around at the places that God was laying on my heart. I then gathered about 40 people around me who were enthusiastic about seeing things not just happen in church kids, but in unchurched kids, because the church I was in was predominantly church kids. A new church started with 40 people to reach unchurched kids – we had more than 200 children on the first night.

The Fraserburgh project takes place on Friday evenings at 7 p.m. during term time.[5]

Analysis

In interview, David, the leader of the Fraserburgh project, was clear that the project's aims were to nurture the children in an age-appropriate way and to bring those children through to be leaders in their own right. These twin aspects of nurture and leadership development permeate the whole project. Of this first aim, David used the metaphor of a nest of chicks and the brooding mother:

> Everything that a nest speaks of is what I want for these kids, until one day when they are older we begin to push them out of the nest and into the deeper things of God... It speaks of warmth, so when the kids come we want them to feel warm and accepted. It speaks of strength and protection – I protect the kids that come. The mother feeds the chicks – I like to feed them on the things of God, Bible stories, life issues. The mother loves those little chicks and we love these kids.

Some of these concepts were restated in interview with Miriam, a Fraserburgh project leader who commented, 'The main reason for the Fraserburgh project is to reach unchurched kids and for me it's about showing them love. We exist to show the love of Jesus to these kids.' These emotive words recurred in many of the conversations I had at this project. David, when asked about his motivation speaks of 'my heart going out to unchurched kids'. David recounted the story of a new child:

> I was in Sunday school one day and I stepped in for a teacher and I was taking the register. The sixth kid was new and I asked the kid his name, and he told me his name, and I asked him where he lived, and when he told me where he lived. The other kids laughed, and something inside me broke that day and is probably still broken, and they laughed because he came from the poorer part of town, where they didn't come from, he didn't go to the same schools that they went to, he didn't have the same lifestyle that they had, and I believe with all my heart, God allowed me to feel what he felt.

David suggested that the Friday night project is 'easy stuff, gentle stuff; there are times of worship but we are waiting until the kids get older'. Certainly, the programme reflects the metaphor of chicks in a nest. The talks covered various topics, but the two most easily recognized were discussions on the difference between Bible stories and fairy stories and the need to avoid behaving foolishly.

This model of Christian nurture was further shown in the Saturday morning programme that involved free play[6] – activities such as bouncy castles, football, basketball, face-painting, dance workshops. David sums up the philosophy succinctly when he stated, 'This is about more than Jesus loved you and died on a cross for you. Sowing seeds is about showing care, concern, love, warmth and acceptance. Saturday morning is quality time of getting to know the children.'

The transfer system from the children's programme to the youth programme also shared these 'nest' characteristics. There is an overlap of a year where children are allowed to continue in the children's programme (the nest), but may also begin to attend the youth programme (learning to fly). It means that children still have a place of security within the children's programme while they get used to the different world of the youth group.

While there is much evidence that nurture is a major part of the Fraserburgh project programme, there is also a strong emphasis on young people and training them as potential leaders. David commented:

> We are very big on the kids who come through the programme as soon as they are old enough – gone to secondary school – in

bringing them back as junior leaders... On Monday night we have a programme which is worship, prayer, ministry, group studies of the Bible – discipleship. Also taking them on the road and stuff,[7] giving them an opportunity to do stuff.

While child evangelism was an important factor here, it was clear that the training of young people as new leaders was also important. However, a more careful analysis suggested that not only was the training of young people as leaders important to the Fraserburgh project, everything else was subservient to this agenda. I recorded in my field notes:

At 3.30 p.m. the room begins to fill, not with children, it will be some time before they arrive, but with primarily young people. Teenagers who have come straight from school, the majority wearing their school uniform. Over the course of the next hour the sound system will spring into life, blasting 'Jesus you are the Light of the World'.[8] Microphone leads emerge from boxes, and a teenage boy who clearly knows what he is doing assembles leads to microphones and positions them expertly. School uniforms are replaced by T-shirts and sweatshirts festooned with the logo of this Children's Outreach Project. Chairs that were stacked around the sides are assembled into three columns facing the front with a circle of chairs gathered at the back. In all, just over 230 chairs are set up. Disco lights are set on the stage and multicoloured shapes flicker on the walls, shapes that are enhanced by the addition of a smoke machine.

Fig 4.2 A teenage leader at the Fraserburgh project prepares the prize table

Three teenage girls spread a golden tablecloth over a table at the front right hand side of the hall. It is the prize table. It is adorned with activity books, stationery sets, art equipment, sandals, skipping ropes, money boxes, frisbees, sport bags, games, umbrellas, goalkeeper gloves, kites, children's jewellery – the items are arranged and rearranged as the girls debate the most attractive setup (figure 4.2). It is all happening in accordance with a well-orchestrated plan that I as the observer am not privy to. At no point is it directed, no one is telling anyone else what to do. This is clearly a well-practised procedure. Everyone knows what needs doing, and it is done – occasionally there is a shout of 'David, where does this go?' There is no sense of this being a chore. These teenagers are serving this project, but they are laughing, chatting and enjoying while they do so.

The Fraserburgh project was a training ground for teenagers, but there was an element of co-dependency. The Fraserburgh project was practically run by the teenagers. David stated:

My young people are very much aware that they get freedom, I'm out nearly every night with my young people; before every event that we do they know that they've got to set things up and get things organized.

There were adults present in the Fraserburgh project, but their role was to train the teenagers in the task of ministering to the children and to ensure that the teenagers were provided for. For example, a group of adults arrived at 4 p.m. but went straight to the kitchen; they were there to feed the teenagers, not to play specific roles in the programme itself.

David's commitment to his young people was clear. The children go home by 9 p.m. but David stayed on with the young people until after 11 p.m. They went to a local all-night bakery together, they ate, they talked, they played football and they sat in corners strumming guitars.

This subservience to the primary goal of training leaders was never more notable than in the children's programme itself. There was a difference when David was not the person at the front. The children were more restless, the direction less precise. When challenged on this, David commented:

If I do everything, then leaders can feel unused and their own gifting is never developed. Therefore I have made a conscious decision to sacrifice the programme a little in order to allow and train people to do what I do. This will eventually benefit us as we look to send teams out into local villages to plant similar Children's Outreach Projects. How can they learn if they are not given a chance?

David restated this when asked what were the most exciting thing he had experienced in the Fraserburgh project. He responded, 'The joy for me is when people take ownership of it. The biggest joy is seeing someone who came as a five-year-old and who are now fifteen and standing up there and doing the story.' If more evidence were needed that the goal was primary leadership development, at the half-way point half the leaders present, primarily teenagers, left the room. They were retiring to the downstairs room to prepare the following week's programme. David explained:

Because of the success of our junior leader programme, we have more leaders than we need. So we have two teams, one team will be out preparing next week's programme and one team will be running this week's programme.

The children's programme itself was used to suggest to the children that they can, and should, be teenage leaders in this project. At the end of his talk to the children, David asked:

Who would like to be a leader here? For every leader that is here, one has left. They made a choice. They chose to walk away. Tonight is your opportunity to choose. Let's close our eyes. If you want to choose God, don't look around, just stand.

David commented, 'It's not about the event, it's about the process.' There was clearly a very definite process of bringing children from the children's programme into the youth programme and into the church. The Fraserburgh project has cultivated this desire to be a leader. David highlighted the situation:

We have one guy who was in hospital last week because he broke his leg on a trampoline and he's lying in the hospital and he's saying to the nurses, I can't be here, I need to be somewhere at 6.30 to pick some kids up. That guy has had a horrendous upbringing, but I've just made him a junior leader, he's waited for years for that. He's just like lots of kids who come through our programme – you

ask them what they want to be when they're older and they'll say
they want to be junior leaders.

There was also a real sense that this was a church vision to draw young
people through the programme and, through a process of involving
them and giving them appropriate responsibility, see them added to the
church. The senior minister was present throughout the whole evening,
but there was no suggestion that he was checking up on his workers. When
questioned, he was clear that the Children's Outreach Project is an integral
part of the church and the Sunday congregation reflects this. On an average
Sunday evening the church congregation numbers approximately 120
people, David estimates that 80 per cent of those gathered are young people
and that the majority came through the Children's Outreach Project.

The goals of the Fraserburgh project were being achieved. At 11 p.m.
on the Friday evening, with the church building still full of teenage leaders,
David began to point to various individuals. He explained how some have
come out of situations of extreme domestic violence. Others had parents
who were drug addicts. Many of them were unchurched children aged
five and six when they first attended the project in 1996. They had been
working hard since 3 p.m.; they were leaders in the children's programme
that had nurtured them. In David's words, 'This is more than a children's
club. This is about much more than the children.' Some of the graduates are
now training to be church leaders at theological college; others are already
leading churches in their own right.[9] Throughout 2008, David launched
several new Children's Outreach Projects in nearby villages, led by the
young people he had been training over the previous years.

Fig 4.3 A teenage leader after leaving the gunge tank

THE LEEDS PROJECT

Project name: *Kids Klub*
Location: Leeds, England
Denomination affiliation: Ecumenical
Leader: Bernie Fell

Fig 4.4 Part of the catchment area for the Leeds ecumenical project

The Leeds project is set in a northern English city. According the 2001 census, the urban area in which the project functions has a population of 443,247 and is one of England's core cities. Like many other cities, the crime rate is above the national average.[10] Leeds is regarded as the fastest growing city in the UK and has a diverse economy with the service sector now more dominant than the city's manufacturing industries. New tertiary industries such as retail, call centres, offices and media have contributed to a high rate of economic growth since the early 1990s. Nearly 100,000 people work in financial and business services.

The strength of the economy is further indicated in many parts of the city by the low unemployment rate.[11] However, these are not the areas that the Leeds project targets. The Leeds project works primarily with children in the inner city, characterized by its streets of dense, terraced housing in the north and 1960s high-rise housing blocks in the east. Some parts experienced rioting as recently as 2001. The areas house both large Asian and sizeable Afro-Caribbean communities, but there is also a strong Irish contingent. The areas in which the Leeds project operates suffer the social problems typical of similar areas throughout the UK.

The Leeds project began life in 1999 with one church running a children's programme. The programme grew to approximately 100 children, but the church building was not big enough to accommodate any more. Bernie, the leader of the Leeds project explained how the problem became an opportunity:

> We were at our limit with the building and also at our limit with workers. We had a team of about 20. So we started to ask and think what else could we do, there was no hall big enough and there were loads more kids out there. That's when we started to explore working with other churches, and we looked for a model of churches working together. But there wasn't one. At the same time as we were thinking, there was a visit to the city by Bill Wilson from Metro Ministries New York. After his visit we put a sheet of paper at the back and said if anyone's interested in doing what Bill is suggesting with unchurched kids put your name here. We got a few churches out of that and started working with those churches. It took about a year of planning [from February 1999 to March 2000] until we eventually launched a city-wide kids' club in March 2000. We started with one group, but that grew very quickly, so now we do two groups, one downstairs in the main church hall for 8 to 11s and one in the upstairs hall for 4 to 7s.[12]

On 4 March 2000 the Leeds project met for the first time. It takes place on Saturday mornings and is situated in the city centre, only a few hundred metres from shopping centres, car parks, bustling shoppers and diligent retailers. The building it uses belongs to a local free church which meets there on Sundays. It is loaned to the project free of charge – the team also has permanent offices based there – but only a few of the leaders attend this particular church on Sunday. This is an ecumenical project. Eighteen different churches have invested people or finance (or both) in the running of this weekly event.

Analysis

The programme at the Leeds project was well themed.[13] There were twenty-five minutes of songs, during which the children become quite restless, but the communication of the Christian message (from Matthew 7) flowed seamlessly from one leader to another, with the children sitting attentively throughout.[14] The project was led by Bernie who stated in interview, 'I've been here since day one, I am the founder.' It was a well-polished operation and it was clear from observation and interview that Bernie was not just the founder; she was also the director of this project. There were undoubtedly co-leaders: Sarah looked after the children aged eight to eleven, Laura the five to sevens, and Lizzie looked after schools ministry. Nevertheless, Bernie was clearly the overall leader and she ran the project with careful observation to detail. She commented:

> If someone is doing some teaching, then they'll practise the teaching, and they'll get the teaching okayed – we set that up early on, people know that their teaching will be critiqued before they do it. Musicians will be practising. Dramas will be rehearsed. All this between 8.30 and 9.00 a.m. Volunteers are asked to be here at 8.30 a.m. at the latest.

This was partly because Bernie sees the communication of the Christian message as important, but also because she understands that the whole project communicates and therefore appearances are important. As one of the buses[15] returned from collecting the children, one of the younger leaders was leaning against a wall; Bernie instructed her not to do it – she was supposed to be up and attentive, ready to greet the children.

Fig 4.5 Feedback from the Leeds project website

The Leeds project was a multilayered project. The Saturday morning programme represented only part of the Leeds project; it was supplemented by a weekly programme of visits to all the children on the registers[16] and regular input into the city's schools. Of the visiting, Bernie commented, 'They are making relationships, so to a child the visitors are the most important people, not who is on the stage doing the mad stuff, it's the people who are spending time with them every week.'

It was difficult to believe that these leaders were from eighteen different churches, such was the sense of community between them. These were not people who were new to each other (although there were some recent additions); this was an established team whose members looked after each other well, and it was clear that denominational doctrinal differences had been laid aside to form a cohesive, functional group. Bernie commented, 'The ecumenical nature is a plus. It has brought unity across the churches. Leaders will recommend the nearest church, not just theirs.'

There is a wide range of positive outcomes in running this form of project ecumenically, in terms of being able to recruit workers from a wider field and in terms of funding.[17] Nevertheless, there are difficulties highlighted, primarily in terms of following the children up when they are too old to attend the project. When I asked Bernie about this, she commented:

> We've got a few young people who came through to be leaders, a few but not many... lots of people are critical when they ask this question, but I really felt God say work with the kids, and it's God's responsibility what happens to them. We do what we can do.

The response was informative; on initial examination, it could be assumed that the ecumenical nature of the project makes it difficult to transition the children into youth projects or into the church. Despite the assertion that 'We recommend the nearest church', it is unlikely that an eleven-year-old is going to walk into a church and join a Sunday morning congregation without some mechanism to get them there. However, Bernie's comments suggested that they disconnect with the children when they move to secondary school, not by accident, but by design. The Leeds project is a project for children only. Bernie informed me that there is an ecumenical project – Space – for young people that has recently started for those over eleven. Bernie commented, 'We try and work together with Space.' However, the delivery of this working together was not sufficient to resolve some of the difficulties with children becoming too old for the Leeds project and leaving with nowhere to go.

One of the leaders in the feedback session before the children arrived told the story of a family they used to visit where the eldest boy was 'very difficult', but they persevered with him. When he was about to leave, his sister starting attending. She also had discipline issues, and she was followed by yet another sibling with more behavioural issues. The leader then explained that although they are all now too old to come, they have a four-year-old sister whom she bumped into when visiting another family and the sister would like to attend. I recorded in my field notes that 'The project has now had consistent input into what is clearly a problematic family for a significant period'. At the time of writing, it was recorded as a positive, but, in analysis, there is a difficulty in working with children for such a relatively short period and then leaving them without support when they are too old. Even if the project later begins working with a younger sibling, there will come a time where there are no younger siblings left and the project loses its influence within that family.

When the Leeds project found a child who came through to become a 'greeny',[18] they looked after them well and a process of Christian nurture took place. They were assigned to a mentor who, in Bernie's words, was 'encouraged to take them out and buy them food and make a fuss of them. And it's not just about the children's club, but about the whole person'.

The project clearly had a positive reputation in the community, even down to the bus drivers who, although employed by an outside company, saw themselves as part of the Leeds project. The driver of bus two had been driving the bus since the project began (figure 4.6). He commented, with a smile, that when the project first began he did not think it would work, but happily admits he was wrong. He clearly enjoyed driving for the Leeds project and volunteered every week for this job. Interestingly, he saw his role as a community worker. He commented on the way he knew many of the children; he saw them here at the Children's Outreach Project, and he would take them on school trips and their parents on trips. On the journey to collect the children, he beeped the horn and waved to the children as he drove.

Fig 4.6 A bus drops off at the Leeds project

The Leeds project was engaged in helping the community in other ways. Bernie stated:

> At Christmas, we give hampers away. We usually have about 100 hampers. The workers decide where they should go. Each worker is allocated a percentage of the whole and the worker decides who he or she should give it to. We ask that the hampers are good, not

everyday stuff, otherwise that would be seen as condescending. Most families can afford to feed the kids, but it's the extras they don't have, so we give the luxury stuff.

It was not just the local community that benefited from the Leeds project. During the morning children's programme there was a presentation of a child the project was sponsoring through Compassion UK.[19] The Leeds project had raised £45.63 so far that term to help support the child they were sponsoring. A picture of the little girl was projected on the screen and underneath was the amount they had raised. After the presentation a collection was taken as the children sang 'I give thanks to my heavenly Father' with accompanying CD backing vocals. Bernie stated:

> We choose something different to give the money to every half term. Last time we did something on street kids in Brazil, because I've been there, so I could talk to the kids about what that actually meant so they could lock into it a lot more. And we always do the Operation Shoebox thing at Christmas and one week it will be 'bring in toothpaste' and another week 'soap'. And they really like that. We get buckets full of stuff.

THE HASTINGS PROJECT

Project name: *Kids Klub*
Location: *Hastings, England*
Denomination affiliation: *New Frontiers International*
Leader: *Chris Beveridge*

Fig 4.7 The town centre at Hastings

The Hastings project is situated in a seaside town in south-east England. The town was one of the Cinque Ports, but its significance as a port declined after the nineteenth century and its main industry became fishing. It still has the largest beach-based fishing fleet in England. From a fishing port it became a watering place and finally a seaside resort in Victorian times.

The area is officially regarded as deprived, with high unemployment rates. Some of this deprivation is substantiated by Chris, the leader of the Hastings project:

> Our kids are pretty much like inner-city kids. They do what they want. They stay out till one in the morning. We have quite a lot of kids who stay away from school or are excluded from school, or go to a specialist school for excluded children. So we have challenging children, many of them come from families where fathers don't live at home, so we have two addresses for them.

The Hastings project is based in this seaside town but is located some distance from the coast in a large rectangular warehouse, which, although not particularly attractive, is nonetheless highly practical for the Children's Outreach Project and the large number of church and community activities that take place there. The Hastings project has been running on Saturday mornings since 1999.

Analysis

Chris, the leader of the Hastings project, was clear that their mission statement is 'Telling children, reaching families'. His statement was reiterated in interview when he stated, 'I want families to hear and respond to the gospel.' Again when asked about his motivation, Chris responded, 'I run the project because I know that there are very few families that are going to church.' When I mentioned to Chris that parents are not the primary focus of other projects, he commented, 'They should be, they're missing a great opportunity to reach families.'

This motivation coloured the Hastings project and as a result the Saturday morning children's programme had elements that were unique to them. Chris commented:

> The first people in on Saturday morning[20] are the technical team, but these are closely followed by Peter and Jill [Peter is 70, a retired caretaker, and the oldest member of the Hastings project team]. They set up the parents' café area at the back of the room – comfortable chairs and tables in a cordoned-off area. From there they head up a designated team who will serve free teas, coffees and juices to the parents who attend.

Parents were encouraged to attend, and when the children were collected on the project's buses, parents also rode the bus. On the morning I visited, fifteen parents (all mothers) travelled to the project on project buses, many of them carrying babies or toddlers.

The strategy was that the teaching programme was presented to the children, but the parents in the parents' area would also listen and respond to what they heard. In reality, the parents in the parents' area are paying some attention to the programme, but they were also involved in animated conversations with each other. Nevertheless, despite the apparent disinterest, three families who were represented in the parents' area came to the Sunday church service for the first time the following day. On the day I visited there were also subtle conversations that suggested that the Christian teaching of the Hastings project was beginning to affect the parents who visited. I overheard the conversation of one mum on the bus journey to the project. She was engaged in telling the story of how the Hastings project team prayed for her the week before to get a washing machine and how someone not connected to the church had given her a washing machine in the middle of the week for no apparent reason. This particular woman had also joined the church's Alpha course, although she would not refer to herself as a Christian.

There was more to the philosophy that underpinned the Hastings project. Chris stated:

> My predecessor only allowed people to visit if they were part of the Kids Klub. Now that is wider, anyone can visit from the church as long as they have a CRB check. So what happens because of that is we have cells [small groups primarily for adults] who own particular council estates[21] and what's started to happen is they meet in community centres and they have their own offshoots projects, so we have a toddlers' club in another area and they do all the visits and do their own thing on Friday.

There was a fine line between the Children's Outreach Project being the most important thing and other activities developing around it, such as shown in the 'coffee boys' project that had developed around one of the projects in the initial survey. In that case, it was clear that the children's club was the main thing and other projects had developed from that to engage with the parents who dropped the children off. There was a hint in the Hastings project that even though the project was established to be the main thing, it was now being used to facilitate a different agenda, that of reaching families. Chris commented, 'Is there an Alpha course we can get them into? If there isn't a follow-up or a follow-on, then I'm not interested.' He was upfront when he stated, 'The main frustration for us is that we work with them for so many years, but so few of them make it into youth group at the end.' It is probable that the new emphasis on reaching families that has been pioneered under Chris's leadership[22] was a response to that frustration, whether consciously or not.

The embedded difficulty with the emphasis on family projects was that the Children's Outreach Project was reduced to fewer meetings during the year. There were only four scheduled *normal* Saturday meetings in the autumn term – the following week the hall was being used for a barn dance.

Nevertheless, there was no inference that the Hastings project was not important and there was a consistent programme of visiting each of the children every week and of ongoing input into local schools by means of school assemblies. There was also evidence within the Hastings project that others were being trained and developed to continue the project. The style of leadership being developed was empowering rather than restrictive. I noted in my field notes that even though Chris was on bus one, the leaders of bus one did not defer to him. They were clearly capable of autonomy. This was highlighted by a conversation I overheard between Chris and another leader regarding the new discipline structure of 'three strikes and out' – if a child misbehaves continually to the point of being warned three times, then they are banned from the project for a set period. Chris seemed concerned that one of the children had been banned, but he ensured that he did not undermine the decision of his leaders by criticizing the decision publicly.

There were concerns with the quantity and quality of the teaching being given. I observed Rob, the assistant leader of the Hastings project, tell the story of Peter and John healing the man at the gate Beautiful in Acts 3. There was a wheelchair projected on to the screen as he told the story. The story was told quickly with very little attention to detail. The application was strongly presented:

> The Bible says if we call on Jesus' name amazing things will happen. If anyone here this morning is unwell, Jesus can heal you. Put your hand on the poorly part and we will pray. Lord Jesus, we know that you are powerful and amazing, heal these people today. Take away their pain and any sickness so that they will feel 100 per cent better.

The overall time used for specific teaching was between ten and twelve minutes. There was no request for feedback from the above prayer; for example, the children who were sick were not asked if they felt better.[23] There was almost a sense that Rob was doing what was expected of him – that is, prayers for people to be healed – but with no real conviction or confidence in the effect; therefore, he made no request for a response in case it was shown that the prayer for healing had not worked. The call for healing by Rob was only one of the many aspects of the Hastings project that exhibited a particular charismatic Christianity.[24] This is not presented as a negative; in many ways it was in keeping with the observations of Old Testament practice highlighted in the introduction – biblical Christianity presents a God who does things. This presentation of a God who does things and who is active was further shown in the programme when MC Tempo[25] was given some minutes to entertain the children. His singing, dancing, rap combination received a mixed response, but it is clear that when he told his personal story, the children were fully engaged. He told the children:

> It was difficult in school, I was bullied, my parents broke up and I
> was deaf in one ear. But a friend of mine had become a Christian
> and asked could he pray for me. He did and I was amazed that I
> could hear again through both ears. I realized that I had sinned
> and there was nothing I could do. I needed God's grace to forgive
> me and asked Jesus to come into my life and save me.

It was unclear whether the children would understand words such as
'grace' and 'sinned', but they were clearly interested in the life story of a
Christian.

Before leaving this analysis of the Hastings project, it is worth stating
that the project is part of the Newfrontiers network of churches. The survey
revealed that four out of the top ten largest Children's Outreach Projects in
the UK were run by Newfrontiers churches (see Chapter 3). On examination,
there are two primary emphases embedded within this denomination that
explain the phenomenon. Firstly, most denominational churches employ
a children's worker because they have children who need teaching;[26]
Newfrontiers advocates a policy of employing children's workers to gather
children. They have an evangelistic focus on work with children and not
only a pastoral one. Secondly, there is a particular emphasis on launching
and maintaining Children's Outreach Projects that flows from the overall
leadership of the denomination. At their 2004 national conference there
were sessions outlining how to launch and sustain a Children's Outreach
Project. In a magazine article in early 2007,[27] Terry Virgo, the overall leader
of Newfrontiers, stated:

> Is more policing the solution to a breakdown of law and order
> on inner city housing estates or is that merely pushing down the
> swelling? Surely the solution is to demonstrate and teach an
> alternative lifestyle by bringing love and care in practical ways, or
> to teach youngsters through such initiatives as children's clubs.

It is this twin motivation of seeing the children's worker as a key member
of full-time staff and the denominational leadership's desire to compel
their churches to run children's clubs that explains why Newfrontiers has
so many Children's Outreach Projects attached to their churches.

THE LIVERPOOL PROJECT

Project name: *Kidz Klub*
Location: *Liverpool, England*
Denomination affiliation: *Frontline Church (Independent G12)*
Leader: *Dave Sharples*

Fig 4.8 A typical street in Liverpool

From the mid-1970s onwards, many of the core industries in Liverpool – the docks and traditional manufacturing industries – went into sharp decline. The advent of containerization meant that the city's docks became largely obsolete. In the early 1980s, unemployment rates here were among the highest in the UK. In recent years, the economy has recovered and has experienced growth rates higher than the national average since the mid-1990s. However, this is still a comparatively poor city. A 2001 report by Consolidated Analysis Centre Incorporated (CACI) showed that it still had four of the ten poorest postcode districts in the country.[28] The Liverpool project works with many families who are economically challenged. Dave, the leader of the Liverpool project, describes its start:

> After running two holiday clubs and various after-school events, the church had made contact with over 100 local children. But

there was a problem. Whilst the kids were enthusiastic about the games and craft activities being offered, when it came to the 'God Slot' it was a different matter. Their attention spans were short and apathy and indifference were the usual response. It was fantastic to have contact with so many unchurched kids but we couldn't see how a hunger for Jesus was going to be birthed within them. How were we to see kids won for Jesus still following Him through their teenage and adult years? It was the question for which few we had met had found an answer.

We began to pray and ask God to show us the way forward. That's how we came into contact with the work of Bill Wilson and Metro Ministries in New York. Metro had been working in the ghettos of New York City since 1980 and by the time we contacted them, were meeting with 13,000 children a week. Lives were being transformed and a thriving teenage work and adult congregation had grown from their kids' ministry.

Their two-pronged approach, combining an action-packed, relevant, gospel-filled programme, with a strong emphasis on building personal relationships with the children was yielding lasting fruit. We visited New York and gleaned all we could and in 1993 we launched using the same principles that we follow today.

The Liverpool project is a thirty-minute walk from the city centre. It meets in a converted factory which is the home of a large independent free church where most of the Liverpool project's workers are members. Six buses of varying sizes (double-deckers to twenty-seat minibuses) pick up the children for this project from around the city; some will travel for twenty minutes or so from the project venue.

Analysis

The Liverpool project had many similarities with the Slough and Windsor project, and some consideration was given to whether it was necessary to include it in the final report. The Liverpool project had a reputation for being the largest Children's Outreach Project in the UK.[29] This may have been true at one time, but during the field research period (2007) both the Slough and Windsor project and the Leeds project had higher attendance.

However, one factor stood out when considering this project that makes it worthy of inclusion. On first examination, it could be thought that it was the quality of its presentation (presentation defined in the narrowest terms of the ninety-minute presentation to the children on Sunday afternoon). However, closer examination showed that it was not the quality of the programme but the charisma of the presenter that made the Liverpool project a worthwhile study. Many of the features will be reserved for the concluding chapter, but there are some observations that can be made here.

Initial encounter with the Liverpool project was not positive. I was able to walk into the building in which several hundred children would soon gather without being challenged. The programme that was due to start at 3 p.m. was showing no signs of getting under way at 3.10 p.m. When Dave, the leader of the Liverpool project, eventually entered the building, he had to ask for a volunteer to operate the lights! Nevertheless, the Sunday afternoon programme that was beginning to look decidedly chaotic suddenly burst into life when Dave was handed a microphone and invited the children to come in.

This was clearly a personality-driven project. Dave is on the stage throughout the whole ninety-minute presentation. He had various co-leaders who shared the stage with him and are then replaced by a new co-leader, but Dave was the common factor. During the more structured teaching part of the programme, a female leader told the story of Joseph and used a video clip for part of the narrative, but Dave sat on the stage affirming her words with 'Yes, that's right!' While Dave was on the stage my field notes recorded that 'The children are fully engaged with the programme'.

Watching Dave was like watching Freddie Mercury at Wembley Stadium, such was the level of charisma being displayed; Dave can sing, rap and dance, and the children clearly loved him. However, if his persona was that of a rock star, his message was that of an evangelical revivalist preacher preaching in the American Bible Belt. When talking about the Old Testament story of Joseph and his ability to resist the advances of Potiphar's wife, he stated, 'God was with Joseph. God made him a winner because he lived for God. God was with him.

Fig 4.9 Children at the Liverpool project sit and listen to Dave speak

God is with us when we live for him; he makes us winners, not losers.' The message was delivered with great intensity (figure 4.9). The children were in no doubt that Dave thought the message was serious and worth listening to. It was delivered with utmost conviction, to the point that when a young girl dared to disrupt the teaching by talking to a friend, Dave asked her to leave. He then instructed a female leader to escort her to the entrance where she would wait until the end of the programme.

However, when another leader stepped on to the platform to tell the final story, the downside of this personality-driven project became obvious. The final story was that of a boy who wanted to be in the top sports teams for his college and he got there because he worked hard and someone believed in him. The story was told with both words and projected pictures. The theme of being a winner because someone believed in you was embedded in the story, but the children were not interested; they listened best when Dave was at the front and he was not the one telling this story. As a result two balloons were burst as the children grew impatient and disruptive.[30]

The project was founded by Dave and grew around Dave. However, such is his ability and charisma that it is uncertain whether anyone else could hold this project together in his absence. As part of the presentation, Dave invited Chris up to share his story. Chris was in his late teens and, until recently, was in trouble with the police. Then he attended the church that this project is a part of and became a Christian. In his words, 'I gave my life to God.' Dave used Chris's story to illustrate a point:

> Let me tell you what happens when you do not live for God. You see the teenagers who stand on the street corners with the gold jewellery and the best trainers. They look good, but they are selling drugs. They are losers... When we do what God wants, we are winners.

Personal stories were important to the Liverpool project. The website is dedicated to showing that it really works. One such example listed is that of Leigh:

> In our first ever report, Dave talked about nine-year-old Leigh Davies who was living in one of the most rundown, drug-infested blocks of flats in our city, Leigh attended the Liverpool project every single week; not only that, he accompanied Dave through the urine-soaked corridors of local housing blocks to visit other children. Rain or shine, Leigh was there and the faithfulness he

showed as a child is still evident in Leigh's life today. As Leigh matured, he progressed from the kids club to Youth Alpha and it was here that he made a firm commitment to Jesus. Leigh has not had it easy; his older brother has been in prison for dealing drugs and Leigh lives in an area where the mere mention of Jesus produces ridicule. But Leigh has stuck at it. In that first report, Dave said his dream was that one day Leigh would grow up and minister to kids who were just like him and he's doing just that. Sixteen-year-old Leigh is an adult member of our team. His faithfulness and commitment are second to none. So much so, that next year at college he is training as a sound technician, so he can use his skills to serve the church.

These personal stories are used to show the children what has happened to others who were like them, to show them what is possible. Because of the area the Liverpool project operates in, there were many children who would relate to the stories of Chris and Leigh and for that reason the stories were undoubtedly very effective. The story of Leigh also illustrated the processes involved within the Liverpool project. There is progression possible from the children's club and into other projects. Dave commented:

We have over 70 teenagers, who were introduced to the gospel through the children's club and have grown up with it, worshipping with us on Sunday mornings, their lives changed by the truth they heard as kids.

The story of Leigh mentions Youth Alpha, a course developed by Holy Trinity, Brompton, for the purpose of discipling young people. Alongside this, there were also initiatives to communicate the Christian message to the parents of the children who attended. Dave stated, 'Whole families have been added to the church and we have 150 mums and fifty dads come to our evangelistic Mums' and Dads' nights each term.'

Youth and parent events were not the only way the Liverpool project communicated with the community outside of the children's club. There was also a concerted programme of visiting local schools to take school assemblies and a large programme of home visits. Dave commented:

The club is only effective, however, because it is combined with the home visits. Each week, every child who attends is visited by a team member. They befriend families, build relationship and, by

meeting the kids on their own territory, they demonstrate God's
love in action.

Dave estimates that they make 1,500 home visits every week during term
time. The children were also encouraged to help the leaders with visiting,
and during the programme Dave reminded them that they could receive a
red T-shirt if they consistently help a leader. There was also a yellow T-shirt
available for those who helped with bus collections.

Even though the children of the Liverpool project were some of
the poorest in the UK, this did not stop the project focusing on those who
might be in a worse situation. To this end, the Liverpool project supported
a charity called House of Grace[31] in Thailand. During the programme
Dave informed the children that money they gave helped build the House
of Grace orphanage. Now he would like them to give so the children at
House of Grace can go to the seaside. Dave delivered this information with
his usual level of passion:

> I cannot send them to the seaside without your help. It is going to
> cost, but everything worth doing costs. We have £18 so far and I
> am going to empty my wallet in to the collection. How much do I
> have? £7.50. That's going in.

When the offering was complete (the children gave as they sang along to a
quiet song), Dave stated, 'God is proud of you when you help others.'

At the end of the programme, as the clear-up operation took place,
one of the sound team who had arrived to set up for the evening church
congregation was a little unhappy at the way the microphones have been
used and commented that when the new microphones came they would be
hidden from the children's club! It was an interesting statement and may
suggest that not all the members of the church are happy with hundreds
of children being in their building on a Sunday afternoon. However, it is
just as possible that the sentiments only represented the feelings of this
particular soundman.

On the Liverpool project website Dave commented (quoting from
Galatians 6:9), 'We know that if we don't grow weary of doing good, at the
proper time we will reap a harvest if we do not give up.' However, there
were some indicators at the Liverpool project that the team is weary. The
move from Saturday to Sunday was to give the leaders more free time.
However, the move has caused a large reduction in the number of children
attending. There was not a particularly large staff team there when I visited,

and my ability to walk into the building unchallenged was indicative of the reduced staffing. A leader running a children's club in West Yorkshire commented, 'I've observed this project regularly for almost ten years – I think the programme they are running now is a shadow of what it was in its heyday. The original pioneering team have all grown older, married and had kids.'

The Liverpool project was still an excellent example of the genre, but it is struggling to reach the heights of its reputation. However, the Liverpool project was more than a Children's Outreach Project. The Liverpool project has had more influence than any other project in replicating its model of child evangelism throughout the UK. On its own website, it claimed:

> Over the past five years, the vision has been replicated literally hundreds of times around the country. From 20 kids meeting in rural Cornwall, to 400 praising God at Leeds, every club represents another community being transformed. By networking together, we're able to offer each other support, ideas and encouragement.

While the project itself may have been experiencing difficulties, it has nevertheless extended its influence throughout the UK and beyond.

Notes

1. There are interviews with others recorded from these four projects, but they were in many ways opportunistic interviews and not intentional. The intention was to interview the leader only.

2. Of the Children's Outreach Projects that stated that there was an outside influence, 34 per cent said that the Liverpool project had been an influence on them in the creation of their project.

4. For example, the leader of the church of which the Slough and Windsor project is a part used to be a journalist, and he has taken the time to write up a typical evening of visiting the homes of the children with the project leaders. I used this document as a source document.

4. BBC News, Thursday, 3 June 1999.

5. It moved to 6 p.m. in autumn 2008.

6. Friday is used for teaching and Saturday for free play.

7. By 'on the road', David is referring to his practice of taking young leaders with him when he goes to other churches to model the running of a Children's Outreach Project.

8. 'Jesus you are the light' – from the album *All of My Days*, Citipointe Church, Queensland, Australia.

9. One of them now leads a youth work project in Edinburgh.

10. Based on Home Office statistics 2006.

11. Information for the first paragraphs is drawn from City Guides and Local Council.

12. Based on the initial questionnaires and subsequent visits to projects, it can be concluded that the Leeds project is amongst the largest projects of its kind in the UK. Only the Slough and Windsor project has similar attendance figures.

13. When I visited, it was Oompa-Loompa day – all the children were dressed in orange and played games involving Oompa-Loompa dances.

14. A more detailed examination of the communication is undertaken in Chapter 8.

15. The project collected the children using six buses.

16. There are over 1,000 children on the register.

17. This is not only because lots of different churches contributing to the running costs, but also because many grant-giving organizations are more likely to support an ecumenical project than they are a project run by a single denomination.

18. This is what the Leeds project calls their teenage leaders because they wear green T-shirts.

19.. Compassion UK is a Christian organization that allows individuals and groups to support children in poverty in other countries through a child sponsorship programme (www.compassionuk.org).

20. After Chris who arrives at 7 a.m.

21. In the sense that they were responsible to pray for those areas and arrange occasional events.

22. The project began in 1999. Chris has been involved since the start, but took over as leader in 2002.

23. On the way home the girl commented that her sore throat got better when they prayed.

24. 'Charismatic' is an umbrella term used to describe those Christians who believe that the manifestations of the Holy Spirit seen in the first-century Christian church, such as miracles and prophecy, continue today. The word charismatic is derived from the Greek word χαρισμα ('gift') which is itself derived from χαρις, ('grace' or 'favour') which is the term used in the Bible to describe a wide range of supernatural experiences (especially in 1 Corinthians 12–14).

It is also noteworthy that the children in the Hastings project are all encouraged to have their Bibles with them. The Hastings project works in partnership with the Bible Society to ensure that 250 children receive a hard-backed Good News Bible every year.

25. MC Tempo is a rap artist and Christian evangelist based in Brighton.

26. Or often babysitting!

27. *Firstline*, Newfrontiers Magazine, January to March 2007.

28. www.caci.co.uk

29. On the initial questionnaires, most projects listed the Liverpool project as the largest, with guesses on the number of children attending ranging from 400 to over 1,000.

30. The balloons are a common way of keeping control within children's projects. The children are told that if they talk during 'silent seats' (the formal structured teaching time), then their balloons will be burst. If they lose all their balloons, they do not receive any prizes.

31. An orphanage located in the mountains of northern Thailand. House of Grace was founded in 1987 to protect and care for tribal girls that are at risk of being sold into prostitution in Bangkok (www.houseofgracethailand.com).

Chapter 5

THE SLOUGH AND WINDSOR PROJECT

Having gathered data from the projects in the last chapter using interviews and intense contacts, this chapter looks in detail at the Slough and Windsor project by means of interviews and ethnography over a period of six months. From this position, the research then moves on to compare Raikes' model with the in-depth analysis of the twenty-first-century models.

INTRODUCTION

Project name: *Kidz Klub*
Location: *Slough and Windsor, England*
Denomination affiliation: *Kings Church International (Independent G12)*
Leader: *Paul Bristow*

Fig 5.1 The contrasting areas of the Slough and Windsor project

The Slough and Windsor project is unique in that those who attend are drawn from two distinct areas. These areas are significantly diverse in terms of economics and ethnicity. According to the 2001 census, the combined population of the two areas was approximately 200,000.

The first area is predominantly white British. It is an affluent leafy suburb south of the River Thames and is most famous for its royal connections and historic castle. This is in stark contrast to the second area, which is among the most ethnically diverse towns in the UK, with 30 per cent of the population Asian and 5 per cent Afro-Caribbean. Only 50 per cent of the inhabitants described themselves as Christian in the 2001 census (compared to the national average of 76 per cent).[1]

Hundreds of major companies have sited in this town over the years, attracted by its proximity to London Heathrow Airport and good motorway connections.

The Slough and Windsor project started in March 2001. Paul, the leader of the project, left a well-paid job in the City of London and became a full-time children's worker in September 2000. He describes the project's beginnings:

> I spent my first few months researching other kids' clubs and that is when I discovered Kidz Klub Liverpool. I went up there and saw what I saw and knew I wanted it. We started in 2001 by targeting two very different and distinct suburbs. The weeks leading up to it we had been to many schools. We launched with two buses, and on that first day 285 kids turned up. Over the past six years we have grown to six bus routes, and we visit over 1,000 children every week.

The Slough and Windsor project is one of the largest Children's Outreach Projects (if not the largest) in the UK. Paul commented, 'On a good week we get 300 children and on a spectacular week we would see 450.'[2]

In interview Paul made an astute comment on Children's Outreach Projects when he stated, 'Increasingly I've learned that kids' clubs are an excellent win tool, and evangelistic tool, but it has to be coupled with other things to make it effective, in our view, primarily cells [small groups].' The Slough and Windsor project had understood that although Children's Outreach Projects are a proven method for reaching large numbers of children, they do not have a proven record for keeping children in their programmes for significant periods of time. All the Children's Outreach Projects visited that had over 100 children also had a large turnover. The Slough and Windsor project visited 1,000 children each week, but the overall database contained the names of 5,000 children who had attended the project at one time or another.

Paul's terminology was also noteworthy; he talks about the need for other activities to make the children's club effective. This was unlike the Leeds project which saw its ability to communicate to boys and girls as the primary focus and had only a limited focus on what happened when the children were too old for the project. Paul had a long-term view of children's work. The Hastings and Liverpool projects also had an emphasis on helping the children carry on into a youth programme, and the Fraserburgh project coupled this with a leadership development programme. However, it was the Slough and Windsor project's particular attention to following through that set it apart from the other projects.

THE SATURDAY CLUB

It is 8 a.m. on a cold, damp morning in early summer. I have made the ten-minute journey from the town centre to this youth centre on the edge of town. As I enter the hall, there is already much activity; the whole team is there from 8 a.m. (with the exception of a few who may have slept in!). The hall is in the process of transformation. Coloured banners adorn the walls bearing pictures of, amongst other things, the *Simpsons* and the project logo. Wooden benches are placed in the centre forming two columns for seating. Props are prepared, varying from the blowing up of numerous balloons and the making of cloaks for the superhero theme to the wrapping of giant presents for the Christmas programme.

The sound system is in mid set-up, sound checks take place;[4] video projections are tested, the image is clear; the lighting rig is tested. All this is the work of the technical team, those who wear black T-shirts with the Slough and Windsor project's logo. The other team members wear blue shirts with matching logos. The logo shows the name of the Children's Outreach Project and also the name of the church of which they are a part.

Fig 5.2 Backdrop for Superhero theme at the Slough and Windsor project

At the front of the hall is the stage, brightly decorated with a colourful backdrop (figure 5.2). The most prominent piece of furniture is a large wooden board featuring the words 'Dr Snot's time machine'. There is also a prize table set up to the left of the stage. The prize table contains dolls, light sticks, *Toy Story* merchandise, colouring pens and a whole host of other items. There are also three balloons positioned in line with the first row of benches and three balloons positioned in front of the second.

Paul is not here today, but the morning will follow the same routine. Luke, the Slough and Windsor project's co-leader calls the team together. He explains the theme of the day. Today they will be teaching the children that they should not follow others in doing wrong that and if they stand for what is right, God will bless them. There is a brief run through the programme, but Paul has e-mailed copies of the running order to all the team the Tuesday before. There is an opportunity for the team to share news. One of the team tells of how when they visited a particular house on Thursday, the parents commented on how their children had come home from the project and were praying for them aloud. These are unchurched parents, but they found the experience of being prayed for by their own children both amazing and heart-warming. The team then spend time learning the memory verse for the day; it will be sung to the tune of 'Sk8er Boi' by Avril Lavigne.[5]

When the practices are complete, there is a time of singing (the project uses the word 'worship') and then thirty adult leaders break into small groups to pray.[6] There is often a short talk, with a motivational slant, but not today.[7]

By 9.20 a.m., the finishing touches have been made to the hall and six buses depart to pick up the children. Each bus has a bus captain and a team of helpers. Roles are allocated:[8] one person will look after registers, another will collect fees,[9] another helps direct the driver, ensure the bus arrives at and leaves each stop on time. As we approach the first pick-up, there is a short prayer meeting on the bus. In common with the Leeds and Liverpool projects, the programme begins the moment the first child steps on to the bus.

The bus I am on today, a double decker, is collecting from one of the most economically and socially depraved estates in the area. As we approach the first stop, there is only one boy waiting; he gets on, pays his fees and takes a seat at the very back. He is also handed a raffle ticket for the money jump.[10] The bus will be filled from the back to the front before starting to fill the upstairs seats. Just as I am beginning to think this is it for this bus stop, a boy and three little girls pour out of a nearby house.

All three girls look under seven, and all of the children are clutching their memory sheet handout that has been delivered to them in the week.[11] A child enters the bus who has not been for a while and the leaders make a special point of acknowledging them and asking how they have been.

As the bus fills, several children have golden sheets instead of the ordinary memory sheets. Paul comments:

> One of the biggest complaints we get from the children is that they never get picked for the games. So we came up with the idea of the golden memory sheet. Each visitor has one per round and they can give the children a golden sheet and they are then guaranteed to get picked for a game.

When I ask the bus leaders about the practice, they expand on the reason for giving the golden sheets. They will sometimes give the golden sheet to children who they know are having a difficult time at home or finding school difficult. One of the children getting on to the bus has a birthday today, but he has remembered that he shares a birthday with one of the leaders – Natalie; he has brought her a birthday card. The relationship with the leaders is clearly very important. When I ask the children why they come, among the usual comments of 'because it's fun', 'because I like the songs', 'because I learn about God', there are also comments such as 'because Natalie is there'.

The bus now has over fifty children on; this will rise to 108 by December. They play a game called 'The crowd says'. It is a form of 'Simon says', but modified for today's theme. The object is *not* to do what the crowd says. After the game there are songs; 'Everywhere we go, people want to know, where we come from'. The children shout at the top of their voices; this is followed by 'Three kids went to Klub, three kids went to Kids Klub, three kids, two kids, one kid and their memory sheet...' and 'Who's side are you leaning on' to close the medley.

By 10.20 a.m. the bus arrives, the children are counted off, they queue up outside and then at 10.30 a.m. they enter the hall, boys and girls in two lines. The boys and girls will be sitting on separate sides. While it is clearly easier administratively to separate the boys and girls, the practice does invite some negative comments, as well as the obvious difficulty that there was rarely an equal mix of boys and girls in any of the projects visited. However, the solution may not be as simple as the ones proposed by the Fraserburgh and Hastings projects either. Fraserburgh and Hastings use three teams with the teams being made up of those who arrive on certain buses – for example, in one of the projects, bus one becomes the blue team. The advantage to this system is that although one team can be the clear winner, the other teams can come equal second, allowing an element of healthy competitiveness without the need for a single losing team. The major disadvantage to this is that because the buses collect from different areas of the town, some poorer and some more prosperous, the children end up split not according to gender but on the basis of socio-economics, where, for example, the green team may be made up of all the poorer children.

At 10.30 a.m., the programme begins. The leader shouts, 'Is bus one here?' Bus one responds loudly. 'Is bus two here?' This goes on for six buses. Luke and Natalie are hosting the programme this morning. Paul comments:

> Most weeks I am the key person to host the event, but increasingly I am bringing on more people to host with me. They have been co-hosting for many years, but I'm increasingly stepping back and allowing a host and co-host to do it.

Luke and Natalie prove to be amongst the best leaders I have seen in the projects observed. They are clearly confident in their roles, and the programme combines elements of fun and excitement with control and order. They count down from five to one and then the programme[12] gets underway. The music is loud and pulsating, the lights flash, leaders run around with water pistols, the children shout and laugh.

There is an ongoing competition between the boys and the girls. The points are projected on to a screen at the front. At the end of the welcome, the rules are explained. There are three rules:[13]

1. *Stay in your seats*
2. *Obey your leaders*
3. *The whistle means silence*

The children are asked, 'Why do we have rules?' Many hands are raised. One boy responds, 'So we can have fun.' This is clearly something the Slough and Windsor project has taught on in the past. The team leaders for the boys, Mike and Dominic, are introduced, as are the team leaders for the girls, Sarah and Emily. The children are asked, 'Who's the best?' There are huge cries of 'Boys!' and 'Girls!' Then the whistle blows. There is instant silence. Rule 3 works!

There are sound/music links between each item. Unless the whistle blows, there is rarely silence. The children then recite the 4Points to the tune of 'The Real Slim Shady'.[14] The 4Points recited are:

1. *God loves me*
2. *I have sinned*
3. *Jesus died for me*
4. *I need to decide to live for God*

The Slough and Windsor project has produced the 4Points in the form of a small booklet. Large numbers of these booklets are available on each bus. According to Paul, 97 per cent of the project's children are from unchurched homes.

They then recite this week's memory verse. It is based on Exodus 23:2 but has been embellished to read:

Don't follow the crowd and do
what God doesn't want you to.
Be a leader and in doing good,
stand up for what you know you should.

It is recited to the tune of 'Sk8ter Boi', but the teaching of the verse is hampered slightly because the team leaders are not as familiar with the words as they could be.[15] Points are awarded for the team that sings the verse the best. The practice of changing the lyrics of a popular song to Christian lyrics is not new; the practice has been attributed to the mid-nineteenth century and William Booth of the Salvation Army, although it is probable that the practice existed long before this.

The next programme item involves a character named Flamey Amy.[16] Amy walks on with a baby on her back – the baby is one of the smaller children dressed in a nappy! The children obviously enjoy the feature, and there is much amusement at the dressed-up child. Amy is charged with looking after the baby and the children are to tell the leaders if she does not. In true pantomime style, Amy neglects her role, the baby escapes, falls into a swimming pool and needs to be rescued by the leaders. This is the cue for the first of the themed baby games.[17]

The baby crawls off, but the children are told that the baby has lost several things in the pool (a ball pool). The children chosen to play the game must retrieve them. Four boys and four girls are chosen to collect items from the pool in relay formation (those waving their golden memory sheets are given priority). In the time allowed, the boys collect five items, the girls only three. Loud music plays throughout the games.[18] The boys win and the scores are projected at the front. There is a further allocation of points to the team cheering the loudest.

Flamey Amy is again charged with looking after the baby. This time the baby crawls off into a bin. This is the cue for game two. Several bins are brought out; there is a baby doll in one of them. A girl is chosen to guess first. If the child guesses the incorrect bin, then one of the female leaders will get a cream pie in their face. Unfortunately, on this occasion, the child guesses wrong and, to the children's obvious delight, the leader receives a cream pie in her face. The boys then attempt to guess. They choose correctly so the other female leader gets a cream pie in the face!

It is now 11 a.m. and Luke invites the children to stand. The praise party (this is the terminology the project uses for this section) is beginning. The first song is 'Superhero';[19] the children sing the words and copy the actions. The words are projected on to the screen and the music is provided by a backing track. The praise party section receives a mixed response from the children. The leaders are completely engaged in the songs and actions, which encourages many of the children to join in, but there are still some children (primarily boys) who seem disinterested in singing.

'Superhero' is followed by 'Gonna jump up and down',[20] again with projected words and music from backing tracks. The leaders do actions that the children copy. Next comes a remix of 'The Birdie Song', with the lyrics 'a little bit of this and a little bit of that and praise his name'. The next song is 'Supernatural'[21] and finally the only slow song, 'Super Strong God',[22] to which the children sway in time with the music.[23] Similar selections of songs were sung in all the large projects visited.

The praise party lasted fifteen minutes and now Flamey Amy is back on the stage. Amy has lost the baby again, but this time they find baby

Fig 5.3 A messy game at the Slough and Windsor project

eating sweets. This is the cue for game three. The children have to guess the number of sweets in the jar. The leader responds to the guesses with 'Higher' or 'Lower'.

When eventually the number is guessed (and it takes at least five minutes!), the leaders begin to hold their noses. It would appear that baby has dirtied his nappy. A 'nappy' is produced that is covered in brown stuff! This turns out to be chocolate and the final game involves eating the chocolate. The girls are deemed to have eaten the most and get the points.

The leader then announces that it is time for 'Silent Seats'. It is just after 11.30 a.m. and the children are instructed by Natalie:

> Everybody needs to sit with their hands on their laps. If you are completely silent, then a leader will put a sweet in your hand. If you get a sweet, do not open it. If you talk, your balloon will be burst. If all three of your balloons are burst, then your sweets will go to the other team. There is also a mega prize. This will go to the perfect child. All eyes on the person with the microphone. Let's hear what God will say to us today.

There is some interesting psychology at work here. The silence for this part of the programme is in direct contrast to the noise/music that preceded it. It has the effect of causing the children to listen attentively. Luke begins his talk and every child sits in silence and looks at him. He retells the story of Daniel 3, the story of Shadrach, Meshach, and Abednego and the fiery furnace. The story is well communicated; it is told dramatically and without the need to use visuals to support the storytelling. The story is used to reintroduce today's theme of not listening to the crowd.

The balloon of one boy is burst at the end of the story. However, the bursting of the balloon in this project says more about the standard the leaders require of the children during 'Silent Seats' than it does about the children who are, on the whole, sitting very still and exceptionally silent.

The Bible story is followed by another leader talking about how important it is not to simply do things because others do. She makes the join from the biblical narrative to her exhortation with the words, 'Do you see what happened there? They refused to do the wrong things.' She continues, 'If our friends smoke, it doesn't mean that we should. If our friends steal, it doesn't mean that we should.'

The next speaker gives a personal account of the time when she used to dress like her friends, which was fine, but also to steal like her friends, which was not. She adds, 'When I said I wouldn't steal any more, they all started to follow me. They followed me in doing what was right. That's what happens when we do what's right.'

The three presentations have all communicated the same message, but in slightly different ways. Combined with the memory verse and memory sheet, there is little doubt that on a cognitive level the communication is good.

The final talk involves the story of Scruffy the Cat. Scruffy is rescued by Sophie, but Sophie's two other cats are unkind to Scruffy. Instead of being unkind to them, Scruffy forgives them and, as a result, the other cats change and become kinder. There are pictures that show what is happening as the story is told, and the combination of word and pictures helps the story communicate well.[24] The story is good, and words and pictures work well together, but I am unsure whether the story was necessary. The extra input in the form of the story may well have detracted from what had gone before it. Nevertheless, when Luke asks for a response – saying, 'Guys, God can help you do the right thing. The Holy Spirit can help you do the right thing. Stand up if you want us to pray for God's help to help you do the right thing' – 80 per cent of the children stand and repeat a prayer along with Luke.

The level and subject matter of the teaching time will be considered in detail in Part 2, but some preliminary comments can be made. To the uninitiated, the contents of the majority of the programme could fall into the category of moral teaching. Paul comments:

> We find that their level of understanding of salvation is really limited, and although they make the response, it is only through discipleship that we see more. Nevertheless, they learn to stop lying and to tell the truth. They learn not to follow the crowd when the crowd do wrong.

Luke makes this comment even more forcefully:

> The goal of the children's programme is to teach important morals with a Christian background. So they don't have to be Christian to come along, they don't have to be converted to come along and they don't have to be converted to stay. But I think everyone needs to hear that if they're stealing they should stop, if they are lying they should stop and tell the truth, that they should be friends with everyone, and they should not to get angry too quickly.

In many ways, this is in keeping with the nest metaphor presented by David in the Fraserburgh project. The children's club is the place for gathering and basic teaching, and the teaching of more substance takes place at a different time or when the children reach a different age. In the case of the Fraserburgh project, the children are taught more in-depth Christian teaching when they reach the youth programme; in the Slough and Windsor project this in-depth discipleship takes place in small groups. However, to think that the Slough and Windsor project children's club is not about converting people to Christianity would be a mistake; there were many occasions on my visits when children were asked to respond to the 4Points or to stand if they wanted to become Christians.

By 12 noon, the children are gathered back on to their buses for the journey home. While the buses are out, people who have not been part of the children's programme, but who are part of the church, will arrive and start clearing up. This is not where the church meets, but it is clear that the whole church owns this event. The clean-up operation is intensive; there are lighting rigs, sound cables and projection screens to clear away as well as the seating and general litter generated by the children.

There is more singing and games on the bus journey home and then they eventually calm down with a game called 'Sleeping lions'. All the children are encouraged to sit as still as possible; the quietest and stillest get the prizes – some of the children actually go to sleep!

There is an incident with an upset girl on the way back, but Natalie talks to her and soon resolves the issues;[25] another child is sick, but an improvised sick bag was found in time to save the upholstery. The incident requires a conversation with the child's mum, but only to make her aware that her child is poorly. It has become clear that in each of the projects the strength of its leaders is a significant factor. The Slough and Windsor project has a significantly high number of good leaders who are capable of a high level of autonomy. This project is not unique in this, but it is an excellent example of leadership development (figure 5.4). When I asked Paul about his role in the Slough and Windsor project, he stated:

> I am the holder of the vision and I try to instil that vision into the heart of my team of volunteers; a leader of volunteers, a motivator of volunteers, trying to spur them on and keep them motivated. These are my roles. Keeping them keeping going on. The honeymoon period for many is long over and it's the weekly hard graft that is the key. So I'm the motivator of my team.

Fig 5.4 Some of the Slough and Windsor project team

The fact that the Slough and Windsor project has many motivated leaders who can articulate the aspirations of the children's club is indication that Paul is fulfilling his role.

Natalie, the bus captain, also runs two small groups that meet midweek; this church refers to small groups as *cells*. One of teenage helpers states that he would like to run a children's cell. Natalie tells him that he must complete a course at the church first (the church call this course 'the school of leaders'), but also encourages him and says that it is a great idea.[26] The subject of cells is brought up on numerous occasions. Most of the workers at the Saturday children's club are either small group leaders or part of a cell themselves – the church aims to encourage both so that its leaders are in a cell and also lead a cell. Paul emphasizes that position:

> We're very much in transition and we have 200 people who have graduated the school of leaders. As a church, we see every member as a potential leader. The way we will explode in growth is by seeing every member lead a cell and be in a cell. Then lead those members to be cell leaders themselves. Therefore, we have 200 people who are embarking on leading cells [as of December 2007].

By 1 p.m. the buses have returned and the venue is clean. Teas and coffee are available together with a range of homemade cakes. Debrief begins at 1.20 p.m.[27] with an analysis of the things that did not work or need improving. A range of areas are identified:

- Water guns need replacing – they are not producing enough water!
- The young leaders are encouraged to be an example in the praise party. Paul encourages them: 'We need to be a good example; you are not here to look cool.'
- Reminders are given that bus captains are responsible for their bus boxes that contain the prizes, sweets, etc.
- Leaders are asked to ensure that they do not wear clothes that cover their project T-shirts.

The analysis then moves to those things that are going well:

- The ongoing drama with Lilly is mentioned.
- Dominic's object lesson.
- The increase in the new bus route. The route is growing by two to three children a week.
- The praise party is commended, but Paul comments that he is looking for a way to take it 'from praise to worship'.
- Sam, a junior leader, is commended for being excellent on the bus route.
- Shannon has become a junior leader for the first time today. There are rules to govern who can become a junior leader. Shannon is part of Naomi's small group; she is in school year 9 (the guideline is year 8 or above).
- Some of the visitors comment on what they have seen on their visit. They are all positive and include 'the way that Dominic prayed for a girl who was unwell on the bus, and she felt better'.

The feedback, both positive and negative, has not come from Paul; it has come from the other leaders/workers. They have learned that to improve what they do, they need to be self-critiquing, but when they are pointing out errors in others, they have clearly been taught (almost certainly by example) to do so in an affirming manner.

During the feedback time, the area Paul is most concerned with is the return of the new registration forms. Some of them are not finding their way to the silver box where they should be deposited; this means the necessary addresses are not put on to the computer that generates the visiting lists, so children are not being visited. It is an isolated event, but

Paul is nonetheless passionate about it. 'The form represents a child,' he announces. Paul knows that the registration forms allow the project the opportunity for wider contact with the child and with the child's family. This is achieved by a strategic programme of home visits. The importance of this was highlighted earlier in the day; on the final bus stop at the Saturday children's club, nobody is there to collect the child. The bus waits. Eventually Granddad turns up to collect the boy. One of the leaders mentions that this little boy's dad is in prison so Granddad is helping the family. This is information that the leader has discovered on a home visit the week before. Because of this, it is important to understand the significance of home visits to the Slough and Windsor project.

HOME VISITS

It is 3.45 p.m. on a Friday in October, but it feels like a summer afternoon. The sun is still shining as I pull into the local secondary school where nineteen-year-old Natalie works. She has allowed me to come with her as she visits the children this evening. She has a full-time job at the school, but still finds time to run a small group for teenagers in the week, work at the children's club on Saturday mornings, attend church on Sundays and visit over ninety children on Friday evenings.

There is a ten-minute drive to one of the poorest parts of the town. The car is parked and at 4 p.m., the visiting begins. Natalie has her arms full of A4 sheets of paper, which show the project logo, some information about this week's children's club, a space for colouring and this week's memory verse; she refers to it as the memory verse sheet. She also has general information leaflets with registration forms in case she meets children who have not been before. My job is to carry the toy that all the children who attend tomorrow's club will receive – a ball that glows in a variety of colours when it is bounced. It is an opportunity for participant observation!

This is Natalie's second week in this area. She has taken it over from someone who did not have the time to do it effectively. She comments:

> He wasn't able to start until 7.30 p.m. and we are asked to finish visiting no later than 8.30 p.m., and because he had so little time he would just post the leaflets through the door. So I'm here to sort out the list and do some pruning and maybe get some of the children to come back.

Paul explains this system of pruning:

If a child hasn't attended for five weeks, we ask them what's up
and are there any reasons they are not coming. Sometimes there
are reasons, not being picked for a game, which we can fix with
a golden sheet, or bullying that we can address. Where we find a
genuine lack of interest, we explain to the child that we are going
to stop visiting but they are always welcome back.

We walk into the run-down estate. Natalie checks her list and we walk
towards the first door. She knocks. A woman in her mid-thirties answers.
She takes one look at Natalie's project T-shirt and shouts, 'Nic!' and walks
back in. A girl of about eight years of age emerges from the house. Natalie
tells her that she was missed last week and asks if everything is OK. She
shrugs and then talks to Natalie about school and friends. She takes the
memory verse sheet, promises she will be there waiting at the bus stop in
the morning and plays with the toy before returning it. Natalie tells her that
tomorrow is superhero day and children who dress as superheroes will get
the opportunity to do the money jump. The conversation is ending when
the girl asks, 'Can I have the golden sheet this week?' Natalie looks down
the register and tells the girl that she is keeping the sheet for someone who
has been every week. The girl shrugs, says goodbye and walks back into
the house, closing the door behind her. The whole visit has taken three to
four minutes.

The next visit is across the street. This time the roles are reversed.
The boy being visited says nothing and the parent talks incessantly. She
tells Natalie that she has pulled her thigh. Her son stands there, saying
nothing. He looks at tomorrow's toy, takes the memory verse sheet, but
continues to stand in silence. Eventually goodbyes are said and the door
closes. Natalie informs me that they are a Christian family who attend a
local church. The boy is in one of the project's small groups.

This is the general pattern of visiting. Sometimes the parent remained
and chatted, sometimes they withdrew leaving the child to talk; on a few
occasions both remained to chat. The visits were all averaging three to five
minutes in duration. Paul comments:

We visit a thousand children, but actually have contact with four
thousand people. A visit could be a minute, the next could be ten
minutes, the next thirty minutes. Thirty-minute visits are rare, but
where there is a need, we will respond.

Natalie then spots an error on the register. The computer has printed off a child who had stopped coming, but she decides a visit might be in order anyway. He answers the door and the project T-shirt is enough to help him with recognition. In contrast, this is not the first time, and will not be the last time, this evening when my lack of T-shirt is greeted with a mixture of curiosity and uncertainty. Natalie tells him he has been missed before breaking into the usual pattern of giving the memory verse sheet, showing the toy, mentioning superhero day and checking the child will be there in the morning. The boy says he will come and we move on.

As the sun begins to drop, we enter a block of flats. We enter by pushing the tradesman's buzzer and someone pushes his or her buzzer to let us enter. The corridors are cluttered with bikes, buggies, dogs and piles of bricks! The mother who answers at the bottom flat says her children are playing with the children in the top flat, and since they are also on the list, it is to the top flat that we venture. We knock on the door and a girl answers. She shouts to her mum that it's the children's club. This is received with a general response of indifference from the mother, but a scurrying of feet from one of the other rooms as now four girls arrive at the door to get their memory verse sheets. Some of the girls came last week for the first time. They are chatting to Natalie and playing with the giveaway toy when mum emerges. She is in her late twenties. She looks at the girls, nods at Natalie and then there is a sudden realization: she notices for the first time that all four girls are there so nobody is looking after the baby on the bed. She rushes in, shouting her annoyance at the girls. The baby is fine! One of the girls had won a prize the week before for bringing these other girls for the first time; her prize was a *High School Musical* CD and she says she has been playing it all week.

As we venture back down the stairs, the girls follow us. A very large boy (large but still in primary school) joins us on the walk down and then another boy arrives. When we emerge back on to the street, Natalie has become the Pied Piper with seven children in tow.

As we turn the corner, there is a large gang of teenagers (more than 30) who, we later discover, are gathering for a fight that is to take place on a nearby common. Despite the peer pressure of the large gang, many of the boys still say 'Hi' to Natalie. Many of them have been to the project in the past. There is an important point worth noting here: even the children who do not stay at the projects are positively disposed to the church in their teenage and adult years. Paul illustrates with an account of a family that he visited:

One family that I visited was on one of the roughest estates in the area. We visited this family two or three times and Mum was open to us. There were three girls and a mum. One week I was invited in and we had the privilege of leading that mum and the three girls to the Lord.[28] The week after that I met Dad. Dad was built like a train, he had tattoos everywhere, skinhead. You could see that he was really eyeing me up and suspicious of this guy in his home. But as we got talking he just warmed up and that night we discovered that he used to come to a Sunday School that we used to run as a church in the seventies.[29] He knew several of the key leaders in the church. I took him down the pub, got to know him, eventually led him to the Lord. He did the school of leaders. This is someone who could hardly read or write and he graduated with distinction from the school of leaders. He's now a bus captain. And then he brings his best mate in, who is also built like a train, and he too had attended one of our Sunday schools. These were seeds that had been sown many years ago when they came along to our Sunday Schools when they were young.

The connection with the church through the Sunday School several decades earlier had given Paul favour with these men.

Another child walks up and asks if he can come the following day. He hasn't been before so Natalie asks to be taken to his parents where she explains what the children's club is and gives the mum a registration form, containing bus pick-up times, that will need completing.

We are heading for another house, but the children from the house pull up in a car. The little boy in the car has not been coming for a few weeks because he has been at his grandmother's, but he will be coming tomorrow. A man comes out of the house carrying a new baby – the baby is the brother of the boy who comes to the children's club – and I assume that the man is the boy's dad. I get it wrong: the man is the baby's dad, but he is not the boy's dad. Relationships are complex here. In some of the houses the door is opened by mum's new boyfriend, an assumption based on the fact that it would not be possible for the person standing in front of me to be the father of the child we are visiting – some of the men were only in their late teens or early twenties. In other houses, the position was reversed and older dads clearly had younger girlfriends. The situation was further emphasized in the homes where there were children present who all had different ethnic backgrounds but nonetheless had the same mother. At one of the houses, we are informed that the child will be coming every second week because she is at her dad's some weeks. This was not an isolated case.

At one house we chat to the uncle who is visiting. He has driven up from London. We talk for five minutes on the doorstep. Some of the children have moved and the registers carry the wrong information so adjustments are needed. One of the children is adamant that he does not want to come anymore and Mum asks that his name be removed. At one of the homes we have a long chat about secondary schools in the area. The girl who attends the children's club is in school year 6 and will have to make her decision on what secondary school she would like to go to soon. Mum is interested in our opinions.[30] Natalie shares her knowledge of local schools and we chat about selective schooling and the eleven plus exam for some time. Paul comments, 'Our heart is to visit every child and visit the family. We do see it as a family visit. We visit one kid, but we do see it as a family visit for in the house will be brothers and sisters, aunties and uncles.'

We call on two Polish children who have just started coming to the children's club. They take the leaflets and the parents indicate that the children are enjoying coming along very much. The ethnic diversity within this project is worth observing. Wes, the leader of the church, records a personal reflection on a visit he made with Sarah, one of the projects leaders:[31]

> Perhaps one of the most surprising and notable developments of the evening was the warmth of the welcome that we received in three Muslim homes where parents and children greeted us. They insisted we come and sit and chat. The Pakistani lady told me that Sarah and others from the church really cared from 'inside here' – pointing to her heart. 'We are Muslims,' she said, 'but we have not seen this before.'

Wes Richards sums the situation up when he comments that the ethnic diversity of the area reflects the 'multi-racial microcosm of the world that God so loves'. This Christian group is keen to engage with these groups of other faiths.

It is now 7.30 p.m. and we return to the car to drive to another nearby estate – via McDonalds Drive Thru! It is quite dark and Natalie informs me that we should aim to finish in the next hour. It is difficult to assess whether the final area we are visiting is better or worse than the last estate. The dark certainly makes it more ominous. It is a mixed area. At some of the houses we call at the younger children have already gone to bed, but at the house two doors away children of the same age are playing in the street and kicking the refuse bins over. At some houses, the welcome is exceptionally warm. One child asks Natalie if can she bring her Bible tomorrow; at another house a girl, knowing Natalie has a matching bracelet to hers, asks Natalie to wear it the following morning. But several doors later a teenage boy, who answers the door bare-chested, informs us that his brother didn't like it and will not be coming again.

At one of the houses, the youngest boy has had cancer and the church has been working and praying with the family. The boy has two sisters; the youngest girl comes to the project and brings the boy with her. He is very thin and needs some help with toileting, but it appears that the cancer is in remission. Dad is not in this evening; he is at an Alpha course being run by the church that runs this project. The support and prayer that the family have received during the son's illness has made the dad curious about Christianity and he has gone to hear more.[32] The eldest girl used to be part of Natalie's small group for teenagers, but because her brother got cancer and looked as if he would die, she stopped coming. However, recently she has been sending text messages to Natalie, and Natalie is hopeful that she will return to the small group.

We are at our last visit of the evening. We go into the house. Dad is sitting on one chair and mum is sitting on another. The floor is covered with rubbish; piles of books and newspapers lie everywhere. The room is a complete mess, everything looks old, and there are layers of dust everywhere. It is uncertain why the house looks this way. Dysfunctional parents, lack of finances, lack of interest? However, there on the sofa is a little girl. This is the environment in which she lives, and every Saturday she catches the bus to go to the children's club. She never misses. Her home is a scene of despair, and it is a stark reminder that even though the Slough and Windsor project draws from a wider socio-economic spectrum than any other project, it understands the inbuilt bias that its senior minister stated in interview: 'This church has a heart for the poor and the marginalized.'[33]

The variations in the conversations that take place on a round of this sort are vast, and some of them are quite sobering. On Wes's report of his visit with Sarah, he experienced the following:

- A conversation with a teenager who wanted a confidential chat with Sarah as she had suffered a serious sexual assault a few days earlier and wanted to move on.
- A mum who invited us in and told us about how unhappy her young son was about his parents' break-up.

- Sarah re-established contact with a mother of three who had been a victim of domestic violence in a relationship that had now ended. She told Sarah how much help she was getting from a course on parenting, held by one of the women in the church. Another mum, with kids all around her, had earlier told us the same thing.
- We had a long chat at another house with one big sister, a single mum and her three teenage friends. We talked about a close friend who was in prison and she asked if we would 'christen' her baby.

By 8.45 p.m., nearly five hours later, the visits are finished. We have called on over ninety children and talked to countless parents and guardians. However, the effects are obvious and quickly quantifiable: the following day the majority of the children are waiting at the various bus stops on the route, dressed as an assortment of Spidermen, Supermen, Wonder Women and an Incredible Hulk, and alongside them are a whole range of characters with cloaks but no other identifiable superhero markings. One child has come as SpongeBob because the theme is telling the truth and SpongeBob never tells lies!

The little boy who had not been for some time but had promised to come back does. 'Nic' is also there. There is a little girl is at the bus stop with Bible in hand, ready to show Natalie. Both Natalie and the little girl have forgotten to wear their bracelets; both promise to remember next week. The little boy who had cancer is there with his sister; their dad who was at the Alpha supper is waiting with them.

In addition, to demonstrate how relationships are formed, Natalie was able to stand at the front of the bus and point to each of the children on the bus and call them by name. The connection is more than attendance at a project on a Saturday morning: she knows where they live and has had conversations with their parents, she has met their younger and older siblings, and she will visit them every week for the thirty-five weeks that the children's club runs each year. However, she is just one of dozens of workers from the Slough and Windsor project who visit on Thursday and Friday evenings; this is how it is possible to visit over 1,000 children every week.

However, home visits are not the only way this project is keeping its connection with the community. Paul informs me, 'We are active in nearly twenty schools. And each school we are active in, we visit once a term. We come up with one assembly a term and we repeat that assembly twenty times.' It is the added dimension of schools ministry that is explored next.

SCHOOL VISITS

At 8.45 a.m. on a weekday in October I arrive outside a primary school, fifteen minutes away from the Slough and Windsor project's Saturday venue. As I sign in at reception and collect my visitor's badge, children are enquiring why I am there. I tell them I have come this morning with the Slough and Windsor project. The news is greeted with euphoric shouts of 'Yes!' and 'Cool!' When I enquire why they are so excited, they respond, 'Because they play games and do good talks and it's fun.'

The Slough and Windsor project team arrives. This morning's school assembly is being conducted by Luke and Ceri. Although the team varies, Luke is the constant. They are escorted to the hall where they quickly set up a video projector and put on their project T-shirts.

By 9.05 a.m. the hall is filled with over 300 children. They have come in quickly and quietly and have been placed with military precision into a 10 x 15 metre space. They sit in silence, facing the front, with teachers lining the edges. 'Good morning, children,' the head teacher begins the assembly. She spends some time commending the children on how well they have behaved so far this week and introduces Ceri and Luke. Luke tells the children his and Ceri's names and then greets them again with 'Good morning, boys and girls'. The children respond, 'Good morning, Luke, good morning, Ceri.'

Luke then proceeds to pull some items out of a bag, announcing, 'I've just had a birthday and I got the most amazing presents. Let me show you them.' He pulls out a flowery hat and puts it on, and the children laugh. He then shows them his stripy socks, which are greeted with more laughter, and finally he produces his patterned boxer shorts, which produce hysteria! Luke looks upset and chides the children, saying that these presents are precious to him. He then asks the children what is precious to them. There are various answers, but Luke is clearly surprised by the response because instead of listing the expected Playstations™ and iPods™, the children give answers such as 'My mother is precious to me' or 'My brother and sister are precious to me'. Nevertheless, Luke recovers well and commends the children on naming people instead of the things and objects 'that others schools did'.

He continues, 'Today we are learning that we are precious to God.' The words 'I AM PRECIOUS TO GOD' are displayed on the video projector and all the children repeat the words.

It is then time for a game. An item is displayed on the screen along with three prices; the children must put their hand up to guess the correct price for the item. The picture shows a speedboat. The options are a) £960,950 b) £1,500,950 or c) £1,230,950. When Luke says 'A', several hands go up. Several more go up for 'B', but the majority opt for 'C'. Luke announces the answer is 'A'. There are cheers and groans. The game repeats for an iPod™ and then for an England football top. The children are getting very excited, but there are enough teachers on the edges to ensure control is maintained.

The projector again projects 'I AM PRECIOUS TO GOD'. The children chant the words. Now three boys and three girls are invited to the front. They take it in turns to draw small flags from Luke's black bag. Various flags come out – Canada, Japan, USA, Holland, Norway, UK. The children are asked, 'Which country is the best?' and then Luke shows the children the empty bag and adds, 'I'll show you which God loves the best.' The children take it in turns to place their small flags back into the bag. When all the flags are placed back in, Luke then draws out of the bag one large flag made up of all the smaller flags and shows the children the empty bag. There are audible gasps. He states, 'To God all are the same. All people are precious to him, no matter what colour, or country or age.'

The words 'I AM PRECIOUS TO GOD' are displayed on the screen and the children repeat the words together again.

Luke walks to the side and Ceri walks on. She tells the story of the Lost Sheep from Matthew 18, counting the sheep, 'One, two, three… twenty-six, twenty-seven… eighty-nine, ninety, ninety-one… ninety-seven, ninety-eight, ninety-nine. Oh no, there's one missing!' The story is told well and the children are focused on her. She concludes with the comment, 'When we are far from God, he comes looking for us', and invites the children to close their eyes to think about this. Ceri prays:

> *Dear God, thank you that you love every boy and girl.*
> *Help us to remember that we are precious to you*
> *and that you look out for us and keep us safe.*
> *Amen.*

Ceri commends the children's behaviour throughout the assembly before handing back to Luke. Luke then mentions the Saturday morning children's club and asks who has attended in the past; 40 per cent of the children raise their hands. The fact that less than 5 per cent are regularly attending reinforces Paul's observation that the Saturday children's club is a great *reaching* tool but not an effective *keeping* tool.

Luke outlines what a Saturday at the children's club is like and then offers a further incentive:

> Everyone who comes on Saturday will get a glow-in-the-dark
> bracelet, but those who come for the next five weeks will be
> entered in a draw and you could win a DVD TV, a mountain bike
> or a PSP. At the end of school today you will get a leaflet to take
> to those who look after you that tells them about the children's
> club and also a list of bus times and where you can catch the bus.
> Hands up if you would like to come.

Eighty per cent of the hands go up. The children are then asked to say
'I AM PRECIOUS TO GOD' one more time as Luke hands back to the
head teacher. The school then sings 'Count your blessings' to a Caribbean
rhythm, to conclude.

In terms of the school assembly being a way of adding extra children
to the children's club, it is partly successful. Only a small percentage of the
80 per cent who indicated a desire to attend actually do so. However, to
think of the school assembly as a way to add children to the children's
club is to take too narrow a view of the project's schools work. As the
children exit the assembly, I ask the head teacher what she thought of
the assembly. She comments, 'It was inspirational, the message reached
the children and it was fun and entertaining.' The Slough and Windsor
project has provided an act of worship at the start of the school day. If
no children came to the children's club as a result, the assembly still has
value. Paul comments, 'The school assembly is a privilege and we serve
that school with a good assembly.' For the Slough and Windsor project, a
child coming to the project as a result is a bonus and not the primary aim
of doing the assembly.

The Slough and Windsor project is multi-layered. Some of its
activities are primarily aimed at reaching children, others at keeping and
others at helping the community. Most of the activities have a combination
of all three. The children's club is a way of reaching the children with the
Christian message, as are school assemblies. However, school assemblies
also provide a way of interacting and engaging with the wider community,
as do the home visits, primarily with the families of the children who
attend. In turn, the analysis of the home visits showed that they are a way
of keeping the children and providing pastoral care.

SMALL GROUPS

Nevertheless, the real work of keeping the children and of Christian
discipleship takes place in small groups. Paul commented that, in order to
be effective, the children's club needed the addition of cells. By cells, Paul

is referring to the small-group programme for children. The language is strongly phrased – effectiveness is based on the incorporation of children into small groups for the purpose of Christian teaching and pastoral care. Paul states:

> We launched the children's project six years ago [2001] and those children are now in our youth programme. Four years ago we ran a summer camp for the youth, 40 young people attended. The following year it was 98. The following year it was 132. Last year it was 250. All from this church. And our kids' club is a key element in where these young people have come from. This year [2007] our goal is 500. But it looks like we will get to 370.

The philosophy of incorporating young people into cells was launched in 2004. Luke, one of the leaders of the project, comments on a cell that he runs and the boys that were added to it because of the youth camp:

> I have four boys who are in my cell group and they have grown up through children's club and are part of youth. They have been away on youth weekends with church and were invited into my cell two years ago and they have been with me for two years. Two of them are young leaders in the children's programme, one of them visits with me.

In order to understand this small-group programme necessitated a visit to one of the cells.

It's early November, evidenced by the large number of fireworks exploding overhead. I have travelled to an ordinary-looking house in an ordinary street in one of the areas that the Slough and Windsor project collects from. I have come to watch a children's small group in action. I arrive just before 6 p.m. and am ushered into a comfortable living room occupied by the leader of the small group, whose name is Frankie. His wife and their two young children (aged five and three) are also present. The small-group programme began in 2006. Paul comments:

> Last year [2006] was the first year we launched children's cells. We did a kids camp last July and fifty children went on that camp and we placed all those children and all church children aged eight to eleven into a cell group which meets weekly. It will either meet in a Christian home or it may meet in a community centre. We have

one example of three girls' cells that all meet in a community centre on Sunday afternoon; they meet as cells and then come together for a game or whatever.

The boys who make up Frankie's group begin to arrive at 6 p.m. There are only three of them this evening; some are missing through sickness, but Frankie's wife mentions that the group is 'very dependent on parental support to bring the boys'. The group is made up of boys from the church and boys from the Saturday children's club. They take off their shoes and make themselves comfortable on the furniture. One of the boys still has the letter and number written on the back of his hand identifying which bus he was on at this mornings children's club and which bus stop he got on/off at. The boys are all in their last year of primary school or first year of secondary school. However, the group has no age limit; it is the hope of the Slough and Windsor project leaders that the boys will stay in this group and with this leader as they continue through their teens and into their adult lives.

This is Jake's first evening here. He has come through the children's club and over the summer he attended the project summer camp. It has been a goal of the Slough and Windsor project to incorporate the children who attended the camp into small groups throughout the autumn and the inclusion of this particular boy is evidence that it is working.

Frankie begins with a prayer: 'Dear Lord Jesus, bless this evening, Amen.' Frankie's wife and children remain as part of the activities, and the whole group has a family feel because of that. Frankie's wife comments that 'This is Frankie's thing really but we have all got to know the boys'.

However, it is clear that the family ethos that has been created here is a particular strength of this group. There is little doubt that other groups led by single people or teenagers (who lead many of the cells) are positive, but there is an extra dimension to the warmth and hospitality evident in the group that will inevitably make it more attractive to the boys who attend.

The activities start with a game of Pictionary™. The boys take it in turn to draw men from certain professions, while the other boys try to guess what the profession is. There is one sheet of paper at the centre and all the boys gather on the rug, looking on. They guess gardener, carpenter, police officer... all no. Fire fighter... yes. The game continues for a few goes, including a man standing next to a building drawn by Frankie's five-year-old son. Builder, the boys guess. Frankie's wife and daughter are also watching with amusement.

It is time for another game. They throw a dice. When they get a six or a one they are given a piece of a puzzle to construct. The dice lands on a three and Frankie's daughter exclaims loudly, 'I'm three.' When all the pieces are gathered, they form a picture of David Beckham.

The game moves seamlessly into the teaching time with Frankie's words: 'Just as you put that picture puzzle of David Beckham together, Jesus often put people back together.' He tells the story of the paralyzed man and his encounter with Jesus (Mark 2). The story is creatively embellished – the paralyzed man is given a name, the friends of the man are given extra character attributes – but the core of the message remains unchanged. Frankie's three-year-old daughter has been sitting on his lap throughout the story and it is all very relaxed, but the boys are clearly listening. Frankie talks about the paralyzed man's sins being forgiven and spends some time explaining what this means. He defines sins as the doing of wrong things, but reassures the boys that Jesus will forgive them if they ask him. The story is further applied as Frankie states:

> Sometime we can feel overwhelmed by the disasters we see on TV or the things that go wrong in our lives. But just like these friends who had a problem they couldn't deal with brought it to Jesus, we too can bring our problems and things we can't deal with to Jesus.

Frankie reinforces his point by talking about the fact that their family car had broken down and they could not afford to fix it, but they brought their problem to Jesus and the car started working again, saving them money they really didn't have. The practical example of a real-life situation involving ordinary people serves well to convince the boys of the authenticity of the message.

Frankie then informs the boys that it is time for prayer. They pray for those who are feeling a bit poorly and they ask Jesus to help them bring their problems to him.

It is now 6.40 p.m. and time for cake! The boys are led to the kitchen for some of Frankie's home-made cake and a drink of juice. The group is marked by informal Christian teaching in a relaxed, homely environment. They chat around the dining table before returning to the living room ten minutes later for another game. This time the game is called 'Topic'. One player chooses a letter – on this occasion it is 'M' – and the next player chooses the topic – this time it's, 'Things found at a fun fair'. They write as many things as possible within a specified time.

The game continues until 7 p.m. when Frankie enquires, 'Does everyone here have a Bible?' The boys nod. They are then handed a little notebook and asked to read Mark 2 themselves before next time. The group meets weekly; in the summer the inside games are supplemented with some activities in the garden.

The group is due to finish at 7 p.m. but some parents are caught in the traffic that has developed outside because of a nearby firework display. Some of the boys leave, others settle down to wait for their parents, and Frankie's wife puts the final ten minutes of *Strictly Come Dancing* on the television. The family feel with its relaxed atmosphere continues, and twenty minutes after the scheduled finish time the last boy eventually leaves.

NOTES

1. The recent influx of Polish immigrants, many of whom are Roman Catholic, is likely to change these figures substantially in the 2011 census.

2. There were just under 300 children on my first visit; this number often rose to 400 and sometimes dropped to 250. Attendance peaked in December with just over 450 children.

3. Wolcott (2005, p. 196) describes this as 'writing with panache', which sometimes feels contradictory to the academic nature of the research. There is an element within ethnography that redefines the nature of academic writing.

4. Complicated further by the seasonal specials where a live band is used consisting of electric guitars, keyboards and drums.

5. The verse changes every week and so does the tune. One week in October, they sang 'Stop lying and tell the truth' (Ephesians 4:25) to the tune of 'The farmer's in his den'. In November a military chant was used for 'God is with us all the time, he's our leader yours and mine' (2 Chronicles 13:12). In December they sang 'I will love you with a love that lasts for ever' (Jeremiah 31:3).

6. On other weeks, they stay together and individuals pray out loud for everyone present.

7. In October 2007, Paul spoke from Exodus 34. He made the comment that we need to go up the mountain (figuratively) and spend time with God so that we rely on God's glory and not our gifts. He listed three effects of encountering God:

> The person is changed
> The person carries the authoritative word of *God*
> The person becomes attractive to others without diminishing their authority

In December Paul spoke from Isaiah 9:2. He commented: 'Our children and families walk in darkness, but Christ is light. Let us pray that his light shines in their hearts today. Many children will be coming for the present today, but what we will do is pray that the Holy Spirit will make them aware that God's love lasts for ever.'

8. Over the period of observation, the roles were rotated so that everyone on the bus was able to perform all the roles required. The intention was to ensure there was never a time when the absence of a leader would cause difficulties. This was put to the test in mid-November when Natalie was absent. The bus leaders all assumed different roles and the bus functioned without difficulty.

9. Of the five projects visited, this is the only project that charges, although Paul is quick to point out that no child is ever turned away because of financial reasons.

10. The owner of the winning raffle ticket will have the opportunity to jump along a stick that has pound coins glued to it. The further they jump, the more pound coins they can win.

11. The week's memory sheet advertises the project, gives information on what will be happening that week, and has a colouring competition area and wordsearch. The memory verse sheets are shown in Appendix 7.

12. It is more accurate to say that *this part* of the programme begins. The Slough and Windsor project, in common with most of the projects visited, believes that the programme begins the moment the first child sets foot on the bus.

13. Most of the projects visited operate a similar system of rules. The Fraserburgh project is slightly more elaborate with the rules spelling the word WINNER:

> **W**atch your attitude
> **I** am here to learn and have fun
> **N**ever disobey a leader
> **N**o toilet visits during the story
> **E**veryone is important
> **R**emember the balloons

14. Song by Eminem.

15. The verse and the tune changed every week, and over the period of observation this was the only week when they had not learned the tune effectively.

16. Characterization/theatre plays an important part in the presentation of the Slough and Windsor project. In the weeks following, Lily the nice girl in her nice dress would be introduced (she cried a lot because she couldn't find Superman!), and Supergran (who was powered by Lucozade™!) was brought on as the theme for the games. In later weeks Superman and Lily will plan to go on a date but will cancel to see some fireworks – an opportunity for the leaders to show some indoor fireworks (primarily exploding coke bottles!). But the date will eventually take place... leading to an eventual marriage! On other weeks, Bin Man Ben also made an appearance, as will a giant snowman. Some of the other projects also used characterization. The Fraserburgh project featured the adventures of Jake and Ruby, two characters with puppet heads, filmed getting into situations in the children's neighbourhood, visiting shops and following unsuspecting people! The film was then shown to the children. And the Liverpool project featured a costumed individual called Strapman who sneaks out from behind the stage and places cream pies in the leaders' faces.

17. Themes were an important part of the programme; as well as this baby week, in the autumn term there was a superhero theme when many of the children and most of the leaders came dressed as superheroes, and the Christmas theme where Santa hats were in abundance.

18. Songs such as 'I love you when you call' by The Feeling and 'If this don't make you jump' by TBC were used. Also, when the boys won a game, 'The boys are back in town' by Thin Lizzy is played, and when the girls win a game, 'Girls just want to have fun' by Cyndi Lauper.

19. 'Superhero' © Hillsong Kids.

20. 'Gonna jump up and down' © Doug Horley.

21. 'Supernatural' © Hillsong Kids.

22. 'Super Strong God' © Hillsong Kids.

23. During my visits to the Slough and Windsor project I saw a variety of

different songs being used for the praise party, including 'Our God is great big God' (Vineyard Kids). 'Hey, hey I want to praise you', 'Put your hands in the sky' and 'Lovely jubbly' © Doug Horley. And for the Christmas event, 'Jingle bells', 'Rudolph the red-nosed reindeer' and 'We wish you a merry Christmas'.

24. The teaching segment always followed a similar pattern, a verse from the Bible, a Bible story, several illustrations/object lessons and then a fictional story to finish. More examples are given from a sample week in October, November and December (the programme is consistent, but at some points in the summer, the programme takes place in the open air).

October

The verse for the day was a paraphrase of Ephesians 4:25: 'Stop lying and tell the truth.' The Bible lesson used to illustrate this is the story of Zacchaeus from Luke 19. The emphasis is placed on Zacchaeus being dishonest and taking more than he should in taxes. When Jesus came to Zacchaeus, Zacchaeus had to change.

The first illustration for the day involved a balloon filled with shaving foam. Every time a lie was told, a little more air was blown into the balloon until eventually the balloon burst leaving the liar covered in foam. The message was that if we continue to lie, eventually we'll get found out and look foolish.

The next illustration was given by a woman who was a primary school teacher by profession. She told the story of the little boy who deliberately told a lie and she had to ask him three times before he told the truth. Her point was that, by lying, not only was he in trouble for the original offence (going into the teacher's cupboard) but he was now also in trouble for telling lies.

The final illustration involved a photograph of a family consisting of two sisters, a brother and a mum and dad. The illustration involved one of the sisters. Firstly, she told her father she was going to the park but she went somewhere else instead, so her father no longer trusted her (the father was cut off the photograph); then she lied to her mother, so her mother was cut off; and later she lied to her brother and sister. Eventually everyone was cut off. The illustration was used to illustrate that lying destroys relationships and isolates us.

The final story involved a nutty professor and Paul the project leader. The story involved the professor shrinking the project bus and hiding the fact from Paul. The professor tells more lies to cover his lie, and it is only when the professor tells the truth that they can work together to solve the problem, find the missing shrunken children and bus, and restore them to normal size. The whole story was told with pictures of each of the scenes projected on to the screen.

The children were then invited to respond by lifting a hand if they have lied and repeating a prayer to start to put things right. The prayer states:

> Thank you that even when I tell lies you still love me,
>> but help me to put the lies right and to tell the truth,
>> and for those who keep telling lies,
>> help them to learn to tell the truth.
>> Amen.

November

The verse for the day was a paraphrase of 2 Chronicles 13:12: 'God is with us all the time, he's your leader yours and mine.' The Bible lesson looked at 1 Samuel 16 and 17 and the account of David and Goliath. The principle was that God would lead and guide David. The Bible lesson is told by one of the junior leaders and is told without pictures. The narrative is presented with enthusiasm and good storytelling style, and the children are engrossed.

The lesson is further stated by reference to the *Forrest Gump* movie where Forrest is running and others are following, but he doesn't know where is going! Another person pretends to be stuck on a climbing wall and someone stronger and more skilled helps them down. This is followed by a personal account from one of the leaders who used to be a fan of Bananarama and copied their clothes, their music and attitude, but she realized she was wrong and they turned out to be very poor leaders who are not around today. The illustration concluded with a warning that although others may let us down, God will never let us down; he will always lead and guide us.

The teaching time concluded with a story about root ants and the Cyberspace Cadets who ended up in trouble by not following their more experienced leader, Sergeant Wilson. The emphasis was on staying close to God who will always lead us safely.

The children were asked to respond to the teaching time by standing if they wanted God to be their leader and praying a prayer after Luke. The prayer said:

> Dear God, thank you that you love me, thank you that I am important to you.
> I'm sorry when I do things wrong and make other things more important than you.
> Help me make you the leader of my life, be my best friend,
> and help me to live for you.
> Amen.

December

The verse for the day was Jeremiah 31:3: 'I will love you with a love a love that lasts for ever.' The Bible lesson looked at the arrival of the angel to Mary in Luke's Gospel, and commented that Jesus is Immanuel, God with us, which means that God's love is always with us.

The lesson is then further emphasized by a leader talking about the Andrex puppy. She asks a child to hold the toilet roll between her fingers so that it can unwind. She comments that the adverts are great and the dog runs everywhere, but in reality the toilet roll will eventually run out, no matter how long it is. At that point the toilet roll in the child's hand finishes. The leader comments, 'But God's love is not like that. It never runs out.'

The next illustration involved a leader walking on holding a baby. He comments that babies 'make smells' but their mums still love them, no matter what. Even when we do wrong things, God still loves us.

Paul pulls the threads together at the end of the programme and comments, using the 4Point structure:

God loves you no matter how bad you've been.
We've all sinned, we've all done things wrong.
Jesus died for you, to show how much he loved you.
Boys and girls, you need to make a decision to live for Jesus.
If you are making that decision today, pray this prayer after me
(somewhere in the region of 400 children repeat the prayer):
Dear Lord Jesus,
thank you that you love me and will love me for ever.
I'm sorry for the bad things that I've done. Will you forgive me?
I thank you that through Jesus I can be forgiven. Forgive me today.
Jesus, come into my heart today, I want to live for you.
Amen.

Paul then instructs those who have prayed this prayer to make sure they tell their mum or dad that they have asked Jesus to be their best friend. He also tells them that they should start talking to God, the thing that Christians call prayer.

25. Primarily to do with a disagreement with two other girls.

26. The recording of this incident is in keeping with Wolcott's (2005, p. 92) advice to capitalize on the bursts and be especially observant about capturing little vignettes or short (but complete) conversational exchanges. The subtle emphasis on cells permeates all of the Slough and Windsor project.

27. On some days, debrief is delayed because Paul spends time with the many visitors to the Slough and Windsor project. The visitors are generally there to see the Slough and Windsor project in operation with a view to starting their own similar projects, although leaders from other existing projects sometimes visit to see what ideas they can incorporate into their project (one of the team from the Hastings project visited during one of the weeks). The largest team to visit in my time of field research was a group of more than ten people from Swindon.

28. By this, Paul refers to those praying a prayer to become Christians.

29. In interview with Wes Richards, the leader of the church of which the Slough and Windsor project is a part, he recounts the Sunday School at the time the men in the story attended:

We've always had a thriving children's ministry. There were twenty-five branch Sunday schools meeting in the week in hired halls throughout the town. They would average 1,000 children a week in combined attendance. We would do Sunday school outings that would end in centre spreads in newspapers. The roads would be lined with coaches. On one occasion we chartered a whole train to take all our kids to Barry Island.

To this extent, Wes suggests that the children's ministry is the rediscovery of the work that once existed and not a new thing. He comments: 'It wasn't until our fiftieth birthday [the church was pioneered by Wes' father in 1943] that we felt God tell us to go back to our roots and re-pioneer children's work.'

30. As my daughter was also about to move from primary school to secondary school, I had researched the subject and had plenty to contribute to this discussion.

31. The integration between children's club and church can be seen on multiple levels within this church, but the fact that the senior minister is visiting children's club families is one of the strongest indications of the holistic ecclesiology being outworked here. Commenting on the ministry, Wes states: 'To take Paul on and pay the transportation budget each year has made us move on other priorities, it has made us stand in faith because we don't want to give ground on it. It has institutionalized the value of children's ministry right at the core of the church; it is growing from strength to strength. We are seeing now not just the immediate response of children, but they are growing up and staying. We are working on consolidating our children and I think we now have about 150 children in cell groups. And we are trying to consolidate the parents.'

32. Sadly, since writing this report, the boy has died. Many members of the family continue to attend the Children's Outreach Project and church.

33. 25 September 2007.

PART 2

CONNECTING WITH THE UNCHURCHED CHILD

Having considered Raikes and the pattern of child evangelism that he developed, and an overview of child evangelism in the twenty-first century, and having made a detailed examination of five key projects, this section moves on to interpretive comparisons. These interpretive comparisons focus on areas of theology, sociology and practice.

Chapter 6

THEOLOGY

It has already been noted that as soon as the Clapham Sect and others began to develop Sunday Schools, the original model of Sunday School was modified and the need for a personal conversion experience was strongly emphasized.[1] This lack of overt evangelism within the original model was a deeply concerning factor for the early Evangelicals and caused many to conclude that Raikes' model was primarily to teach literacy to the masses.[2]

As the nineteenth century ended, Evangelicalism pervaded nearly all the Sunday Schools. The need for every boy and girl to have a personal conversion experience was intrinsic to the Sunday School movement as it entered the twentieth century, as highlighted in the article produced by the Revd Frank J. Gould writing in the Birmingham Sunday School Union quarterly record of 1903:[3]

> But after all the business of the Sunday School is salvation. Let me ask then, are there more lives won for Christ? Are conversions more frequent than they were? This is the great question, for if we have not increased our main result, our profit is not much to boast of. A scholar is either won for Christ or lost to Christ, and a little learning more or less is nothing compared to eternity.

All of the Children's Outreach Projects examined in Phase 3 (Chapters 4 and 5) have a clear emphasis on the children undergoing a conversion experience. The Slough and Windsor, Hastings, Leeds and Liverpool projects have a prescriptive approach to evangelism and conversion that is presented in a formula the projects call the 4Points. The Slough and Windsor project uses a booklet to present these 4Points, and the Leeds and Hastings projects use a card. The Liverpool project uses four shapes to explain the four points (figure 6.1). In interview, the leader of the Fraserburgh project outlined a different model of evangelism, a nurturing model that he presented using the metaphor of the nest; however, when I observed the project in action, his co-leader (possibly unaware of the nest metaphor) presented the theology that underpins the 4Points to the children. The 4Points state:[4]

1. God loves me

2. I have sinned

3. Jesus died for me

4. I need to decide to live for God

Fig 6.1 The Liverpool project uses these four symbols to represent the 4Points

There are issues surrounding the formulaic approach to evangelism presented by the Children's Outreach Projects, and specifically a strong theological debate concerning the second point 'I have sinned'. Paul, the leader of the Slough and Windsor project, sums up the theological position of all the largest Children's Outreach Projects (in practice if not in stated theology): 'If the child is of an age of understanding, they are responsible for their own sin, and they are not saved.'[5] To clarify the position of the Children's Outreach Projects examined, it is not that the child has sinned or will sin; it is that the child's intrinsic state is sinful. This issue necessitates some discussion on the spiritual state of the pre-evangelized child.

Fig 6.2 The 4Points display at the front of the Slough and Windsor project

THE SPIRITUAL STATE OF THE PRE-EVANGELIZED CHILD

Traina[6] suggests:

> The history of the theology of childhood might well be cast as
> the history of the struggle to preserve and express Augustine's
> doctrine of original sin without ending beliefs in both divine justice
> and divine mercy toward the weak and vulnerable.

The use of the phrase 'Augustine's doctrine of original sin' is necessary;
it is Augustine's doctrine of original sin[7] that has provoked such strong
debate. Until the fourth century the prevailing view of original sin was
represented by the views of Chrysostom[8] who wrote:

> Newborn babies are innocents, wholly without sin. Infants may
> belong to a corporate human nature, which in its wholeness is
> mortally wounded by original sin and the will of which is weakened
> and prone to personal sin, but they are still innocents.

To clarify, Chrysostom wrote, 'We do baptise infants, but they are not guilty
of any sins.'[9] For Chrysostom, baptism represented the public acceptance
of the child by the faith community.

Meyendorff[10] further comments on original sin before Augustine's
formulation as 'an inheritance essentially of mortality rather than sinfulness,
sinfulness being mainly a consequence of mortality'. In light of this, an
understanding of the formation of this doctrine is necessary. Although
history has rightfully noted that Augustine first formulated this doctrine,
the process by which he drew this conclusion is worthy of exploration.

Shortly after his ordination in AD 396 Augustine, preaching on the
slaughter of the innocents,[11] concluded that even though they were not
baptized, God had some 'good compensation' for them. This statement is a
long way from the conclusion that he would eventually reach towards the
end of life: that the holy innocents were condemned to eternal damnation
but he hoped their punishment would be gentle.[12]

The journey between such extremes is not an overnight one. The
change in doctrinal stance and his eventual position is arrived at through
much reflection, study and emotional angst. In his letter to Jerome,[13]
Augustine wrote, 'But when we come to the perils of the suffering of
children, you must understand that I experience great difficulties for which
I have no answer.' By the beginning of the fifth century Augustine argued,

'The feebleness of the infant limbs are innocent, not the infant's mind.'[14]

Augustine argued that unbaptized infants occupied a state between depravity and innocence. This is a state that Stortz[15] refers to as, 'non innocence'; she further comments that Augustine's Confessions draw together the idea of stages of development from infancy to childhood to adolescence with greater degrees of guilt and accountability attributed to each of these stages. By 415[16] Augustine had concluded that an infant's lack of baptism would mean they were condemned.[17] There is an observed development in Augustine's doctrine, but the end is without ambiguity. Hall[18] observed:

> Augustine developed the idea of original sin, which means the sin people are born with... the child is born stained, and must be washed clean. Each is therefore born guilty. What they are guilty of is Adam's sin.

It must be remembered that doctrine is rarely formed in a vacuum and the doctrine of original sin is no exception. Augustine's view is formed through observation and study of New Testament texts and against the backdrop of refuting what he saw as the heresy of Pelagius.[19] Stortz[20] summarizes Augustine's observational conclusion:

- Even infants show sinful tendencies.
- Adam's transgression, which implants in his progeny an alien sin, accounts for those tendencies.
- Baptism remedies those damnable tendencies and should be conferred as early as possible.

Although it is important not to assume that baptism is the cure for alien sin and damnable tendencies, it is the beginning of the cure.[21] Within Augustine's theology, baptism only bestows on the baptized admittance to 'the hospital of grace, where one spent a lifetime convalescing'.[22]

It would be easy to dismiss Augustine's argument based on fairness, as many have tried to do.[23] However, Augustine's arguments are too embedded within modern theology to avoid engagement with him on this basis. If we replace the third point above with the words 'A personal conversion experience is necessary to remedy this sin', then we have a clear statement of the position of the Children's Outreach Projects (and much of the evangelical church) at the commencement of the twenty-first century.

Although Augustine's conclusions were partly formed through

observation, he would assert that the main basis for the formation of his doctrine of original sin came from a careful study of the New Testament, particularly Paul's letter to the Romans;[24] Romans 5:12, 18 was used to present the core of Augustine's argument.

Many elements of Augustine's argument can be dismissed without much discussion. For example, in reading Augustine's writings, specifically his writings against Pelagianism, it becomes clear that much of the debate is to do with the translations used. Pelagius' translation used the phrase sin 'came into'[25] the world through Adam, although Augustine's translation used the phrase sin 'penetrated'[26] the world through Adam. Stortz[27] comments, 'For Augustine the word dripped with sexual meaning: the contamination spread from Adam's semen.' In Augustine's view, the spread of Adam's sin is by sexual reproduction.[28] However, although both Latin words are a legitimate translation of the Greek word εἰς [29] (*eis*), the word εἰς does not carry sexual connotation.

There are further issues with regard to translation. Augustine[30] wrote:

> In whom[31], that is, Adam, all have sinned. He [Paul] used the masculine (*in quo*) though he is speaking about the woman, because his reference was not to the sex, but to the race. So it is clear that all have sinned in Adam collectively, as it were (*quasi im massa*). He was himself corrupted by sin and the race that he begat were all born under sin. From him therefore all are sinners, because we are all produced from him.

Meyendorff[32] clarifies:

> The last four Greek words were translated *in quo ommes peccaverunt* ('in whom [Adam] all men have sinned'),[33] and this translation was used in the West to justify the guilt inherited from Adam and spread to his descendants.

However, such a meaning cannot be drawn from the original Greek. Moo[34] agrees that if 'the one man' is the antecedent of the pronoun, we have then an explicit statement of original sin: 'in whom [Adam] all sinned'. However he continues, 'This interpretation, and others that rest on a similar grammatical basis are unlikely. For the two words probably function together as a conjunction.[35] The phrase may then mean 'from which it follows'. *Today's New International Version* of the Bible translates the phrase 'consequently'.

Augustine's main opponent, Pelagius, held that Adam's sin has absolutely no connection to our sin, other than through sinful example. However, to draw this conclusion is to ignore the textual evidence completely. Several issues are not as straightforward as Pelagius asserted and need further consideration. Moo[36] writes:

> Paul says nothing explicitly about how the sin of one man, Adam, has resulted in death[37] for everyone; nor has he made clear the connection, if any – between Adam's sin (v. 12a) and the sin of all people (v. 12d). What he has made clear is that the causal nexus between sin and death, exhibited in the case of Adam, has repeated itself in the case of every human being. No one, Paul makes clear, escapes the reign of death because no one escapes the power of sin.

Several questions need to be addressed. What is the relationship between Adam's sin and the sin of subsequent individuals? Why do all people without exception sin – and this statement must apply to children also ('all sinned', v. 12d)?[38] In addition, how is it that Adam's sin leads to the condemnation of all people?

There is almost universal agreement amongst commentators that Paul most often uses the word *sin* to refer to the sinful acts committed by individuals. Wesley defined sin as 'the guilt that stems from a culpable act traceable to the unethical conduct of a morally responsible person'.[39] Fitzmyer[40] writes:

> The verb Hemarton[41] should not be understood as have *sinned collectively* or as *have sinned in Adam*, because they would be additions to Paul's text. The verb refers to personal, actual sins of individual human beings, as Pauline usage elsewhere suggests (2:12; 3:23; 5:14,16; 1 Corinthians 6:18; 7:28, 36; 8:12; 15:34), as the context demands (vv. 16, 20), and as Greek Fathers understood it.

Further to this, the Bible does not teach that a single transgression changes the position of a person from *in Christ* to *in Adam*. Instead, the Bible teaches that to move from being εν χριστω must involve a conscious decision to terminate relationship as paralleled in the Garden of Eden narrative. Hall,[42] in particularly impassioned words, writes, 'The idea of infants being guilty at birth and deserving damnation is repulsive, and leads to an improperly superstitious view of the necessity to baptise infants.'

Others have argued that what was inherited from Adam was a sinful human nature, a particular bias towards sin. It is an argument that will be presented by both Luther and Calvin. The argument suggests that Romans 5:12 refers to individual sins committed in history, as a necessary result of a corrupt nature inherited from Adam. Spiritual death can then be attributed to the sinning of each individual and to the sin of Adam – Adam causing the corrupted human nature that makes sin an inevitability. Judaism also denies the form of original sin suggested by Augustine and embraces its own version of sinful bias that it terms the *Yezer Hara*. Robinson[43] defines Yezer Hara as 'the impulse common to the race of Adam'. Also, there are certainly Old Testament examples where the actions of individuals can appear to have a representational character – being regarded as the actions of others at the same time. The most obvious example is Achan's sin of Joshua 7 that resulted in the death of hundreds of Israelites.

Undoubtedly, the notion of a sinful bias may seem to resolve some of the tensions of Romans, but to advocate this view would involve making many assumptions. In the Achan narrative, Achan is not strictly representative of his community; instead, the narrative focuses on how Achan's sin causes Yahweh to remove his blessing and as a result people die in battle. Further to this, the doctrine of Yezer Hara suggests that Adam already possessed sinful nature before he sinned – some would suggest it caused him to sin. On that basis, the concept of Yezer Hara should be questioned.[44] In addition, the text itself would have to read 'one man's trespass resulted in the corruption of human nature, which caused all people to sin, and so brought condemnation on all men'. Although it is possible that Paul would want us to assume these additions, he has given us little basis for doing so.

Therefore, although it may be an attractive proposition to conclude that Romans is resolved with an understanding that humankind inherits sinful nature from Adam, it would be to attribute more to the text than is actually there. It is also difficult to reconcile this with a doctrine of free will. How can a person who will inevitably sin because of innate sinful nature be truly free? And those who express concern that justice is not served by Augustine's doctrine of original sin when a person is found guilty of sin they have not committed, must surely be likewise concerned by the unfairness of a system where sin becomes an inevitability.

Having discussed both Augustinian doctrine and the notion of inherited sinful nature, a third way may now be suggested. The difficulty is not with Romans 5:12. The text in modern translations is self-explanatory: death (total death, as explored earlier) came to Adam because of his act; all people likewise experience death (total death) because of their own personal act of rebellion against God. After the parenthesis offered by Romans 5:13–17, 18, then continues Paul's argument to state that Adam's act brought condemnation for all, just as Christ's act brought justification for all. It is suggested that the groups affected by Christ and Adam are not commensurate, but that Christ affects those who are his in the same way Adam affects those who are his. This view has the additional factor of being consistent with Paul's further writings in 1 Corinthians 15:22 and with subsequent comments in Romans, such as Romans 8:1 However, this interpretation of Romans is often undermined by inconsistencies. Moo[45] suggests:

> When we ask who belongs to, or is *in*, Adam or Christ, respectively, Paul makes his answer clear: every person, without exception, is *in Adam* (cf. vv. 12d–14); but only those who *receive the gift* are *in Christ*.

The suggestion is that all human beings are automatically 'in Adam' until they make a conscious choice to 'receive the gift'. There is no logic to this argument, and neither does it follow the very narrative that Paul is expounding – that of Adam. Adam is clearly seen to be *in Christ* until he makes a decision to sin. Romans 5 gives context and biblical example (Adam's personal fall in Eden) to demonstrate that far from being born guilty of Adam's sin, or being born with inherited sinful nature, the child is born *in Christ*, and only as a result of a conscious decision to walk away from being *in Christ* do they become positionally *in Adam*.

Because of this, it is suggested that the Augustinian view of original sin cannot be sustained through a study of Romans; furthermore, a doctrine that attributes actual sin and judicial guilt to the child at conception is without validity and should be rejected. However, despite this rejection and the clear flaws in thinking, Augustine's doctrine of original sin is still a strongly held belief today[46] and its doctrinal basis is adopted and propagated by the Children's Outreach Projects visited. However, the reason for this may have more to do with denominational affiliation and church tradition than theological reflection.

If Augustine had provided the structure for this way of thinking, Aquinas provided the building. Traina attempts to present a balanced picture of Aquinas but in reality Aquinas' theology began where Augustine's concluded. Aquinas stated, 'All who are not baptised are subject to the power of demons.'[47] He also shared Augustine's belief that baptism was the beginning of the process that, with continued prayer, teaching, self-discipline and sacraments, may eventually result in salvation.

It was from Aquinas that for the first time there is a clear suggestion that baptism remits sin, both 'original and actual'. The idea is embedded within Augustinian theology, but is not stated as clearly as it is in Aquinas.[48] Of course, this did not deal with infants who die before baptism. It is at this point that Aquinas develops what must be seen as the cruellest of doctrines. Aquinas declares that although they are not deserving of damnation, since they are incapable of *actual* sin, they are also undeserving of salvation, since they still bear the stain of *original* sin. They are therefore consigned to the *limbus puerorum*, or children's limbo, where they are denied intimate union with God but spared the physical, spiritual, and psychological pain of hell; as innocent bearers of original sin, they neither deserve nor expect heaven.

As repugnant as these doctrines of *limbus puerorum*[49] and Augustine's original sin[50] may sound, they would be ratified in subsequent councils[51] and would remain the prevailing Roman Catholic view into the mid-twentieth century.[52]

Despite various challenges to Aquinas' doctrine of children's limbo, Augustine's doctrine of original sin faced no significant challenge until the twentieth century[53] and the writings and work of two significant theologians. The first of these is Karl Barth.[54] Barth rejects transmission of sin as an extremely unfortunate and mistaken doctrine that would rule out a human agent's responsibility for the evil he or she does or becomes.[55] He tackles and resolutely opposes the doctrines of original sin and *limbus puerorum*, leading Werepehowski[56] to write:

> Barth opposes this fusion, stressing instead that children are bearers of a promise of grace by virtue of God's will to make them, and all humanity, covenant partners in Jesus Christ... Like all human creatures, they possess impulses and desires that must be respected and ordered to responsible existence. Under no circumstance should they be respected and ordered to responsible existence. Under no circumstances should they be identified with an inherited strain of original sin.

For Barth, sin is not an inherited principle but a conscious act.

A more recent challenge to the doctrines of original sin and *limbus puerorum* has come from within the Roman Catholic Church through the twentieth-century theologian Karl Rahner.[57] Rahner, a Jesuit, was clearly influenced by Ignatian spirituality,[58] and for him the concept of *limbus puerorum* was simply unacceptable. Many have argued that without his intervention *limbus puerorum* would have become church dogma at the Second Vatican Council.[59]

Rahner rejected the doctrine on the basis that it was not something that could be sustained scripturally or ethically, and it was not in keeping with what he saw as the character and nature of God.[60] Rahner[61] supported this position further with his theological position: 'if someone knows nothing about baptism or is unable to receive it, divine life nevertheless lives, in the innermost heart of this person, as proffered or as freely accepted divine life.'

Rahner's view is considerably more optimistic that that of Augustine, the Reformers or even the Council of Trent, since he recognizes also that although children are born into a history of sin, they are also in their origins encompassed by God's love through the pledge of grace, which, in God's will to save all humankind, comes in all cases and to everyone from God in Christ Jesus.

Rahner suggests that original sin is only sin in an analogous sense;[62] it is not sin in the actual sense. It is a return to the pre-Augustinian view, the view that has prevailed in the Eastern Orthodox Church for two millennia.

The conclusion from these paragraphs must be that the newborn child is untainted before God. However, does all this in itself challenge the assumptions of point 2 of the Children's Outreach Projects' 4Points? The answer is not necessarily. The assumption that everyone sins – defined as not living up to God's standards – is the reason that many Christian services start with acts of confession and absolution. The 4Points themselves may be perfectly legitimate. The theology underpinning point 2 and the way point 2 is presented is the issue – it is the theology behind the statement. This goes one step further in the application of the 4Points. The Hastings project uses a card to enable the children to respond to the four points. It reads:

1. *Father God I thank you that you love me*
2. *I'm sorry I have sinned*
3. *Jesus thank you that you died for me*
4. *Help me to live for you*

Although the card could be a useful tool, the difficulty is that it is used as a once-and-for all response to the 4Points.[63] Before the children complete the cards, they are seen as not Christian. After completing the cards, they are seen as Christian, or *saved*, or having received *salvation* (the terminology varies). When several children stood to respond to the 4Points in the Liverpool project, the leader Dave quoted Luke 15:10 and informed the children that there was rejoicing in heaven over the decision they had made. At the Hastings project Chris stated:

> The 4Points is what happens when people become Christians. God loves me, I have sinned, Jesus died for me, I need to decide to live for God. So becoming a Christian means knowing God loves you, being sorry for the things you've done wrong and realizing that Jesus died for those things, and you can have that relationship with God. But you need to make that decision.

The problem with this was highlighted by Bernie, the leader of the Leeds project, when she stated, 'If we did the 4Points a month later, 99 per cent would probably respond again.' The 4Points are presented in such a way that they assume that before the children choose to say the 4Points, they are not Christians; after they have said the 4Points, then they are. However, what will be shown below is the Children's Outreach Projects themselves have no consistent theology with regard to this. The Slough and Windsor, Hastings and Liverpool projects are far more pragmatic in theological terms, suggesting that before the children stand and make a response, and undergo their own personal conversion experience, they are not Christians. The Fraserburgh and Hastings projects are far more reluctant to state that. It is this need for a one-off personal conversion experience and the evangelistic process that will now be explored further.

CHILD EVANGELISM AS CHRISTIAN EDUCATION

Most definitions of evangelism will involve a greater or lesser level of imparting information; words such as *proclamation, spreading good news* and *preaching* dominate.[64] There have been many challenges to defining evangelism in this way. One of the most recent is from Abraham,[65] who contends that this way of understanding evangelism as imparting information is a recent development:

> The process began with Wesley and Whitefield in the eighteenth century; it was developed by Charles Finney and his imitators in

the early part of the nineteenth century; it was perfected by D. L. Moody and Billy Sunday in the last half of the nineteenth century; it has been tempered and qualified by Billy Graham in the last generation; and it has now received a whole new lease of life with the arrival of the so-called television evangelists.

However, to suggest that the model of evangelism defined by proclamation and response is an eighteenth-century construct is to ignore most of Paul's missionary journeys[66] where this pattern is clearly in evidence, and to ignore the etymology of the word *evangelism* itself. Nevertheless, to suggest that the only model of evangelism is that which consists of a single individual loudly addressing a crowd, as modelled by Paul and the other examples listed by Abraham, would also be wrong and show a misunderstanding of what is meant by announcing good news. Although the announcing of the Christian gospel in a stadium by a famous evangelist such as Billy Graham is a completely valid form of evangelism, so is the one-to-one announcing of good news modelled by Philip in Luke's account of the meeting between Phillip and the Ethiopian eunuch.[67] More relevantly, what is also encompassed within this definition is the man or woman who stands in front of a group of boys and/or girls and announces what Stott refers to as 'gospel events'.[68]

It must not be overlooked that *bringing of good news* is an equally valid etymological definition of evangelism. There is embedded within this definition the idea that the person who does good in the name of Christ may be performing an act of evangelism without the use of words. It is the form of evangelism suggested by the New Testament book of James; it allows the definition of evangelism to encompass acts of Christian service. This definition of bringing good news could also encompass the miracles recorded by the New Testament writers and writers of church history – they too are in effect acts of evangelism as they bring good news. They proclaim without words the Christian message. It is therefore reasonable to conclude that projects involved in feeding those who cannot feed themselves properly, or homework clubs, or after-school projects for those whose parents are not at home at the end of the school day, are acts of evangelism.

Evangelism therefore can be said to encompass the bringing or announcing of gospel events through proclamation, acts of Christian service and/or miracles. Nevertheless, most New Testament examples of acts of service[69] and miraculous signs[70] act as platforms for some sort of proclamation of Christian doctrine. In light of this, it can be concluded that although evangelism may have many facets, the combined factors of etymology, Scripture and experience suggest that proclamation and announcement are the predominant forms.[71]

That which has been termed the announcing of gospel events was referred to by Raikes as catechism and, in the twenty-first century, is often termed Christian education. The words proclaim or announce may unfortunately continue to invoke pictures of John Wesley addressing the crowd, but, as has been seen, this is only a small aspect of the overall use of the term. There could be little doubt that evangelism does involve the communication of knowledge. It was Hegel[72] who suggested, 'To describe religion as something wholly or even essentially of the feelings is to misrepresent its true character.' Despite this dynamic evolution of Christian spirituality, it does not prevent the area of catechism from causing consternation. Added to this, it is child evangelism under discussion.[73] Since the eighteenth century, many have suggested that children are simply incapable of understanding Christian catechism. They believe evangelism should be confined to adults; the argument is that the announcement of a Christian message is a form of indoctrination. However, far from trying to avoid the term, Copley[74] embraces it and writes:

> None of the commentators, interestingly, raise the questions of whether indoctrination by omission is possible. A child from a home in which religion and God are never mentioned and encountering a curriculum in which they do not occur, except perhaps *en passant* in history lessons, may not only have no belief on God, but may view the entire question of God as unnecessary and irrelevant, even incomprehensible... Surely this too is indoctrination, as it has very effectively fixed habits and dispositions without engaging the child's active powers. The child genuinely means it when she says that she does not believe in God, that God is unnecessary. She has no ability to critique this view or to see how it has been so successfully implanted.

Copley brings a clear understanding that all children experience indoctrination. Some are exposed to religious doctrine; others are exposed to atheistic or agnostic doctrine simply by the lack of religious teaching. Copley[75] further emphasizes his point:

> Commentary on indoctrination has tended to emphasize it as a method of teaching rather than as the content or intention

of teaching. Church schools are periodically accused of indoctrination, but illogically, public schools, i.e. 'state schools', as they are often inaccurately known in Britain (no school is directly controlled by the state), are not accused of the mirror image, secular indoctrination. It is often presumed that no religious institution is value free. But no corporation or institution, secular or religious, is value free.

The word *indoctrination* will always have negative connotations, but the idea that children are – and should be – exposed to a wide range of beliefs and practice is well made by Copley. There are those who come from perspectives other than theological who question the need to expose children to religion at all; still others from the social sciences who doubt that children have the ability to understand what is being presented. However, far from dismissing their comments, it is important to evaluate the contribution they may make. The theological task must not only be concerned with the interpretation of religion but also with the interpretation of other disciplines that offer interpretations of religion.[76] The work of structural theorists and their theories of cognitive development in children are important and the following paragraphs will review their findings.[77]

The man most often acknowledged as the founder[78] and most famous exponent of structural theory was Jean Piaget,[79] a European psychologist who studied children's cognitive growth and abilities. Piaget suggests the stages of a child's cognitive development, listed in figure 6.3.

Piaget believed that the way children understand their world is determined by the cognitive structures that develop sequentially as they grow. He hypothesized a state of harmony or equilibrium, which is achieved as particular cognitive structures develop. However, as cognitive growth continues, the things and people in the environment are seen in a new perspective. This introduces what Piaget termed 'cognitive dissonance'. Elements of the child's mental picture of the world no longer fit, so the child actively works at reconstructing his or her picture of the universe, reordering the elements present to provide equilibrium again; the development needed to restore equilibrium has, in effect, moved the child to a new cognitive structural stage.

Piaget's structural stages became the building blocks for future research into cognitive development. Goldman pioneered the application of Piagetian stages to religious thinking in the early 1960s, although Goldman's research is dated and has been extensively challenged. A more recent example of Piagetian stages applied to faith development is James

1½ to 4	Pre-conceptual	• imitative language, only partially understood • objects seen as stable, not able to grasp changing shapes due to perspective • lacks abstracting ability to perceive space apart from perspective • beginning to distinguish between past, present and future • reasoning is by analogy to experiences
4 to 7	Intuitive	• language and thought still tied to phenomenal experience: words represent child's own experiences and perceptions (a bottle is 'where you put water') • comprehends and can respond to complex adult language, but does not understand such processes as conservation (the transfer of a principle or characteristic across situations) • objects now maintain identity despite changes in position perspective • number sense develops with ability to measure quantity • can compensate fully for perspective changes caused by change in position • time sense is still personalised, and interactions between time, distance, speed, etc. not grasped • great interest in explaining causes of what is observed, understanding of causes still highly intuitive • can trace change in states through complex series rather than rely on impression of a particular observed state
7 to 10	Concrete	• can take others' points of view and integrate their prescriptive with his own • can begin to distinguish variables that cause change and mentally predict changes • capacities to perceive objects, numbers, time, space all significantly developed • mechanical explanations of cause are given priority (clouds move because the winds push) • only now does the ability to think about thought – to explore relations between the real and the possible develop; 'adult' kinds of thinking become possible
10–15	Formal operations	

Fig 6.3 Piaget's structural stages summarized by Richards (1983)

Fowler's *Stages of Faith*. Goldman's research will be touched on, but it is Fowler's work that will form the major part of this consideration of child evangelism.[80]

Fowler built on Piaget's structures to form his stages of faith. The parallels between Piaget's and Fowler's stages, alongside several other

Piaget's Suggested Ages	Ages based on K & A Research	Levinson's Eras	Piaget's Stages	Erikson's Eras	Fowler's [83] Stages
Age 0-2	Age 0-2		Sensorimotor	Trust v Mistrust	Undifferentiated Faith (0)
2-3	2-3		Preoperational or Intuitive	Autonomy v Doubt	Intuitive projective Faith (1)
3-6	3-(4-6)	Infancy, Childhood & Adolescence		Initiative v Guilt	
6-11	(4-6)-(8-12)		Concrete Operational	Industry v Inferiority	Mythic-Literal Faith (2)
11-20	(8-12)-		Formal Operational	Identity v Role Confusion	Synthetic-Conventional Faith (3)
		Early Adulthood (21-35)		Intimacy v Isolation	Individuative-Reflective Faith (4)
		Middle Adulthood (35-60)		Generosity v Stagnation	Conjunctive Faith (5)
		Late Adulthood (60+)		Integrity v Despair	Universalizing Faith (6)

Fig 6.4 Faith, cognitive & psychosocial parallels formed from the amalgam of several tables within Fowler and Richards

important contributors (Erikson's psychosocial research and Levinson's Eras), are shown in figure 6.4.

There are three observations that need to be made on Fowler's research before considering the developmental stages. For Fowler, faith is means by which people experience self, others and the world, in a way that shapes loyalties and commitments, and as grasped in or expressed through their images of ultimate being.[82] Fowler further clarifies, 'Faith is a generic feature of human struggle to find and maintain meaning and that it may or may not find religious expression.'[83] For Fowler, the exploration of faith development is about more than developing religious belief; it is to do with the development of a general world view, which may or may not be religious in form. Interestingly, the majority of the research interviews that Fowler published involve religion, and since this is an exploration of child evangelism, the discussion will be restricted to those cases.

Secondly, Fowler[84] believes that faith stages meet the structural-developmental criteria for stages. In this way, he sees faith as moving from one stage to another. Interwoven with this is the third observation; these stages of faith development primarily involve cognition and epistemology. It can also be observed from the table (figure 6.4) that these faith stages tie in to the stages suggested by Piaget, with the addition of three extra stages (4–6). Fowler suggests that these extra stages could be comparable with Levinson's eras with stages 4, 5 and 6 falling within the eras of early, middle and late adulthood respectively.

Finally, while believing that Fowler and Piaget have made a valuable contribution to their respective disciplines, consideration must be given to the research of Klausmeier and Allen.[85] In their study of concept formation, Klausmeier and Allen carried out extensive developmental tests on children. The results of the study are significant in that, although the children did move from level to level in the sequence predicted by Piaget, there was a difference in the ages/grades at which individuals attained and mastered concepts.[86] It is therefore postulated that since Piaget began his research in the early twentieth century children themselves have changed. Certainly, within the Western world, children are developing *physically* faster, but there is evidence in Klausmeier and Allen's research that children are developing *cognitively* faster. It may well be that children in modern European cities, for example, are passing through the cognitive stages more rapidly than was the case several decades ago.[87] It appears that although Piaget allows for some movement within the ages of his stages, the actual movement is considerable. Although the preoperational and intuitive phases are more consistent, the age that the child moves from concrete to formal operation is far more dynamic. Added to this, although it will be seen that the age at which children enter Fowler's faith stages 0, 1 and 2 are relatively predictable, the age at which they enter stage 3 is not. Moreover, many adults do not move past faith stage 3 and many show characteristics of faith stage 2. In fact, if Levinson's eras are helpful, it is in indicating that the majority of people complete their faith development by the end of the first era.

By the time an average person leaves their adolescent world, their world view has become fixed and inflexible. Since faith development for Fowler is primarily cognitive (directly relational to what Piaget terms 'intelligence'), it is not surprising that when cognitive development reaches the formal operational stage, there is no further faith development. Piaget writes, 'Finally, from 11–12 years and during adolescence, formal thought is perfected and its groupings characterize the completion of reflective intelligence.'[88]

Further to this, the idea that Fowler's later stages match Levinson's eras of early, middle and late adulthood is undermined by the fact that not everyone reaches stage 4. Stage 5 remains undefined in Fowler's understanding – making it difficult to assess whether those in middle adulthood are really at that stage, while stage 6 is reserved for a tiny percentage of the population.[89] Hull writes:

> Stage six persons threaten ordinary standards of survival and self-interest... [They] set up around themselves a zone of freedom that proves to be extraordinarily attractive and creative.[90]

This is undoubtedly why Fowler limited his examples of stage 6 individuals to the likes of Gandhi, Mother Theresa and Martin Luther King![91]

There is no attempt to discredit Fowler's work here; the insights brought by his analysis of stages of faith are significant and eminently useful. Nevertheless, what must be avoided is assuming that the development of faith is something that happens automatically in the same way as physical or intellectual development. This may be the case for children in faith stages 1 and 2, but based on the aforementioned research of Klausmeier and Allen,[92] beyond that stage the age at which faith stage 3 takes place (and for that matter the stage that Piaget's formal operational stage takes place) is not as predefined as the structural theorists may suggest. It would certainly be within the realms of probability for formal operational abilities and synthetic conventional faith (faith stage 3) to be encountered as young as age eight – at least in emerging form.[93] What must also be avoided is the idea that faith stage development is an instantaneous act, in the sense that today the child is at faith stage 1 and tomorrow they are at faith stage 2. There are large overlaps between the faith stages, to the extent that a child or adult may exhibit faith stage 3 characteristics in one area, still be holding on to faith stage 1 in another, but generally work out of faith stage 2. This interweave is much more pronounced in faith development than it is in Piaget's cognitive stages.

There is also a key distinction between Piaget and Fowler. This is summarized by Hull: 'James Fowler makes it clear that doubt is part of the life of faith, for the successive images of faith destroy their predecessors.'[94] Fowler writes:

> Development results from efforts to restore balance between subject and environment when some factor of maturation or environmental change has disturbed a previous equilibrium. Growth and development in faith also result from life crises, challenges and the kinds of disruptions that theologians call revelation. Each of these brings disequilibrium and requires changes in our ways of seeing and being in faith.[95]

Faith development therefore involves changes in the way things are perceived, but more than this. Fowler writes:

> In these kinds of constitutive-knowing not only is the 'known' being constructed, but there is also a simultaneous extension, modification, reconstitution of the knower in relation to the known.[96]

These movements through faith stages may legitimately be called conversion experiences.[97] This process of transformation is in contrast to Piaget's stages where cognition is a process of unbalance and equilibrium as knowledge is added to, or amended, precept upon precept. Within faith development, a person moving from one stage to another becomes something they were not before. Not only is their way of seeing their world different but they themselves are different. To use Hull's words, the way they 'experience self' is different. Westerhoff writes:

> Christians are not made or formed through nurture. Conversion – reorientations of life, changes of heart, mind and behaviour – are a necessary aspect of mature Christian faith whether or not one

grows up in the church.[98]

Westerhoff further clarifies his position: 'To be a Christian calls for numerous experiences of conversion.'[99] This view is in keeping with Löffler's statement that 'Conversion is, moreover, an ongoing, lifelong process'.[100] The vocabulary may be different, but, in essence, Westerhoff is suggesting that the child undergoes various conversions as he or she develops physically and cognitively. Traditionally, the child evangelist is one whose focus is the conversion of children to Christianity. Their role has been primarily involved with those who are not yet Christian. This understanding cannot be reconciled with Westerhoff's assertion that multiple acts of conversion are necessary. Therefore, within the context of this book the child evangelist will be redefined as the one to whom is given the responsibility of aiding children through various conversion experiences. The definition is not, and must not, be restricted to that first encounter with the Christian faith. The label of child evangelist can therefore be extended to the vast army of Sunday School teachers and children's club leaders who work with the same children on a continuous basis. The definition is also not out of place when applied to those schoolteachers who teach Christian education. This is not to say that a person encountering Christianity for the first time is not important, Frank states, 'It has become too common in all the talk about journey and pilgrim models to minimize those crystallizing moments, especially the key one of spiritual birth.'[101] However, it is also important to recognize that for some there will be no time when they remember not being Christian. What is important is that there are ongoing conversion experiences. The language is important and what is being said must be clear. Both Westerhoff and Fowler are talking about conversion in the sense of transformation. Gadamer writes:

> Transformation is not change, even a change that is especially far-reaching. A change always means that what is changed also remains the same and is held on to... But transformation means that something is suddenly and as a whole something else... When we find someone transformed we mean precisely this, that he has become, as it were, another person.[102]

The observation needs making with clarity; otherwise it could be misconstrued as agreeing with Buckland's view:

> Every move towards Christ can be described as a 'decision towards

Christ'. People don't just drift into Christ, it involves decision, but it may, probably does, involve a number of decisions. And we want to affirm them... We want to encourage them to keep on going. That may mean we are encouraging more movement towards the point at which they enter into discipleship.[103]

This reintroduces Attfield's earlier idea of a halfway house between Christian and non-Christian. Westerhoff has room for an ongoing journey towards Christ through ongoing conversion; nevertheless, as soon as the first conversion takes place then the child is deemed, εν χριστω (in Christ). There is no middle ground suggested by Buckland and Attfield; the child is in Christ or they are not. Overall, the Children's Outreach Projects do not fall into this halfway-house position. On the one hand, Bernie, the leader of the Leeds project, is clear that 'The whole of the child's life is a journey, so what they might understand at four they might understand in a different way at seven or eight'. However, she is also clear that once they have stood to accept Christ they are Christians, but she does not comment on their spiritual state before this point. This may owe much to her own experience: she speaks of coming from a Catholic background and making an active decision to follow Christ at age fourteen. She does not use terms such as conversion, or being saved, to describe her own experience, but instead opts for the expression 'Decision to follow Christ'. Chris at the Hastings project also refutes the idea of a halfway house and is clear that the children have transitioned from non-Christian to Christian at that moment of first response and were outside of Christ before this first response:

When they stand and respond to a gospel appeal and they stand and they close their eyes and they know it is a special moment between them and God, when they stand and respond to the gospel, then I have to believe that they are saved. And I believed that they are saved and they have entered the kingdom of heaven, but their level of understanding is woefully short, but God is a God of grace and mercy and I believe that they have entered the kingdom of heaven at that point.

The faith stages themselves will now be considered.

Faith stage 0

Faith stage 0 is paralleled with Piaget's sensorimotor stage. It is described by Fowler as a pre-stage rather than a faith development stage in its own right.[104] However, all are clear that normal development at this point is crucial to the faith stages that follow. Difficulties during this stage, as will be illustrated when phenomenology and the construction of the *God* image is considered later, may hinder or completely paralyze future faith development. Hull, drawing on the psychosocial work of Erikson, writes:

> The characteristic tension, as described by Erikson, is that between trust and mistrust and the result is the achieving of a certain equilibrium or balance of trust. If this is satisfactory, the resulting virtue is called by Erikson 'faith'. In faith the inner and the outer world are acceptably combined and are seen to be mutually engaged in compatible activities.[105]

The failure of this development of faith due to an overdevelopment of mistrust (as a result of neglect or abuse) will lead to stunted development in many areas – in the areas of autonomy and hope, but particularly in the development of faith.

Faith stage 1

Faith stage 1 (intuitive-projective faith) is paralleled with Piaget's preoperational stage. According to Piaget, these children are characterized by egocentricism: in simplest terms, young children simply cannot see things from the perspective of others, their assumption being that the perspective they have is the only available perspective. Fowler writes:

> Children in stage 1 combine fragments of stories and images given by their cultures into their own clusters of significant associations dealing with God and the sacred. Children from non or anti-religious homes show similar tendencies, though their sources of images and symbols may be more limited.[106]

One example of stage 1 faith cited by Fowler was particularly interesting.[107] The subject's name is Sally; she is four and a half and from a home where the parents are non-religious and have gone out of their way to avoid all forms of religion. Nevertheless, Sally had constructed an image of *God*[108] that, although not rich in symbolism, was relatively well developed. She had formed her images from weddings she had attended and the funerals she had seen in television westerns. Sally highlights well the point made by Rizzuto:[109]

> Despite secularisation and religious fragmentation, religious symbols and language are so widely present in society that virtually no child reaches school age without having constructed – with or without religious instruction – an image of God.[110]

Within our Western world, it would be a rare thing indeed to genuinely start from a blank sheet of paper when addressing children with regard to *God*. In whatever form the image has been formed, by the time a child reaches school they have already constructed an image of the numinous – the other – which their culture has taught them to call *God*. This is an image primarily formed by reference to the family and community that has nurtured them, but where insufficient or inadequate images of *God* exist within that family or community, their *God* image will be formed from elsewhere – television being the primary example.

It is tempting to conclude the discussion of faith stages with an analysis of how child evangelism could be geared towards them. However, the definition of evangelism being constructed in this chapter is still limited and undeveloped. These observations will therefore be reserved for the further observations on communication in Chapter 8.

It is worth pausing here to make an important observation. Although there are no difficulties in agreeing with Fowler that stage 1 and 2 children use stories to construct their image of *God*, what must be considered is the nature of those stories. For Fowler and Piaget, stories engage children only cognitively. This is to limit the nature of stories and storytelling. Barton, commenting on stories in the Old Testament, writes, 'Stories in the Hebrew Bible do not exactly teach us duties or virtues, they engage us existentially and can deeply inform our moral life.'[111] This is not only the case for Old Testament stories but for stories in general. They have within them the capacity to engage the listener or reader on a level beyond cognition. Stories have the capacity for transcendence, a capacity to change the listener or reader without them understanding how.

Faith stage 2

Faith stage 2 (mythic-literal faith), paralleled with Piaget's concrete operational stage, is the area where much time must be spent. These are the stages that are seen to characterize school-age children, and also the stages at which many advocates of Piaget's work would seek to avoid Christian education altogether on the basis that the children are unable to understand. Those at faith stage 2 begin to take on for themselves the stories that characterize the life of the community. This is a radical transformation.

The child has moved from egocentricism to community awareness; they are now for the first time able to see things from the perspective of another. They have come to an understanding that their story is interwoven with the story of their community. Fowler writes:

> In this stage the rise of concrete operations leads to the curbing and ordering of previous stage's imaginative composing of the world. The episodic quality of Intuitive-Perspective faith gives way to more linear, narrative construction of coherence and meaning.[112]

Stage 2 is characterized by a move away from existence defined by a series of seemingly unrelated events, to a form of existence that is understood to be a journey. Alongside this, there comes a desire to understand the journey – to bring meaning to the journey. The vast catalogue of stories stored in the previous stage is now added to, and this amalgam is the reference point from which meaning and understanding are drawn. More than simply adding to their bank of stories and drawing meaning from them, concrete operation development allows a child at faith stage 2 to begin to generate their own stories. Fowler writes:

> The convergence of the reversibility of thought with taking the perspective of another combined with an improved grasp of cause–effect relations means that the elements are in place for approaching and retelling the rich stories one is told. More than this, the elements are in place for youngsters to begin to tell self-generated stories that make it possible to conserve, communicate and compare their experiences and meanings.[113]

They have developed the ability to draw meaning from the stories; they have learned how to generate their own stories, and gained with that the ability to compare their experiences and develop a sense of meaning from them. However, the limitation of faith stage 2 is seen in the fact that they have not yet developed the ability to reflect on this story. Their story brings meaning to their journey, but they are unable to step back from the journey and reflect on its value. At this stage, it simply is their journey; this lack of reflection means – to use Fowler's word – that they are *trapped* in the journey.[114]

The individuals interviewed by Fowler listed under faith stage 2 illustrated how fluid the structural development stages are.[115] Allan, aged eleven, exhibits the attributes of a child at faith stage 2, but so does another interviewee in her 50s, referred to as Mrs W. Her interaction with God is based on reciprocity. Hull,[116] talking about stage 2, writes:

> Reciprocity is the fundamental way in which God deals with the world and with people, and this leads to the development of a sense of justice, where God, adults and friends will be expected to follow the rules of fairness.

It is this reciprocal element, or lack of it, that makes the interview with ten-year-old Millie so noteworthy. Fowler comments on the interview:

> It seems likely that here we are getting thoughts that grasp and repeat some things her parent or parents have recently offered her. Yet one judges that Millie is not merely parroting, but that she has passed the meaning they shared with her through the filters of her own structures of knowing and valuing and that we are getting first formulations on these matters.[117]

A large portion of the interview is included. The interviewer has just asked Millie why people die:

> *Millie:* Well, if everybody stayed alive then, I mean, the world would just be so overcrowded. And, and it would make it harder for a family like to lead, to get money, to work, to find jobs and to find food and it would just be hard for the world. So God has to let some people die.

> *Interviewer:* Is it up to God?

> *Millie:* Well, well yeah. But like you know, he has to – let's see. Well, in a way, yes. Because he kind of controls. And I think that probably that – well actually he can't help it if somebody's going to die. Like he can't say that person's good, he can't die. He'd just say well I'm sorry but he's going to have to die. I mean like he can't really help. Like my friend, she had a puppy and he got ran over. And she was so mad, and she says, 'I hate God, I hate God!' And I go, you know, that you shouldn't say that, 'cause God does work in mysterious ways. And you know you never know what's going to happen next. And neither does he.

Interviewer: But is it always the best thing?

Millie: It's always the best thing. Because if that puppy didn't die, then you know, you never know what would have happened next. And usually what God does is the best thing.

Interviewer: Usually?

Millie: Most of the time. All of the time.

Interviewer: Which one?

Millie: All the time he does the best thing and the thing he thinks is best for us.

Interviewer: How does he know what's best?

Millie: Well, it's like your parents. They think they know what's best for you and so they try and do what they think is right. So that's what God does. And usually it turns out that what he does is the right thing.

Fowler suggests that Millie's *God* image is taking the form offered by her culture, both the larger Western culture and the more particular Protestant culture of her family. This may well be the case, but, as Fowler has already acknowledged, 'She has passed these through her own filters… and we are getting first formulations'.[118] What is clear is that this was a ten-year-old who was beginning to function at a higher faith stage. Fowler uses the terminology 'emerging structure'.[119] What must not be overlooked is that many adult churchgoers, if challenged with some of the questions given to Millie – 'Does God decide who dies?' and 'Is it always the best thing?' – would find it difficult to answer the questions.

At the end of the interview, Millie was asked to talk on wealth distribution and what the interviewer termed 'a good definition of capitalism'. Millie may indeed have given a textbook definition of capitalism because it was familiar ground to her, whereas she was clearly facing questions of theodicy and ontology for the first time and having to construct her answers there and then. It may be that it is in the facing of questions such as these, and being gently challenged to answer them, that Millie and those like her will make the transition to the next level of faith development.

Before moving on to consider faith stage 3, it is important to explore the phenomenon of the small group of children who even at this young age (6–12 and younger) exhibit faith stage development beyond that of their physical and cognitive[120] development. Helfaer terms this as 'precocious identity formation' and defines it as 'the child, at conversion, taking on the adult faith identity called for by the religious group'.[121] Fowler suggests this experience leads to the emergence of 'a very rigid, brittle and authoritarian personality'.[122] It would be easy to criticize this unnatural development and speak of it in significantly negative terms, as do both Fowler and Helfaer. However, there are clearly significant Bible characters who would be diagnosed as having precocious identity formation, the most obvious of whom is the Old Testament prophet Samuel. Samuel is brought to the temple, to the aging priest Eli, immediately after his mother finishes weaning him. The biblical narrative states that the boy Samuel ministers before God, assuming some of the priestly duties, and is able to communicate with God from a very early age (1 Samuel 2). The adult Samuel becomes one of the most revered men in Israel and anoints both Saul and David to be kings of Israel. When reading of the unfolding of Samuel's life, he could very easily be characterized using Fowler's words as 'very rigid, brittle and authoritarian'.[123] Although the majority of children will develop faith stages in relation to their age, is it possible that some may develop in a different way that is yet still perfectly natural for them? This is not an attempt to excuse those who would force children into a faith stage beyond that which they have developed into – that would be a form of abuse. The challenge this raises for ministry with children is significant. We are not to try to force children into adult modes of learning or into modes that demand cognitive processes beyond their abilities.[124] Some may suggest that this is simply an opt-out designed to avoid labelling certain biblical characters with precocious identity formation – this may indeed be the case. Nevertheless, the possibility must at least be left open that some children will *naturally* develop faith stages beyond the normal, particularly if they live in and around overt religion on a daily basis, as would clearly be the case with Samuel. Hull, in reference to Erikson's stages, suggests that some of our greatest religious men and women have always paid scant regard to normal stage development:

> This is why, in the lives of the greatest religious men and women, Erikson's eight stages seem somehow to be collapsed or telescoped, so that the individual is drawn across the various

crises more rapidly and perhaps more painfully than would normally be the case.[125]

The distinction between those who can be termed as having precocious identity formation and those who simply are unique is important. If the individual is forced to evolve beyond that which is appropriate, then this is unnatural; if, however, they choose to develop at a faster rate, then this must be considered natural development for them, even though it is outside the normal framework.

Although Fowler does not include children in faith stage 3, this thesis suggests that many children by age eight[126] (school year 4 in the UK) are beginning to exhibit the development of synthetic-literal faith and formal operational cognition. It is not suggested that these areas have fully developed, but instead that they are developing and over the coming years will further develop in each child at a different rate. It is because of this assertion that faith stage 3 paralleled with Piaget's formal operational level will be considered.

Faith stage 3

Hull observes:

> In stage three an interpersonal perspective emerges and the person becomes much more acutely self conscious... The person knows that he believes and strongly experiences the state of faith, but he can seldom tell why he believes, and almost never tells you how he believes.[127]

It is the stage marked by two key features. Firstly, those at faith stage 3 generally exhibit a tacit, or unchallenged, faith. They will hold to a strong set of values, will be able to articulate them and have a strong emotional attachment to them, but they would not have reflected on them. This stage is often evidenced by an unspoken attitude of 'We know what we believe, even if we don't know why we believe it!' It is a stage of unexamined ideology. Stage 3 is demonstrated well by the person on the Alpha course who states with absolute conviction that 'Jesus died on the cross to take away my sins', and then, in the moments of silence that follow, they blurt out, 'But I've never really known what that means.'

The children of the Leeds and Hastings projects demonstrate tacit faith. Chris, the leader of the Hastings project, comments, 'Nearly if not all the children can recite the 4Points.' At the Leeds project the ability to recite the 4Points is the qualification for a game. In many of these cases, the 4Points will represent an unexamined ideology. Tacit faith is shown well in Fowler's interview for this stage.[128] Linda is 15. She has been asked what she believes:

> *Linda*: Well lots of people have done research into religion and they've gone insane you know? I've never wanted to go that much into it. I just want to do what the bible says. Lots of good people think how the earth started and everything, I, only... there's a limit to me, I know that it started from God. God made it and I don't ask any more questions, you know? I'll find out later on.

Linda demonstrated a typical attribute of faith stage 3. She has a system of belief but she will not open Pandora's box and look inside. There is a refusal to examine her faith. Nevertheless, it is in the examination of beliefs held at faith stage 3 that begins the process of development to faith stage 4.

The second area that marks stage 3 is that of the *significant other*. Hull stated that this stage is particularly self-conscious. Fowler writes, 'With the formal operational ability to construct the hypothetical, there can emerge the complex ability to compose hypothetical images of myself as others see me.'[129]

Kohlberg formulated the phrase that best sums up this stage: 'I see you seeing me, I see the me I think you see.' During this stage (it is worth repeating that many adults never leave this stage), the individual is dependent on significant others to see themselves. Their self-image is formed through the eyes of others. With these issues in mind, it becomes clear how significant the significant other is. The concept of the significant other is not dissimilar to Cooley's looking-glass self. Ullman comments:

> Awareness of the self, he argued, evolves indirectly by taking the perspective of others. The self is identical to a social self-concept, namely, to the individual subjective construction of others' judgments of the person which arises out of his or her social interactions with primary groups.[130]

The partial outcome of this must at least be to place a burden of responsibility upon those who would be the significant others. The British Nationwide Initiative in Evangelism (1980) stated, 'What we are and do in this respect is no less important than what we say.' Ullman[131] states the case more strongly and writes, 'The typical convert is transformed not by religion, but by a person.' However, her description of that person as a 'powerful authority figure' is not substantiated by other researchers.[132] This was evidenced at the Slough and Windsor project when I asked a ten-year-old girl why she came; she responded, 'Because Natalie is here.' Natalie is one of the Slough and Windsor project leaders.

There are two comments that need to be made concerning this stage. Firstly, Fowler's assertion that this stage only affects teenagers is rejected. It has been noted that many adults will never leave this stage. It has also been noted that many children as young as eight are emerging into stage 3 and therefore the significant other becomes important to them.

Secondly, the potential and value of evangelism at this stage cannot be overlooked. If the evangelist is able to present God as the significant other, using the New and Old Testament Scriptures, the child develops a picture of God valuing them, loving them, protecting and comforting them. However, there is a very clear warning here. If the image of *God* that has been constructed by the individual is a negative one, then the concept of *God* as the significant other may be damaging. It is for this reason that Christian education has a part to play in the construction of an individual's *God* image.

Some of the faith stage 4[133] characteristics are listed here for the simple fact that although it would be rare for a child to experience this stage, the child evangelist or Christian educator should. Stage 4 is the first stage that is a development beyond normal cognitive development; it is the first stage that cannot be reached simply by an increase in intelligence. To this extent it is discussed here because of a belief that some of the Christian educators in the UK's churches and schools still operate from faith stage 3. The reasons for this are numerous, but Fowler suggests that those who are part of faith stage 2/3 communities – communities where the majority hold to a tacit or unexamined faith – will themselves be restricted to faith stage 2 or 3.[134] Although it is probable that many of the children in the Children's Outreach Projects have a tacit faith in the 4Points, it is also possible that many of the leaders also have that same basis of belief. Often children's workers hold strongly to a stage 3 belief system and have made the children's leader/minister their significant other, and the children's team have become their stage 3 community. To move stage 3 individuals to higher levels of spiritual maturity is often difficult. Hull writes, 'In Stage 4 one is compelled to accept responsibility for one's views, and many people in Stage 3 will resist this.' Hegel leaves no doubt that the transition may be a painful process:

> Hence, the believer is led to realise that his faith is no longer immune to question and that strength of personal conviction alone is not enough to authenticate the truth of the teachings familiar from childhood. The resulting condition is one of spiritual disquiet; the old confidence having been eroded everything may come to be seen as doubtful.[135]

To exist at stage 4 involves knowing what the belief is and why it is held. Those in a faith stage 2/3 community are never challenged to move to this level by either other members of the community or, more importantly, its leaders – for the very obvious reason that it takes secure leadership to oversee a faith stage 4 individual. Hull[136] plainly states:

> The authority of institutions is challenged by people at stage four, and this presents a limit to the degree to which institutions are prepared to sponsor their members. It is in the interest of religious institutions to sponsor their people to stage three but not beyond it.

Fowler lists two key features of a person at faith stage 4: 'the critical distancing from one's previous assumptive value systems and the emergence of an executive ego.' What must not be overlooked in faith stage development is that a move in faith stage causes a change in the person. They undergo a conversion experience. They become someone else[137] – or, more accurately, they become a different them.

The idea of the executive ego is interesting. To use Fowler's imagery of the river, stage 1 children are egocentric; they are only aware of themselves and they do not see the river. Stage 2 children are aware of the river, of the stories they are part of, but possess no ability to step out of the river and observe themselves from the riverbank – this ability is reserved for those at stage 3. Children at faith stage 2 are the fish of whom Culkin[138] spoke when he suggested, 'We do not know who discovered water, but we are certain it was not a fish.' Children at stage 3 have the ability to stand on the riverbank and observe, but do not yet have the ability to reflect on what they see. However, the executive ego of stage 4 enables reflection on what is being seen and experienced – those at faith stage 4 are what are sometimes termed 'reflective practitioners'. To take Fowler's river imagery to its conclusion, faith stage 5/6 then can best be described as an ability to reflect on all the issues from a purely objective position, to see all sides of the argument and to weigh them all equally.

An understanding of the stages of faith is important. Fowler writes:

> Put negatively, to approach a new era in the adult life cycle while clinging too tightly to the structural style of faith employed during the culminating phase of the previous era is an anachronism… such an anachronism virtually assures that one will settle for a narrower and shallower faith than one needs.[139]

Fowler presents guidelines against which faith development can be evaluated. What should not be overlooked is that they are guidelines. Due to the nature of emerging stages, the development from one stage to another may vary by as much as five years from child to child, and, as has already been shown, some adults may never develop beyond stage 3.

Part of the role of the child evangelist must therefore be to proclaim the Christian message in a way that it can be understood by the audience, but, at the same time, their role is to help facilitate faith development within the children – that is, to allow them naturally to convert from one stage to another through clear Christian education. Although it is possible for the Children's Outreach Project to proclaim a Christian message that can be understood, the large venue of the Children's Outreach Project is not the place to help facilitate faith development. This leads to the conclusion that the large Children's Outreach Project forum should be backed up with a small-group programme (such as the one in the Slough and Windsor project) or some follow-through project (such as the one at the Fraserburgh project). Without these forums for more personal/individual nurture, faith development will be difficult and the Children's Outreach Project itself will quickly form into a faith stage 2/3 community.

CHILD EVANGELISM AS ENCOUNTER

To this point, the focus has been almost exclusively cognitive: evangelism defined as Christian education. For many, a cognitive understanding of Christianity constitutes child evangelism in its entirety; they suggest that, whatever its specific content, spiritual education is clearly a matter of teaching so that students will change by adopting and growing in certain processes, attitudes, values and even beliefs.[140] Nevertheless, others have suggested that to define child evangelism only in terms of cognition and epistemology is to miss an area of fundamental importance. Richards writes:

> Children are able to generate spiritual insights that they arrive
> at intuitively, which can be expressed in faith responses. How
> tragic if we were to dismiss the intuitive insights of children and
> their acts of faith as somehow irrelevant to nurture because the
> theological concepts they express are not 'really' understood.[141]

The New Testament is clear: the disciples met Jesus and then began to
understand who he was; they *encountered* him before they began to
understand him (Acts 1:1). When, in Matthew's Gospel, Peter states that
Jesus was the Son of God, Jesus attributed this discovery not to a process
of learning but to revelation from God.[142] Michael Ramsay[143] said, 'Christ's
earliest followers came to him first and then, out of that experience, did
their theological reflection.' Bushnell makes the same point with regard
to children when he writes, 'We are to understand that a right spirit may
be virtually exercised in children, when, as yet, it is not intellectually
received.'[144] Fowler, although basing his faith stages on cognition, hints
that there may be something more when he writes:

> We encounter another set of limitations of Piaget's and Kohlberg's
> approaches as we build on them to understand faith. This has
> to do with the role of imagination in knowing, their neglect of
> symbolic processes generally and the related lack of attention to
> unconscious structuring processes other than those constituting
> reasoning.[145]

However, Fowler's method of research does not reflect this. Piaget suggests
that children may appear to understand certain things intuitively, but he
insists that unless they can explain the reasons for their conclusion their
understanding is artificial. For Piaget, the test of true understanding
is awareness of how a particular conclusion was reached. A child may
intuitively grasp the right answer or make a valid response, but, for Piaget,
'real understanding' requires the ability to explain.[146] It is the defining, and
potentially the most limiting, feature of Piaget and the structural theorists
that follow him;[147] for Piaget, unless the child can explain what he knows
in a reasoned and logical way, then the child's knowledge is invalid. There
is no room within Piaget for knowledge that is derived from intuition,
subconscious structuring or transcendent encounter. A system based purely
on reasoned knowledge that can be explained does not accommodate what

Hegel refers to as 'an intuition of the infinite transcendence from which our entire existence derives'.[148] Hegel goes further and talks of 'a primal belief in God which may not unreasonably be called intuitive'.[149] He concludes that it is therefore perfectly legitimate to speak of knowledge that is 'spontaneous, original and immediate'. Hay and Hunt drew a similar conclusion, that humanity is spiritual by biology/nature rather than by society/nurture.

Christians, while wanting to acknowledge the positive contribution that the social sciences have brought to an understanding of *God*, nevertheless stress that *God* is more than the product of the child's mind, but is a living being who has chosen to reveal himself. To this extent, Hegel[150] presents the concept of universal religious consciousness[151] and further states, 'No longer is God an unknown being far off; he has made himself known to man not merely in nature or the events of external history but through man's own inner consciousness.' It is possible that this universal religious consciousness is a contributory factor to the formation of such an established *God* construct amongst Fowler's interviewees, even when they had not come from an overtly religious environment. This universal religious consciousness, it is suggested, is the very thing that allows *God* to be encountered. Hegel is adamant that this ability to encounter *God* is not a purely cognitive process: 'it is a work of the divine spirit, not a discovery of man.'[152] Rahner writes:

> I think that people must understand that they have an implicit but true knowledge of God perhaps not reflected on and verbalised – or better expressed: a genuine experience of God, which is ultimately rooted in their spiritual existence, in their transcendentality, in their personality, or whatever you want to name it. It is not a really important question whether you call that 'mystical' or not.[153]

It could be assumed from Rahner's comments that the word *encounter* used for this experience should not be understood as that which the individual has met externally, but is more to do with becoming aware of that which is within; in effect, to begin to recognize that which has already been encountered.[154] However, although acknowledging the truth of this, encounter cannot be limited. There are many biblical references to suggest that although God has made himself known, he continues to make himself known to individuals through further encounter.[155] What is notable is that within these biblical references to further encounter there is often the acknowledgement that the person *encountering God* is not doing so for the first time – they *recognize* what/whom they encounter.

The concept of encounter is embraced readily by the postmodern mind because it is devoid of authority structures and allows each individual to develop their own personal religion. However, this is both its strength and its weakness. Copley[156] highlights the integral difficulties with the approach:

> It looks dangerously like becoming either the moral exultation of the self or else a synonym for the aesthetic... The self expects to be titillated, enlarged, enhanced, affirmed, as a result of the exercise... Having rejected a God-centred approach it has become a self-centred approach.

Of course, it could be suggested that what Copley highlights as fault is exactly the motivation behind tens of thousands of people attending church services every week!

The language of encounter in many people's thinking falls into the area of spirituality and away from religion. Copley explains the distinctions:

> Spirituality seems by its nature to lie outside the boundary of definition; it can be made neither definite nor 100%. Religions in contrast are too often defined and frequently made to appear like static belief systems.[157]

However, the word *spirituality* should not be discarded too quickly, for within it, as Fox[158] points out, 'lies the mechanisms to displace patriarchal control and pessimism with hope'. Fox[159] prefers the term *Christian spirituality* to *Christian religion* for the very reasons that Copley suggests: the word *religion* communicates that which is rigid and static. More importantly, the freedom to explore, question and critique inherent within the word *spirituality* facilitates more freely children moving through faith stages 2/3.[160]

Hull, although generally agreeing with Hegel, allows an important progression in the formation of this exploration of child evangelism. He writes, 'Not only does the formation of the sense of God lie in early infancy but its origin is related to the formation of the view of the self.'[161] Rizzuto suggests:

> The fantasy of the child certainly adds colour, drama, glamour, and horror to the insignificant moments as well as to the real tragedies

of everyday life. It is out of this matrix of facts and fantasies, wishes, hopes, and fears, the exchange with those incredible beings called parents, that the image of God is concocted.[162]

Both Hull and Rizzuto propose that at this point the children have not experienced a real *God*; Rizzuto concludes that the child's *God* is simply the concoction of childhood experience. Hull suggests that many will go on from this projected *God* to a belief that there actually is a real *God* in whom they can have faith.[163] Although there are important points being expressed here, particularly with regard to the child's construction of *God* being imperfect, there are assumptions embedded within the views being expressed that need challenging. It must be equally valid to suggest that although universal religious consciousness allows children to encounter *God*, because the image of the *God* they have encountered is so heavily interwoven psychologically with their development of self, the construct of the *God* they have encountered will be unclear[164] or even marred. Nevertheless, even though the materials the child has used to construct their image of *God* may not give the most accurate representation, embedded within the construction is the real *God*.

Many factors contribute to the child's development of self. Freud[165] suggests that the image of *God* is based upon the actual father and formed through the social experiences of child and father. Jung suggests these images are formed through relationship with the mother. The natures of these relationships are considered by Erikson under the heading of 'Trust v mistrust'. Many external factors will also contribute to the formation of the child's construct of *God*, not least of which will be the child's interface with traditional religions, particularly if this is part of the home environment. If the experience at home is of a moralistic and punitive type (God won't like you if you don't say your prayers), the child is likely to hear traces of such attitudes in the public life of their church, where the sound of such traces may drown out other aspects of religion. [166]

However, although Hull is correct to point out the difficulties and dangers that have the capacity to damage the child's understanding of *God*, this must not be seen as a fait accompli. Rahner points out that the very things that threaten to deform the *God* image are the very things that can bring awareness of the *real God*. Rahner acknowledges that in the majority of cases:

> Only one who has been able to learn that the names 'mother' and 'father' stand for protecting love to which he can unquestionably

trust himself – only he will find the courage trustfully to give the name 'father' to that ineffable and nameless source which upholds him in being, to recognise that he has not been swallowed up by it, but that he has found the very source of his own existence in it and has been empowered by it to be really and authentically himself...[67]

He also acknowledges:

It is precisely possible that a lack of protection, a lack of that sheltering solicitude and security which comes from the love of one's parents, may actually serve to spur us on to the metaphysical quest for one who will provide us with our ultimate support, who will sustain and protect us.

Rahner continues in the same vein and suggests that even those who have never managed to achieve a close relationship with a parent based on 'love, protection, and security' may find those very things in the concept of God's fatherhood. It is a wonderfully optimistic view, which works on two levels. Not only does the individual have a healthy view of *God*, but also they can now draw from that construct of *God* their understanding of how they in their turn can be a parent. The human concept of childhood and parenthood is only fully realized when it is transferred to *God*.[168]

With so many factors contributing to the child's formation of self and therefore of *God*, the child evangelist's role becomes one of firstly seeking to understand the child's construct of *God* and secondly of helping deconstruct and reconstruct that image where necessary.[169]

Many of the Children's Outreach Projects are unable to do this because of the number of children present; others have not recognized the need or importance. The co-leader of the Hastings project prayed, 'Lord, reveal who you are to these children.' He has clearly concluded that God was self-revealing, but felt that God could only reveal himself to children when they came to the project. He had not understood the nature of universal consciousness or the possibility that God had already begun to reveal himself. His assumption was that the children who would attend on this particular day were a white sheet on which he could paint his theology. There were further questions with regard to the extent that he actually felt God could reveal himself within the project. During the programme he suggested to the children that God could heal them if they were sick, and he prayed for those who were sick to be healed. He chose not to ask for feedback from the children on the prayers – he didn't ask them what they had encountered. He may have simply forgotten or he may have been uncertain that these children would encounter anything. This omission would cause the children difficulty in being able to express the *God* they had encountered. However, despite the large numbers, some children's outreach projects still negotiated around this difficulty. I recorded the following in my visit to the Leeds project:

> At the end of the morning, Sarah invites the children to pray for the person next to them. Many of them do. Then she closes in prayer, 'Dear God, thank you that you love and help us every day. Help us to ask you for what we need. Amen.' The children who would like to be prayed for are invited to put their hand up. Several children do. Leaders then go and pray with those children as quieter music plays in the background.

It is in these moments that for the first time the children are treated as individuals, with individual needs and individual levels of faith development. It is a small part of the programme, but it is there.

Two disciplines are needed for this task of constructing, deconstructing and reconstructing the child's *God* image. The first is phenomenology. Rickert[170] defined phenomenology as 'that which seeks to grasp the essential significance of phenomena in a meaningful context, a context of normative values, symbols and beliefs'. Dallmayr suggests, 'Phenomenology implies attentiveness to the broad range of experience, a radical openness to all kinds of phenomena irrespective of scientific validation.'[171] Dallmayr's phrase 'irrespective of scientific validation' is important, for within phenomenology the discussion is centred on the subjective experiences of an individual; within this research, the experiences are the subjective experiences of children. They cannot ever be other than subjective because, as Ihde points out, 'All experience is arrived at reflectively'.[172] The child encounters *God*, and this encounter may indeed bring with it a level of understanding that is intuitively received, but it is then within human nature to reflect rationally (according to the child's level of understanding, as outlined in the previous section) on that encounter. Hegel further clarifies this point: 'For although the actual process of reasoning may not be explicit, and may even be obscure or concealed, it nonetheless is there.'[173]

Phenomenology can be an intangible concept,[174] and, in many ways, phenomenology has less to do with its definition and more to do with the context in which it is used.[175] It is Heidegger who provides the suitably focused definition for the purpose of child evangelism. He writes, 'Phenomenology is our way of access to what is to be the theme of ontology.'[176] Phenomenology is the method of accessing what the child has encountered – the way of seeing the image of *God* the child has constructed. It is a complicated process, with a multitude of factors affecting what is perceived, as Hull illustrates:

> I am aware, for example, that God is speaking to me, that I am in the presence of Christ, that I feel I have betrayed the Holy Spirit and so on. I am seldom aware that my emotions of presence, guilt, vocation, betrayal or whatever are part of an on-going negotiation between myself and previous and future selves, of which negotiations the religious beliefs or symbols are the mediators.[177]

It is therefore important that the child evangelist helps the child to bring into the area of consciousness that which they unconsciously know. Often children will hold a particular belief in a strong and intense way but not be aware of it. Moreover, until the belief is exposed for what it is, it cannot be examined.

The child evangelist is therefore charged with bracketing out his or her own understanding and experience to enter sympathetically into the knowing situation of the other person. However, observing the phenomena is not in itself of benefit. If the child is to be helped in the reshaping of their construct of *God*, or, for that matter, affirmed in that construct, then the child evangelist must be involved in *hermeneutic* phenomenology and not just phenomenology – interpretation and not just observation. It is therefore essential that hermeneutic phenomenology should be a consideration in the process of creating the environment for child evangelism.

The second discipline needed for child evangelism has been explored in detail in the preceding section: Christian education. Phenomenology may provide the mechanisms to understand what the child's construct of God looks like, but it will be Christian education that provides the tools for deconstructing and reconstructing the child's image of *God*. The reconstructed image will look like the God of the Old and New Testament, the God of hope and life. Without Christian education, the child has no reference point to understand that they have encountered the God of Christianity.[178] Christian knowledge allows the person to understand what/ whom she has encountered. For child evangelism to be evangelism into the

Christian faith, it must involve Christian catechism. Evangelism is therefore made up of two components: Christian education and encounter.

The 2001 Dearing Report makes a useful contribution to the discussion with its definition of child evangelism in the context of church schools as 'to open up people to what God wants for them'.[179] It is an interesting and useful definition because it suggests that it is possible for schools and churches to become places where Christian education is taught but also where an environment for encounter is created.

Child evangelism takes place, therefore, when church-based children's activities become environments that allow exploration, enquiry and challenge. Nye,[180] commenting on an educational context, writes:

> The teacher has four main responsibilities:
>   1. Helping children keep an open mind
>   2. Exploring ways of seeing
>   3. Encouraging personal awareness
>   4. Becoming personally aware of the social and political
> dimension

Although Nye's four points are expanded and explained in much greater detail,[181] they never move past observation and the exploration of spirituality. This is pure phenomenology; there is no mechanism here to allow the child to better understand their *God* image. A far bolder and more useful model is presented by Fowler:

> Parents and teachers should create an atmosphere in which the child can freely express, verbally and nonverbally, the images she or he is forming. Where the expression is allowed and encouraged, the child is taken seriously and adults can provide appropriate help in dealing with crippling, distorted or destructive images the child has formed.[182]

The statement is simplicity itself, but this is the very heart of hermeneutic phenomenology. The child is invited to present their subjective understanding of the God they have encountered. It is a method that understands that all children have a universal religious consciousness and sets out to present an image of God as revealed in Christian orthodoxy, as presented in the Old and New Testaments and in the Christian creeds. It goes beyond Nye's observational position and allows for misunderstandings or distortions to be explored together against the aforementioned Christian framework. Because the process involves allowing the unconscious to be brought into the area of the conscious, the announcement, to use Kant's expression, must be in keeping with the child's cognitive ability. It is Piaget, therefore, who suggests one of the most developmentally appropriate tools for hermeneutic phenomenology:

> In addition to language the semiotic function includes gestures, either idiosyncratic or, as in the case of the deaf, systematized. It includes deferred imitation, that is, imitation that takes place when the model is no longer present. It includes drawing, painting, modelling.

Faith is a deeply personal thing. What Fowler and, to a greater extent, Hull[183] facilitate is an understanding that faith develops. But this development does not happen best in rigid environments where faith is presented as absolute and cannot be critiqued or doubted. As Hull points out, 'Genuine certainties can only arise through doubt'.[184] Hull is not saying that those who do not have regular doubts concerning their faith have no real certainty concerning that faith; it may well be that those individuals have long since faced that doubt and now established their faith on a firmer foundation. Hull's comments attest to the fact that strong faith develops through questioning and consideration of belief.

All this may seem obvious, but it is often overlooked and, more seriously, often undermined. Parker, Hartas and Irving, writing about Muslim schools, state:[185]

> Knowledge is thus conceived within the context of religion and Qur'anic interpretations, whereas in the western model of education, religious knowledge is constructed as a discipline in its own right rather than a subject which permeates the curriculum and establishes the school ethos.

A body of knowledge is constructed (in this case extracted from Qur'an) and children acquire that knowledge. In this way, Islamic child evangelism may be very different to Christian child evangelism.[186] The pillars of Islam are a set of non-negotiables – Islamic child evangelism is about imparting a set of facts, without critique, into young lives.

The Islamic Education Trust[187] summarizes the key features of Islamic education as:

1. Acquisition of knowledge

2. Imparting of knowledge

3. Inculcating moral values

4. Consideration of public good

5. Development of personality and emphasis on actions and responsibilities.

Undoubtedly, many fundamental Christian faith-based schools educate their children using a similar system. Moreover, as has already been observed, it is the natural tendency of some of the Children's Outreach Projects. But not all. David, the leader of the Fraserburgh project, comments, 'I reckon, to be honest with you, our aim is to sow seeds.' It is a philosophy that gives children the basic building blocks necessary to construct their faith, rather than a philosophy that tries to indoctrinate a group of children with a pre-packaged theology. David further develops this:

> [The Fraserburgh project] is to be a nest. Everything that a nest speaks of I want for my kids' work. So you look at the nest and the mother with the little chicks. It speaks of warmth, so when the kids come we want them to feel warm, accepted. It speaks about strength and protection, I protect the kids that come. I like to feed them on the things of God, Bible stories, life issues. And in the same way the mother loves those chicks, we love these kids.

The Fraserburgh project has built in another morning outside the Children's Outreach Project where the children can come and be with the leaders. David comments:

> But Saturday morning is quality time because the kids come in, they can go to the bouncy castle, they can go to basketball, football, they can get their face painted, and you have leaders talking to them all the time – so sowing seeds is not just about saying Jesus loves you and died on a cross for you. Sowing seeds is about showing the whole care, concern, love, warmth and acceptance.

In the Church of England's *Guidance on RE in Church of England Schools* this is stated as helping pupils to 'respond in terms of beliefs, commitments and ways of living'.[190] This is a clear and valuable step beyond the simple learning of facts. This is reinforced when the document later advocates that children should 'explore and experience prayer and worship from a variety of Christian traditions'.[190]

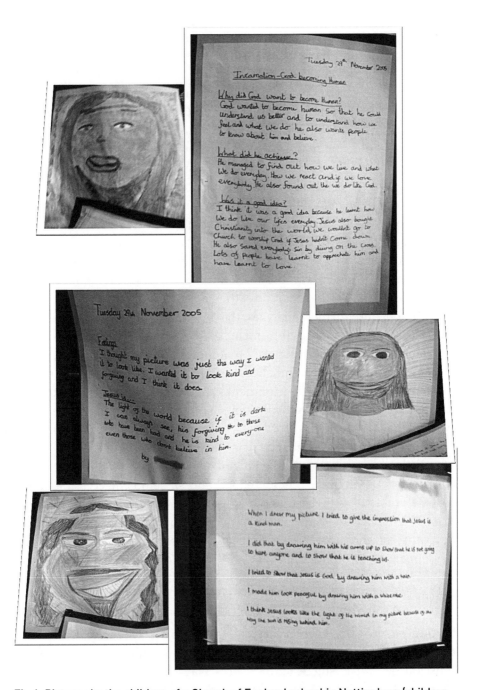

Fig 6. Pictures by the children of a Church of England school in Nottingham (children aged 11)[188]

CONCLUSION

The analysis of both theological tradition and Scripture shows that the child's default state is *in Christ*. However, to use Copley's expression, 'indoctrination' away from the Christian faith is an inevitability for children whose environment is not Christian.[191] Although children born into a non-Christian home may be born in Christ, it is unlikely that they will be nurtured into the Christian faith without some outside intervention. Therefore, whether in thought or action, they will reject the Christ they have encountered, and their spiritual status, using the analogy from Romans 5, will become *in Adam*. Using the terminology of 2 Corinthians 5 and Romans 5, the child is baptized to show that they are in Christ. Baptism is the public affirmation that the child is in Christ, and children who die before they are baptized are already in Christ.[192]

Pridmore used 1 Samuel to show that children are capable of relationship with God in proportion to their physical and cognitive development. Fowler's exposition of the stages of faith builds on Pridmore's observation and further analyzes the interface between cognitive and faith development, although in many ways Fowler's observations are so embedded within Piaget's stages[193] that they add little to existing research in this area prior to his examination of stage 4 faith development (and this is beyond the cognitive development range of the child).[194] It is only in the discussion of the movement from stage 2 to stage 4 – the move out of tacit, unchallenged faith – that Fowler presents a stage that is not arrived at through natural physical and cognitive development.

What is unfortunate is that Fowler does not present clearly the stages beyond this point. Stage 5 is undefined and stage 6 is inaccessible to the vast majority. Nevertheless, Fowler does present clearly an understanding that faith develops, that communication with regard to faith must be developmentally appropriate, and that education involving sensitive challenge can promote that development. Fowler also suggests that movement from one stage to another may legitimately be described as a conversion experience.

However, Christian evangelism is not purely cognitive. Hegel[195] introduced the concept of universal religious consciousness and stated that there is a God who chooses to reveal himself. This universal religious consciousness, it is suggested, is God's way of making himself known. Christian evangelism, then, is the vehicle by which something that has already been encountered is recognized and identified. Although agreeing with Rizzuto that everyone to a lesser or greater extent has a construct of God, it is further stated that this construct is not formed because of the environment, but instead because everyone has a universal religious consciousness. Everyone has had an encounter with God (although it has been shown that an individual may have further encounters with this God). However, it is conceded that environment considerably influences the formation of this construct of God, and as such the construct often contains what Hull[196] termed 'myth and baggage'.

It is this understanding of myth and baggage that necessitates the need to embrace the social sciences and the use of hermeneutic phenomenology in the work of child evangelism. Phenomenology allows access to the child's construct of *God*. Although access is not enough, hermeneutics is then necessary to understand what has been observed. As was observed in the case of Rizzuto's patient Daniel (note 188), however, this is not a straightforward process. Moreover, where there is great complexity, the child evangelist must understand when they need outside assistance.

In light of these observations, questions can be asked as to the validity of the Raikes' model and the model of the Children's Outreach Projects as forms of child evangelism. It has been shown that the early Sunday Schools were places of Christian education and places of evangelism on two levels:

1. *They were places where gospel elements were proclaimed through Christian catechism.*
2. *They were places where good news was brought through the meeting of clearly defined social needs.*

It was observed that the majority of the Children's Outreach Projects surveyed or visited also fulfil these objectives. However, the form of Christian education demonstrated by the Sunday Schools and the Children's Outreach Projects is limited and was primarily to do with the memorization of events, facts and figures. It would be, at best, what Fowler would describe as faith stage 2/3 faith. However, it must be measured against the same method and mechanism of Christian education that is used within the churches themselves. Preaching, teaching and evangelism were (and maybe still are) to do with the imparting and subsequent memorization of knowledge.

No attempt is made to suggest that Raikes and the early Sunday School institutions had systematically thought through the issues involved. Moreover, he was not privy to the development theories of Piaget or the faith stage development materials of Fowler.[197] He was a product of his time and place in history. Nevertheless, because his pattern was not burdened with the constant distraction of needing to see a one-off personal conversion experience, he was able to present biblical truths through catechism, object lesson and illustration that gave the children the building blocks to experience various stages of conversion – although again Raikes would not have understood the concept or the terminology.

Some of the Children's Outreach Projects indoctrinate children with a rigid doctrine, usually involving the presentation of the 4Points. The flaws in this form of evangelism have been pointed out. However, it has also been noted that some of the Children's Outreach Projects have developed beyond this. Some have placed the children into small groups where more purposeful faith development can take place alongside clear and open discussion of what the children have encountered. This is an important development for Children's Outreach Projects.

What this section should also do is alleviate some of the concerns that surround the words *child evangelism*. Some of this is accomplished by avoiding the overemphasis on the one-off personal conversion experience, but this is primarily done by redefining the terminology against renewed understanding. Christian child evangelism should be the process of education and encounter within a safe and secure environment of exploration, enquiry and gentle challenge. It involves guided learning and discovery, and not over-prescriptive impartation of facts. It should be facilitated by the rich and diverse biblical narratives that fill the Old and New Testaments, and in particular the telling of the compelling and captivating Jesus story.

NOTES

1. In 1799 the *Evangelical Magazine* advised parents to teach their children that they are 'sinful polluted creatures' and therefore in need of a personal conversion experience.

2. Compare Cliff (1986, p. 2).

3. The article itself features in Appendix 5.

4. Taken from www.the4points.com developed by the Liverpool project, although the Leeds and Hastings projects also cited the same four points verbatim.

5. This age of understanding is said to be different for every child.

6. 2001, p. 105.

7. This was a predominantly Western church position.

8. John Chrysostom (AD 347–407). Chrysostom represented the universal view prior to the fourth century, but his view continued to be the view held by the Eastern Church even after Augustine's doctrine.

9. Cited from Bettenson (1977, p. 165).

10. 1976, p. 144.

11. Matthew 2.

12. In a final defence of his argument against Julian Bishop of Eclanum (Bastian, 1960, p. 212).

13. Augustine's letter to Jerome, in *Letters of Saint Augustine*, translated by John Leinenweber (1992, p. 190).

14. *Confessions* (1.7), translated by Henry Chadwick (1991, p. 9).

15. 2001, p. 82.

16. Augustine's letter to Jerome, in Leinenweber (1992, p. 190).

17. The fact that Augustine had not always held this view may be hinted at by the fact that church tradition suggest that he was 33 before he was baptized.

18. 2000, p. 207.

19. Pelagius (c. 354–c. 420) was an ascetic monk and reformer. He denied the doctrine of original sin from Adam and was declared a heretic by Augustine.

20. 2001, p. 79.

21. There is some confusion here, but it is possible to read between the lines of Augustine's theology and see that although he did not see baptism as a cure but rather the beginning of the process, he did see baptism as the mechanism to remit sin. The sin of a baptized child – actual and original – could no longer be held against them.

22. Stortz (2001, p. 92).

23. Pannenberg (1999, p. 124) writes, 'It is impossible for me to be held jointly responsible as though I were a joint cause for an act that another did many generations ago and in a situation radically different from mine.'

24. Paul's Epistle to the Romans had been a contributory part of Augustine's conversion to Christianity and his understanding of its theology was therefore particularly significant to him.

25. Latin *intravit*.

26. Latin *intrare*.

27. 2001, p. 93.

28. In the twenty-first-century world of scientific breakthroughs with regard to propagation, Augustine's views seem increasingly anachronistic. It is noteworthy that, for Augustine, Adam is an actual figure and not simply part of an allegory.

29. The word is more often translated 'into' in the New Testament (over 500 times) and never translated with a sexual inference.

30. In *Ep. Ad Romanus*, 5:12, cited from *Creeds, Councils and Controversies* (1989).

31. Augustine is assuming that the relative pronoun in the phrase has independent pronominal force ('which' or 'whom').

32. 1976, p. 144.

33. However, this translation became part of the text of the King James Bible and a major contributor to the ongoing promotion of Augustine's doctrine of original sin.

34. 1996, p. 321.

35. In Paul's three other uses of this phrase (2 Corinthians 5:4, Philippians 3:12; 4:10), the relative pronoun does not have independent pronominal force, but reflects an abbreviation; the phrase as a whole would mean, literally translated, 'upon this, that'.

36. 1996, p. 323.

37. No attempt has been made to deconstruct the meaning of *death* in these passages. Moo's (1996, p. 323) conclusion below is widely accepted:
> He may refer to physical death only, since 'death' in v. 14 seems to have this meaning. But the passage goes on to contrast death with eternal life (v. 21). Moreover, in vv. 16 and 18 Paul uses 'condemnation' in the same way that he uses death here. These points suggest that Paul may refer here to 'spiritual' death: the estrangement from God that is the result of sin, and that, if not healed through Christ, will lead to 'eternal' death. However, we are not forced to make a choice between these two options. Paul frequently uses 'death' and related words to designate a 'physico-spiritual entity' – 'total death', the penalty incurred for sin.

38. Compare Romans 3:23

39. *A Contemporary Wesleyan Theology* (1983, p. 1267) edited by W.C. Carter.

40. 1993, p. 417.

41. Translated 'sin'.

42. 2000, p. 209.

43. 1926, p. 120.

44. It would imply that Adam, created in the image of God, was created with a bias towards evil.

45. 1996, p. 343.

46. However, it continues to be strongly debated. Fox (1983, p. 18) attributes to this doctrine the reason for the negative attitude to Christianity in many churches: 'One reason for this pessimism that leads to cynicism and lack of caring is a fall/redemption religious paradigm that begins its theology with original sin.'

47. *ST* III.71.2.1. *ST* denotes Aquinas' work *Summa Theologica*. The version referred to was translated by the Fathers of the English Dominican Province (1948) and published by the Westminster Press.

48. *ST* III.68.3.

49. Commentators have noted that it led to such practices as concerned parents asking priests to baptize their dead children so they could avoid limbo. Many priests, guided by pastoral concern over theological conviction, baptized children who were clearly dead.

50. The difficulty with the term *original sin* is that it will be defined and redefined throughout history. However, the form and shape of original sin suggested by Augustine and Aquinas would remain the majority position in the Western church well into the twentieth century.

51. Including the Council of Trent in 1546.

52. As recently as 1905, Pope Pius X stated plainly, 'Children who die without baptism go into limbo, where they do not enjoy God, but they do not suffer either.' Cited from *New York Times*, 28 December 2005.

53. It was discussed at the Council of Trent on 24 May 1546 when the general congregation took up the discussion of original sin, its nature, consequences and cancellation by baptism. In the fifth session on 17 June 1546, the decree on the dogma of original sin was promulgated.

54. Karl Barth (1886–1968).

55. *Church Dogmatics IV*.1 (1956, p. 501).

56. 2001, pp. 389–90.

57. Karl Rahner (1904–85).

58. Egan (1992, p. 263) suggests that the Ignatian themes of 'joy in the world' and 'finding God in all things' permeate Rahner's theology.

59. 1962–65.

60. So effective was Rahner's protesting that today there is practically no mention within Catholic Catechism of this doctrine that was so embedded within the Roman Catholic Church for over 700 years. Although there is presently a working party considering the doctrine, the fact that Pope Benedict XVI stated, 'Personally, I would let it drop, since it has always been only a theological hypothesis', makes it unlikely that the doctrine will emerge with any strength in the future.

61. 1992, p. 197.

62. Rahner expands on this significantly in 'Original Sin', *Encyclopaedia of Theology*, Seabury Press, 1975.

63. Resulting in the giving of a free Bible to the child in some of the projects, which must surely question the child's motivation.

64. Definitions of the word *evangelism* are numerous. Barrett (1987, pp. 42f.) lists seventy-nine definitions of the word! The word itself is derived from the Greek word ευσαγγελιζω (*euangelizō*) and literally means to bring or announce ευσαγγεσλιον (*euangelion*) good news. From the New Testament word ευσαγγελιστησ~ (*euangelistos*), it can be shown that the evangelist was the announcer or bringer of good news. W.E. Vines in the *Expository Dictionary of New Testament Words* suggests the literal translation should be *a messenger of good* (ευσ is best translated as *good,* αγγελιστησο as *a messenger*). It is unsurprising, therefore, that modern definitions focus on the proclamation of the gospel or good news message. *Webster's Third International Dictionary* (1990) defines evangelism as 'The proclamation of the gospel; especially in the presentation of the gospel to individuals by such methods as preaching, teaching, and personal or visitation programs'. The Lausanne Covenant (1974) stated:

> To evangelise is to spread the good news that Jesus Christ died for our sins and was raised from the dead according to the Scriptures, and that as the reigning Lord he now offers forgiveness of sins and the liberating gift of the Spirit to all who repent and believe.

One of the most comprehensive definitions comes from Bosch (2004, p. 420) in his book *Transforming Mission*:

> We may then summarise evangelism as that dimension and activity of the church's mission which, by word and deed and in light of particular conditions and a particular context, offers every person and community, everywhere, a valid opportunity to be directly challenged to a radical reorientation of their lives.

65. Abraham's (1989, p. 57) thesis needs careful consideration but it often appears as simply an exercise in semantics. What others have described as nurture or discipleship following evangelism and conversion, Abraham describes as all part of the evangelism process; although this may seem substantially different, for the individual going through evangelism or nurture there will be no actual distinction. His unique contribution however is in his deconstruction of the evangelistic experience as involving six stages of initiation. These are summarised as:

> The communal stage where the person evangelized is initiated into the Christian community, the church.
> The cognitive stage where the convert needs to make the Christian belief-system, as summed up in the Nicene Creed, his or her own (Abraham [1989] picks up on this discussion of the creed in pp. 145ff.). Since rational belief is desired, indoctrination is excluded and a proper place is found for apologetics.
> The moral vision: the moral vision of the kingdom needs introducing to the new Christian. It overlaps with conventional morality but also has distinctive features.
> The experiential dimension: the newly evangelised is encouraged to feel a

sense of assurance and peace.

The reception and development of gifts that help the newly evangelised to serve God.

The appropriation of certain disciplines: Abraham (1989, p. 103) writes, '... as a bear minimum to fast, pray, read the scriptures and participate in Eucharist.'

But theology is often untidy and to try and present the definitive process of Christian initiation in six neat points and suggest that they constitute 'evangelism' is to oversimplify a complex subject and is a long way from the more ad hoc early Sunday School programmes that Raikes developed.

66. Recorded in the Acts of the Apostles.

67. Acts 8.

68. Stott (1975, p. 44) suggests that most New Testament evangelism involved the announcement of good news or gospel events – that God, Creator and Lord of the universe, has personally intervened in human history and has done so supremely through the person and ministry of Jesus of Nazareth who is the Lord of history, Saviour and Liberator.

69. James 2.

70. Acts 3.

71. What is not in doubt is the extraordinary act of service that the Raikes' model of Sunday School performed, with tens of thousands of children taught to read and write. However, while it was not doubted, it was rarely incorporated into twentieth-century models of child evangelism.

72. 1977, p. 31. All quotations within this section attributed to Hegel (1977) are cited from *Hegel's Philosophy of Religion* by B. Reardon, 1977. New York: Macmillan Press.

73. Often this area attracts extreme responses, most recently seen in the chapter on children (chapter 9, titled 'Childhood, abuse and the escape from religion') in Dawkins' (2006, pp. 309f.) book *The God Delusion*. It is a good example of what happens when an academic of proven track record loses objectivity in pursuit of a cause – in this case, discrediting Christianity. He begins the chapter by describing the historical incident of a child taken from its parents for religious reasons; he is obviously highly critical. However, towards the end of the chapter he suggests that children of Mennonite families should be removed! Whatever the rights or wrongs, it is astonishing that a man of this calibre cannot see the contradictions in his own argument. Unfortunately, it is indicative of the style of writing that characterizes this book. It is also unfortunate that Dawkins cannot see that atheism, a position he passionately holds to, is not a neutral position, but is in itself a system of belief.

74. 2005, p. 5.

75. 2005, p. 5.

76. Hull (1985, p. 149).

77. The repeated claim that young children are capable of much more than would be expected on Piagetian grounds does not mean the work of Piaget and his successors have no contribution to make (Hull, 1991, p. 3).

78. The phrase 'most often acknowledged' as the founder is deliberate. In 1762 Rousseau published *Émile*. In it he lists a range of developmental stages, as follows:

> Stage one: Infancy (birth to 2 years)
> Stage two: The Age of Nature (2 to 12)
> Stage three: The Noble Savage (12 to 15)
> Stage four: Puberty (15 to 20)
> Stage five: Adulthood (20 to 25)

Although primitive, particularly with regard to the distinctive development of the female Sophie (involving dressing dolls and moving gracefully, alongside numeracy and literacy) as distinct from the male Émile, Rousseau nonetheless suggests that people develop through different stages and therefore, different forms of education are suitable at different stages of development.

Although in reality, the concept can be found in both the Old and New Testaments. Luke's Gospel records Jesus as growing in stature and wisdom and in favour with God and men, Pridmore (1967, p. 53) also adds 1 Samuel to the list of primary texts relating to children and their spiritual development. He focuses the reader's attention on 1 Samuel 2:21b, 2:26 and 3:19. Any of these verses taken in isolation would not prove particularly significant, but all three verses clearly drawing parallels with physical and spiritual growth would indicate that the writer is making a statement. Pridmore (1967, p. 53) summarizes his position:

> Their importance for our purpose is that they show us that the Old Testament can conceive of a child's growth in stature and in human relationship being accompanied by equivalent growth in his relationship with God.

C.S. Lewis tackles a same theme in a conversation between Lucy and Aslan in *The Chronicles of Narnia*. Lucy sees Aslan for the first time in the new book and asks Aslan if he is bigger. Aslan responds that he appears bigger because Lucy is bigger. And the more she grows, the bigger he will seem. It's a wonderful analogy particularly when most things from childhood now appear very small; it is only God who we see as bigger and more awesome the more aware we become.

79. Jean Piaget (1896–1980).

80. A summary of Fowler's research is cited in the Anglican report, *Children in the Way* (1988, p. 52). Unfortunately, it is written as a statement of fact without critique.

81. Fowler uses Piaget's (1950) ages until they reach formal operation and then resorts to Levinson's eras.

82. Hull (1985, p. 182).

83. 1981, p. 91.

84. 1981, p. 99.

85. 1978, pp. 16–24.

86. There were children aged six who exhibited age twelve development and vice versa.

87. Hull, 1991, p. 3.

88. 1950, p. 136.

89. 1981, p. 185.

90. 1985, p. 192.

91. 1981, p. 201.

92. 1978, pp. 16–24.

93. Fowler himself hints at this when he talked of an *emerging faith stage* in one of those interviewed.

94. 1985, p. 186.

95. 1981, p. 101.

96. Goldman (1986, p. 226) suggests, 'The way in which the mind reviews its old beliefs is by adding new informational pathways and getting them to dominate the old pathways by means of interference.' In effect, the old system of thinking is no longer accessible.

97. There is a caution here in that Fowler (1981) also refers to 'lateral conversion' – that is conversion that happens within the same faith stage. For example, a Muslim may become a Christian and convert from one belief system to another; they have been stage 3 before and 3 three afterwards – the substance of the faith stage has changed, not the stage itself.

98. 1981, p. 190.

99. 1981, p. 191.

100. 1977, p. 8. Astley (2002, p. 181) adds his strength to the view and writes of students 'who need to be challenged to new and renewed commitment and to multiple conversions'.

101. 1998, p. 16.

102. 1975, p. 100.

103. 2001, p. 77.

104. 1981, p. 121.

105. 1985, p. 158.

106. 1981, p. 128.

107. 1981, p. 129.

108. It would be impossible to prove that the image of God that Sally has constructed is based on the God of Christianity and Judaism. At this point, it is only possible to say that Sally is forming an image of *the other* – what Spiro (1966) referred to as 'a postulated superhuman being', as drawn from his definition of a religion as 'an institution consisting of culturally patterned interactions with culturally postulated superhuman beings'. Hegel used the term 'Divine Being'. However, the term *God* will continue to be used, but placed in italics to show it could be replaced by a range of terms including 'other'. However, it is acknowledged that the meaning of the name of *God* is ultimately lodged in the

concrete life of religious communities where the name is deployed (Caputo, 2006, p. 53).

109. Cited from Fowler (1981, p. 129).

110. Rizzuto's study is in the area of object representation. Her thesis relies much on Freud's initial comments of 1909 where he refers to *God* as a personal object. Rizzuto (1979, p. 8) writes, 'For these reasons I think that a comprehensive study of the representational world has to give equal time to *God* as representational object.' Rizzuto's (1979, p. 178) eventual conclusion is: '*God* is a special transitional object because unlike teddy bears, dolls, or blankets made out of plushy fabrics, he is created from representational materials whose sources are the representations of primary objects.'

111. 1988, p. 34.

112. 1981, p. 134.

113. 1981, p. 136.

114. 1981, p. 137.

115. 1981, pp. 143–146.

116. 1985, p. 188.

117. 1981, p. 141.

118. 1981, p. 142.

119. 1981, p. 143.

120. *Cognitive development* is used carefully here – it is not an attempt to suggest that faith development outlined by Fowler is not cognitive – the inference is that the faith stage is on an adult level whilst cognitive development marked by Piaget (1950) is at a child level.

121. 1972, p. 72.

122. 1981, p. 132.

123. 1981, p. 132. 1 Samuel 15 records Samuel killing a foreign king with a sword because he is God's enemy and then severely rebuking King Saul for not doing it himself.

124. Richards (1983, p. 123).

125. 1985, p. 159.

126. Based on the findings of Klausmeier and Allen (1978).

127. 1985, p. 188.

128. 1981, p. 157.

129. 1981, p. 156.

130. 1989, pp. 104–5.

131. In her introduction to *The Transformed Self.*

132. Finney (1992, p. 17), when looking into the reasons why people became

Christians, asked about those who had been influential. The subject referred to 'the teacher (who) was quietly religious and I still have fond memories of her' as a significant factor. It is interesting that this is not a recollection of the things the teacher said. Indeed, it appears that the teacher made no overt references to her faith; it was to do with her character – 'She was quietly religious.'

133. More accurately, they are stage 4/5 characteristics. Fowler (1981) finds it difficult to define stage 5 as a distinct stage.

134. 1981, p. 161.

135. 1977, p. 27.

136. 1985, p. 189.

137. 1 Samuel 10:6.

138. John Culkin (1928–1993).

139. 1981, p. 114.

140. Astley (2002, p. 185).

141. 1983, p. 120.

142. Matthew 16:17. The verse is not ambiguous; it proposes two fundamental concepts. There is a real being that is termed *God*, and that being is self-revealing – he makes himself known. Hegel (1991, p. 15, translated from 1882 original by Sibree) writes, 'In the Christian religion *God* has revealed Himself – that is, he has given us to understand what He is; so that He is no longer a concealed or secret existence.'

143. In his address to those about to become priests, Canterbury, c. 1973.

144. 1847, p. 21.

145. 1981, p. 103.

146. Richards (1983, p. 114).

147. This is particularly the case with Goldman (1964, 1965).

148. 1977, p. 82.

149. In his definition of what constitutes intuition, Hegel (1977, p. 84) chooses to refer to intuitive understanding as knowledge: '"intuitive" knowledge, so-called, from which rationality were *ex hypothesi* excluded would be no knowledge at all.' In the philosophy of Immanuel Kant, intuition is one of the basic cognitive faculties, equivalent to what might loosely be called perception.

150. 1977, p. 87. A similar construct could also be gleaned from Aristotle and Plato and many have suggested is in keeping with the Old Testament book of Ecclesiastes assertion that *God* has placed eternity into the hearts of men.

151. Although this idea of transcendent encounter can also be found in modern philosophers such as Sartre. Sartre (1958, p. 226) suggests that 'The relation between subjects should be one of being and not knowledge, and also one which does not leave one's own being unaffected.' Sartre is quick to point out that this is experience of others of the same type, and is not an allusion to *God* consciousness. Nevertheless, it does open the door to at least the suggestion

that human beings are capable of transcendental experience.

152. 1977, p. 60.

153. 1990, p. 115.

154. Hull (2006) returns to this concept in his critique of *Mission-Shaped Church* (2004). He points out that in regards to inculturation, the report has overlooked the fact that:

> The gospel is already present in the receiving culture prior to the arrival of the explicit Christian faith. There must be some places within the culture with which Christian faith has some affinity. One of the tasks of mission is to identify these points of contact... There is no trace in *Mission-Shaped Church* of the methodology of seeking in the surrounding culture for rumours of angels or signals of transcendence.

It is again the idea that Christian education and mission are about explaining what has been encountered.

155. Isaiah 6 and Acts 9. The Isaiah reference is self-explanatory. However, Acts 9 needs to be read against Paul's own retelling in Acts 26 when he amplifies that this is the Lord whom he has been resisting.

156. 2005, p. 84.

157. 2005, p. 83.

158. 2000, p. 3.

159. 1983, p. iv.

160. Spencer (2003, p. 5), in his research published as *Beyond Belief*, drew a similar conclusion and commented on people's perception of religion versus spirituality. Religion is into control; spirituality freedom. Religion is narrow-minded; spirituality open. Religion is judgemental; spirituality is not.

161. 1985, p. 151.

162. 1979, p. 7.

163. 1985, p. 152.

164. The New Testament Apostle Paul in his first letter to the Corinthians suggests that no Christian actually sees God clearly (1 Corinthians 13:12). Christianity maintains that Christians grow in relationship with God and that the image of God clarifies over time.

165. It is important to note Hull (1985, p. 167) when considering the view of Freud:

> Although the diagnosis which psychoanalysis offers of neurotic religious life may well be extremely perceptive, the total framework within which the analysis is offered is one within which religion can only appear as an expression of immaturity and illness. Not only does Freud show how in particular cases and situations religious behaviour is neurotic, but his whole understanding of religion is only relevant to the kind of religion which is the product of deficiency.

Rizzuto (1979, p. 7) writes:

> Freud himself – contradicting his own findings about the lifelong

importance of the father – insisted that people should not need religion, called it a cultural neurosis, and set himself up as an example of those who could do without it.

Rizzuto (1998) concluded in her later book *Why did Freud reject God?* that Freud's early life and family relationships made it psychically impossible for him to believe in 'a provident and caring divine being'.

166. Hull, 1985, p. 154.

167. 1971, pp. 44–45.

168. Rahner, 1971, p. 47. This is in direct contrast to Freud's (1914, p. 243) fatalism:

> For psychoanalysis has taught us that the individual's emotional attitudes to other people, which are of such extreme importance to his later behaviour, are already established at an unexpectedly early age. The nature and quality of the human child's relations to people of his own and the opposite sex have already been laid down in the first six years of his life. He may afterwards develop and transform them in certain directions but he can no longer get rid of them. The people to whom he is in this way fixed are his parents and his brothers and sisters... All of his later choices of friendship and love follow upon the basis of memory-trace left behind by those first prototypes.

169. There is of course a stage prior to this. The child evangelists must have a clear and confident understanding of their own construct of *God*.

170. 1962, p. 7.

171. 1973, p. 138.

172. 1979, p. 97.

173. 1977, p. 84. Hegel (1977) goes further than this and insists, 'If the science of religion is to be limited to statements like "God is feeling", it is not worth having, and in fact it would scarcely be possible to understand how theology, as rational thinking about religion, should ever have come into existence at all.'

174. The concept of phenomenology and hermeneutic phenomenology could be expanded on significantly. However, the references made and the explanations given are sufficient to highlight this particular area of study.

175. The word is claimed by sociologists, psychologists and philosophers who all maintain that phenomenology is a branch of their particular discipline.

176. 1962, p. 60.

177. Hull (1985, p. 176) goes on to say:

> This is of course, not to deny that I am indeed experiencing God. It is to claim that God speaks in and through the structure, both conscious and unconscious, of our lives and our thinking, and not only or not mainly through the specifically religious symbols and propositions in which the tradition if faith is expressed.

178. It is an interesting thought that universal religious consciousness makes God available to everyone, but it is in the catechistical processes of each religion that the form and shape of God take place. Therefore, the basis of converting

from another religion to the Christian religion is that exact same process of deconstructing the elements of the constructed *God* image that are not in keeping with the Christian God.

179. Dearing defined the wider church's brief as 'To proclaim the gospel; to nourish Christians in their faith; and to bring others into faith'. It is important to note that Dearing's (2001) definition of mission is in relation to the overall mission of the Church. Therefore, from Abraham (1989) and Dearing (2001) it is possible to glean a healthy picture of the overall activity of the church initiating people into the kingdom of God by proclamation of the gospel.

180. Nye (2006, p. 149) is commenting on her research from a decade earlier.

181. pp. 149–59.

182. 1981, p. 133.

183. It is not that Hull's (1984) work is more significant than Fowler's (1981); indeed, Hull's (1984) work is built significantly on Fowler's (1981) research. It is that Hull's (1984) book *What Prevents Christian Adults from Learning?* is specifically written to challenge Christians to address those issues that prevent faith development and in a very real way help facilitate their movement to higher levels of faith.

184. 1985, p. 166.

185. 2005, p. 117. These are Islamic writers. This is not simply a case of a Christian writer suggesting what Muslim schools practise; these are Muslim writers highlighting what Muslim schools practise.

186. The term 'may be' is used because, unfortunately, many Christian attempts at child evangelism still follow the Muslim pattern – requiring children to learn an inflexible and static body of knowledge.

187. www.islamiceducationtrust.org.uk

188. Interestingly, this is the same method that Rizzuto (1979) uses on her adult patients. The adult is asked to draw their image of *God* and explain it. Rizzuto (1979) is working with adults who, on Fowler's (1981) scale, are recognisable as faith stage 2/3 individuals. This assumption is made for the simple reason that there are no signs of 'executive ego' that marks the individual at faith stage 4. This element is important to note. The child has not developed an 'executive ego'; therefore they need to be guided to understand the image of *God* they have constructed. To bring that image from the unconscious to the conscious and then considered with the child evangelist to understand where their construct is in keeping with the Judeo/Christian God and where distortions have occurred that need deconstruction. Further to this, it may well be the role of Christian educators to follow through this process with adults who haven't passed stage 3, although it must always be the goal of the Christian educator to facilitate this move to stage 4 and beyond, no matter what the effect on the Christian community. (It is at the point of the development of 'executive ego' that Hegel [1882] suggests that 'freedom' comes. The assumption is that the stage 4 individual is no longer dependent on others to bring the unconscious into the conscious. The reflective tools of the stage 4 individual allow them to do this for themselves.) Failure to do this can lead to children entering adulthood with distorted images and understandings of *God*. As highlighted by a diagrammatic

representation of Rizzuto's case studies shown in the table below.

	Fiorella	Douglas	Daniel	Bernadine
Category Definition	1. A *God* whose existence is unquestioned, and with whom they have a significant relation.	2. Unsure whether *God* exists.	3. Amazed and angered by those who believe in a *God* who does not exist	4. Struggling with a harsh *God* she would like to get rid of, but can't.
Representation of *God* belongs to:	The latency period with idealizing love for the safe and protective oedipal object.	The anal retentive phase with its ambivalent attachment to the object.	The latency period. But Daniel has a lifelong defence or schizoid nature and as such his *God* finds his limitations in the young man's need for protection against fantasized annihilation.	The anal sadistic phase with its sadomasochistic involvement with the object.
Connection to parents	*God* image mainly drawn from paternal representation, but some components of the maternal in the background.	*God* image from the mother. An image of a kind *God* who nonetheless ignores him and his need for appreciation.	*God* image exclusively from his father, who Daniel sees as the terrifying father of the primal horde.	*God* image is formed primarily from the mother, a relationship which was damaging and emotionally abusive.

Paraphrase of Rizzuto's (1979, pp. 93-173) findings with four case studies represented diagrammatically.

Clearly, the individuals examined have a distorted *God* image. Many Christian counsellors will work with individuals in this position and will help the individual to see the real *God* through the myth and baggage they have developed. Nevertheless, the unfortunate reality is many psychoanalysts will effectively bring the patients image of *God* from the unconscious to the conscious using the methods explored above, will then deconstruct the unhealthy *God* image that has developed, but for many this is the end of the process. No further exploration of faith takes place.

189. 2006, p. 6.

190. p. 10.

191. Modern research into this area was conducted by David Voas (2005, p. 1) who concluded that two non-religious parents successfully transmit their lack

of religion. Two religious parents have roughly a 50/50 chance of passing on the faith. One religious parent does only half as well as two together. There is a fairly constant chance, about 8 per cent that the child will become religiously different from its parents.

192. Some discussion is needed about denominations that do not practise infant baptism. Services such as 'thanksgiving' and 'dedication' are used in many Christian denominations. The thanksgiving service is often offered as an alternative to baptism, or in some cases as a stage before baptism. It is not the same as baptism and is a service completely in keeping with the title; it is a service where people give thanks for the gift of a new life. Often the thanksgiving service will take place in a church, although it may take place in the family's home or even a nearby community centre. The dedication service is slightly more complicated in that the concept is borrowed from Old Testament practice and as such is clumsy. The Old Testament practice was to do with redeeming, or buying back, the child. In practice, the service tends to follow the same pattern as the thanksgiving service. The inference is that those involved in the dedication service are not only giving thanks but dedicating the child to God. As a casual observation, it seems that the 'dedication' should be a more private affair between parents and God.

There is no attempt to undermine these practices here, and it is fully acknowledged that in some ways infant baptism is a construct, based an Old Testament practice (circumcision), albeit a 2,000-year-old construct with clear scriptural foundation! However, this is not about practice; it is about theology. The primary reason that many denominations hold services of thanksgiving and/ or dedication is because they do not believe the child is *in Christ* and will not be until they make a personal commitment to Christ based on a cognitive response and a later stage of development. Infant baptism is the public acknowledgement before the faith community that the child is *in Christ* and is not based on the child's cognitive response but on the child's spiritual state.

Added to this, it is suggested that children/young people need a mechanism to show that they have come to a point of making their own commitment to follow the teachings of Jesus Christ. The Anglican Church uses a service of confirmation. The type of service is not the primary issue, but some form of service that facilitates this rite of passage is essential. Where there is no opportunity for this public communication, substitutes have been invented or borrowed to take its place. The obvious example is the development of the public appeal or the altar call (Abraham 1989, p. 182). Interestingly, the nineteenth-century revivalist Charles Finney (1847, p. 305) makes exactly that link:

> The church has always felt it necessary to have something of the kind to answer this very purpose. In the days of the apostles baptism answered this purpose. The gospel was preached to the people, and then all those who were willing to be on the side of Christ were called on to be baptised. It held the precise place that the anxious seat does now [This was Finney's equivalent to the altar call – a means of responding to the preaching of the word by kneeling at the front of the church, usually as indication that the person kneeling was converting to Christianity] as a public manifestation of a determination to be a Christian.

193. However, it is suggested that the ages of Piaget's developmental stages are in need of revision when compared with research that is more recent.

194. Except in rare situations, where Helfaer talked of precocious identity formation.

195. 1977, p. 60.

196. 1985, p. 151.

197. Although he may have been aware of Rousseau's *Émile*, c. 1760.

Chapter 7

SOCIOLOGY

Although there is universal agreement that the childhood experienced by children living in the UK in the early years of the twenty-first century is significantly different from that of previous generations,[1] there is no consensus of opinion as to whether the quality of that experience is better or worse. Before this can be examined more closely, a sociological framework is necessary to ground the discussion. American sociologists have developed a system of categorization that designates generations in nineteen-year blocks (figure 7.1). Within this system of categorization the children that form the basis of this study fall into two different groups: firstly, the last years of Generation Y (or Mosaics, born 1984–2002) and Generation Z (or Kaleidoscopes, born 2003–2021).

	Year of Birth	Age in 2000	Population Size (2001)
1. Builders (or Boosters)	1927-1945	55 to 73	4.5 million
2. Boomers	1946-1964	36 to 54	12.4 million
3. Busters (or Generation X)	1965-1983	17 to 35	15.1 million
4. Mosaics (or Generation Y or Beepers)	1984-2002	Up to 16	12.6 million
5. Kaleidoscopes (Generation Z)	2003-2021	–	0

Fig 7.1 Five generations of British people (adapted from Brierley, 2000b)

The classifications that are used are inexact and in many ways arbitrary, although they do allow loose identification of specific age groups, to which a set of characteristics that they broadly share can be attributed. However, what is more helpful is the observation made by Cray, Savage and Mayo:

> Generation X is the generation for whom modernity has failed to deliver its dream of progress... It is a hinge generation, raised in modernity but living in 'postmodernity'.[2]

If Cray, Savage and Mayo are correct, then a more simplified categorization of the children who form the basis of this research is possible. This generation of children is the first generation to live wholly in the third phase of modernity (or postmodernity).[3] Some may have inherited characteristics from their Generation X parents, but they have many characteristics that are uniquely theirs. Cray, Savage and Mayo reinforce this with the assertion that Generations Y and Z cannot be understood without first acknowledging the major cultural shift within Western society from modernity to post- (or late)[4] modernity.[5] During the lifetime of these three generations, culture has gone through a transition from an era primarily formed from the eighteenth-century Enlightenment into a new era, which had no name until recently – hence, the proliferation of the use of the term *postmodern*. Bauman comments that 'We have not been here before, so we do not know what to expect'.[6] This may well have been the case had Bauman been writing two decades earlier; however, we have been here for some time now. The basic shape and central values of culture are in place and this is the only culture this present generation have ever known; they were born and live in the third phase of modernity. This generation really is wired differently.[7] It is against this postmodern background that children and childhood will be considered, using the same frame of reference that was used to examine Raikes' England:

- Social environment and influences on the child
- The state of the church

When considering these areas, the average person could be forgiven for assuming that there are no positives. The media chooses to take a negative view on the influences on the child, the hostile social environment for childhood development and the ineffective church that is haemorrhaging children at an alarming rate. Plato once commented, 'The children now have bad manners and contempt for authority... Children are now tyrants.' This quotation is used here to suggest an elementary truth: children and childhood are often presented in a negative light, particularly by academics! Many centuries after Plato, the debate over the nature of childhood continues, although the emphasis has not changed. An example of this was the letter printed in the *Daily Telegraph*[8] written by Sue Palmer and Dr Richard House that contained such emotive statements as 'We are deeply concerned at the escalating incidence of childhood depression and children's behavioural and developmental conditions'. The letter was more disquieting because it was signed by 110 prominent teachers, psychologists, government experts and children's authors, among these Phillip Pullman and Jacqueline Wilson. However, bringing a more balanced perspective, Lord Winston, speaking to *The Guardian* on the day of the launch of the Children's Society's *Good Childhood* Enquiry, commented:

> I have no problem with the initiative – it's an excellent idea – but I do consider that what's happening is some broad sweeping statements that are not justified. It's all very well to say that childhood depression is on the increase, but there are no data to support that (18 September 2006).[9]

Jacqueline Wilson added her voice to the debate and stated:

> We are not valuing childhood. I speak to children at book signings and they ask me how I go through the process of writing and I say, 'Oh you know, it's just when you play imaginary games and you write it all down.' All I get is blank faces. I don't think children know how to use their imaginations any more.[10]

Wilson's (almost Plato-like) quotation is indicative of the current difficulties facing an honest assessment of childhood; it is difficult to get past the sea of cynicism to address honestly the state of today's child.[11] However, this research tried to move past that cynicism and present a more balanced view. A view somewhere between Katz's utopian and somewhat anarchic view that:

> This new machinery is making the young more sophisticated, altering their idea of what culture and literacy are, it is transforming them – connecting them with one another, providing a new sense of political self... children can for the first time reach past the suffocating boundaries of social convention, past their elders' rigid notions of what is good for them.[12]

and the view of Postman[13] and others that challenge newly emerging constructs of childhood by questioning their ontological status; they interpret late-twentieth-century change as a sign that childhood as a social institution is in the process not merely of changing but of disappearing. Both positions adopt an essentialist view of childhood and an unduly deterministic account of the role of the media and technology. Both reflect a kind of sentimentality about children and young people that fails to acknowledge the diversity of the lived experience, and certainly Postman's view fails to appreciate the natural adaptive skills demonstrated by today's child.

While agreeing with the statement made by the church leader of Kings Church International that 'The damage done in childhood is immense and we are reaping that in the problems in society', it is also necessary to note Barna's summary of the present situation when he writes:

> What do the data regarding young people teach us? Many of the statistics that capture the public's attention tell the bad news. Yet if we examine all of the data, from various angles, we find that most kids face a few difficult challenges but generally live safe and satisfying lives.[14]

This is a view in keeping with the findings of the *Good Childhood Inquiry*,[15] that concluded that 87 per cent of boys and girls in the UK were happy. It is also worth noting Caputo's observations on the nature of cultural changes:

> Enlightenment or modernity is a necessary phase, an essential course correction, in working out a satisfactory reconciliation of the corrupting claims of faith and reason. Religious people hold their faith to be the most precious thing they have, and well they should, but everything depends upon understanding the faith that is in you, on thinking it through and thinking it out, in dialogue with others and with everything else that God has given us.[16]

The concept of a course correction – the ebb and flow of culture throughout history – is useful and places modernity, and for that matter postmodernity, in context; the overemphasis on faith without reason, the empirical above the cognitive, necessitated the assertions of modernist/Enlightenment thinkers to bring a balance. However, as with all phases of history, there is an overbalance, and modernism brought with it an overemphasis on rationalism and cognition, and a diminished view of the empirical. It is this balanced sociological perspective of Barna and Buckingham and an understanding of the ebb-and-flow nature of culture represented by Caputo that underpins this examination of influences on the child, their social context and the state of the church within this thesis.

SOCIAL ENVIRONMENT AND INFLUENCES ON THE CHILD

When considering the influences on the child in the eighteenth century, it is true to say that life was simpler. The primary influences on the child were parental, and even secondary factors such as economics were outworked from the perspective of the family. For example, the eighteenth-century child may have worked long hours from an early age, but their motivation to do so was the economic sustainability of the family unit. In 1977, *The Myth of God Incarnate* was published; in it Houlden argued, 'We must accept our lot bequeathed to us by the Enlightenment, and make the most of it.'[17] As Houlden was writing, the Enlightenment world was in decline. The rise of the movement, now generally known as postmodernism throughout the Western world, is a direct result of the collapse of this confidence in reason and a more general disillusionment with the so-called *modern* world.[18] Twenty-first-century life is complicated. It has already been stated that the parents of this generation were primarily a *hinge* generation; they lived in the cusp between the second and third phase of modernity. Croucher suggests that fewer than half of them have lived with both biological parents throughout their childhood.[19] The way they were parented has affected the way they parent; this is demonstrated by the fact that in 2001, 23 per cent[20] of children lived with lone parents[21] and a third of all sixteen-year-olds were not living with their biological father.[22] There has also been an increase in the number of lone parents who have returned to work, undoubtedly encouraged by a range of government initiatives, including an increase in nursery and preschool provision. The type of work being undertaken has also changed in the last three decades. The nine-to-five work pattern has been replaced by more complex shift patterns to facilitate the emerging service industries and the push for convenience, which has resulted in twenty-four-hour garages, supermarkets and fast food outlets.[23]

Withers points out that 'Children will spend weekends or holiday time with the second parent and maybe an entire second family'.[24] The difficulty in reading such statistics is that, as with earlier comments, they are often presented negatively; the statistics stated are representations of data, and they have no moral bias.[25] There simply is no evidence to suggest that children in lone-parent families fare worse than children with two parents.[26] Barna comments:

> You don't need a series of surveys to remind you that life is messy.
> We prefer experiences and conditions to fit together into a single,

easy-to-interpret, black and white storyboard. But this is not often the case.[27]

In the leadership of the Fraserburgh project, there were leaders who had grown up in homes where domestic violence had become the norm and parents were regular drug abusers. The projects at Slough and Windsor, Leeds and Hastings all recorded spasmodic attendance patterns because of children spending one weekend with one parent and the next weekend with the other. (This didn't result in a change of programme: all three projects continued to work through a weekly series despite the realization that many children would only attend every second part.)

It is also important to note Cray, Savage and Mayo's[28] point that 'Generation Y rejects the victim status that characterized Generation X'. Cray, Savage and Mayo are suggesting that the children encountered in this third phase of modernity are more resilient than many writers give them credit for, and they are certainly more resilient than their parents are. Barna observes, 'Their relationships are much more radically integrated and fluid than any generation we have seen before.'[29] What should be avoided is the temptation to treat this uncertainty of life as a problem when it is freely embraced.[30]

It would be easy to assume that this third phase of modernity would result in a return to a pre-modern world view. Toulmin suggests that this movement into the third phase of modernism has brought with it a return to pre-Enlightenment values, specifically, a return to the particular, the specific, the timely and the oral.[31] Nevertheless, this is only part of the process – culture is far more multifaceted.[32] This generation of children now lives in a culture where modernism is no longer dominant, but they have also assimilated characteristics from previous generations, as well as manifesting characteristics that are uniquely their own. Their lifestyles are an eclectic combination of traditional and alternative activities,[33] but there is clearly a move away from modernism. McGrath suggests:

> The new cultural mood, which developed in the 1980s, rebelled against the Enlightenment. There has been a general collapse of confidence in the Enlightenment trust in the power of reason to provide foundations for a universally valid knowledge of the world, including God.[34]

Toulmin is more specific in that he labels the changes that this rebellion entails:

> All the changes of mind that were characteristic of the 17th
> century's turn from humanism to rationalism are, as a result,
> being reversed. The 'modern' focus on the written, the universal,
> the general, and the timeless – which monopolised the work of
> most philosophers after 1630 – is being broadened to include
> once again the oral, the particular, the local and the timely.[35]

The third phase of modernism is also marked by a return to an emphasis
on localized truth. The modernistic philosophy that truth is universal has
been undermined by the complexities of twenty-first-century life.[36] Toulmin
suggests that 'This new phase of modernism challenges the temptation to
generalise'.[37] It marks a weaning off Descartes' assertion that what is true
in one place was true everywhere.

Croucher suggests further interesting characteristics of postmodern
children (full list in figure 7.2). They have learnt to live with ambiguity
and rejected institutions for a more collaborative approach, they have
rejected the construct of absolute truth, and they multi-task naturally.[38] It
suggests that not all people in all cultures and epochs have access to the
same neutral basic conceptual framework, and a localized culture can only
be properly understood when their cultural anthropology and history are
taken seriously.[39.]

---

1. Survivors of the most aborted generation in history

2. The best educated, most travelled and longest-living generation ever

3. The first electronic generation, having already mastered laptops, the Internet,
   CD-Roms, faxes, modems, Nintendo, Sega and PlayStation (they have a
   tremendous ability to process lots of information at once. Playing video games
   while talking on the phone, listening to the radio, doing their homework, and
   making a snack was an after-school ritual for this generation. This 'parallel
   thinking' allows 'multiple tasking'.)

4. The first generation to be raised completely by TV (so 'everything is image') and
   shaped by music: and their lyrics are often passionate and angry, sometimes
   rebellious, mostly honest, sometimes spiritual/religious (there's a pervasive
   longing for reality, healing, community and peace).

5. Having insatiable appetites for junk food, junk films, junk ideas, and junk culture

6. Rejecting institutions (this is a collaborative generation – hierarchical structures
   are out)

7. Affirming diversity and able to live with ambiguity

Fig 7.2 Dr Rowland Croucher's characteristics of Generation X

Not only is truth within postmodernism seen to be specific and localized, it also presented as being timely. Toulmin writes:

> In recent years, the focus of philosophy has broadened to include problems whose rational significance is not eternal but depends on the timeliness of our solutions... Only in the last 25 years, however, have academic philosophers in Britain and the United States generally shared this underlying perception that *meaning* cannot be analysed as a timeless relationship between propositions and states of affairs alone, but must be understood always in relation to one or another larger behavioural context.[40]

This three-pronged philosophy of the local, specific and timely must lead to the conclusion that the concept of absolute truth and morality will struggle for incorporation in a postmodern framework. There is no longer a universalizing meta-narrative; society has moved from story to stories, localized interpretations of truth for the present. Lyon writes:

> The inflated characteristics of modernity, which give rise to postmodern premonitions, relate above all to communication and information technologies and to the tilt towards consumerism. Both are bound up with the restructuring of capitalism that has been under way since at least the last quarter of the twentieth century.[41]

Cray, Savage and Mayo identify one further characteristic when they write, 'There are shifts from producer to consumer, from industrial to electronic society and from sovereign nation states to globalised world... but it is the integration of the three that gives them their profound impact.'[42] Therefore, alongside the return to the timely, specific, local and oral, this present generation of children are also fully immersed in a culture of consumerism, technological media and globalization.

The defining feature of consumerism, as it affects children, is summed up in the word *choice*. Choice lies at the very core of consumerism. The central values of society have moved from progress to choice: the absolute right of freedom to choose. As Bauman expresses it:

> The difference is one of emphasis, but that shift does make an enormous difference in virtually every aspect of society, culture and individual life. The differences are so deep and ubiquitous

that they fully justify speaking of our society as a separate and distinct kind – a consumer society.[43]

This is another factor affecting attendance at church or the Children's Outreach Project. The Children's Outreach Project is one of many options that include ballet classes, music lessons, football matches and uniformed organizations. The days when church attendance was a duty to be fulfilled have been relegated to a bygone age. Nevertheless, it is not only attendance that is affected; the core teachings of orthodox Christianity also become a matter of choice, leading Barna to conclude that, for children, 'The central spiritual tenets that provide substance to their faith are the customised blend of multiple-faith views and religious practices'.[44] Lyon comments:

> When many voices can be heard, who can say that one should be heeded more than another?... When the only criteria left for choosing between them are learned in the marketplace, then truth appears as a commodity. We hear the people *buy into* a belief.[45]

With this in mind, therefore, it should not be a surprise that postmodern children have a hybrid faith; they have selected the elements of spirituality that they prefer, as did their parents before them. Their core values are the result of a cut-and-paste mosaic of feelings, facts, principles, experiences and lessons.[46] Of course, this is completely consistent when the dominant philosophies show that truth is localized and timely. Therefore, Richards, speaking of the churches' response, concludes:

> It seems clear that the living faith to which the Christian community is called demands the ability to apply biblical truth in a constantly changing world, where many varied associations of biblical principles with changing situations is vital.[47]

There is no contradiction here. This is about the application of orthodox Christianity into a variety of settings and over different times. Some may be concerned that this may mean that biblical truth may be applied in different ways in different places, or, for that matter, biblical truth may be applied differently at different times. It is argued that this is exactly what Christianity has always done. Mbiti tries to communicate this thought when he writes:

> We can add nothing to the gospel for this is an eternal gift of

God; but Christianity is always a beggar seeking food and drink,
cover and shelter from cultures it encounters in its never ending
journeys and wanderings.[48]

Children's Outreach Projects are failing to address this as they continue to
present what Fowler categorizes as stage 2/3 tacit faith. Copley reinforces
the point: 'Religions across the planet are constantly evolving, never static,
always adapting to cultures and eras, spaces and places.'[49] This evolution is
demonstrated by the numerous church councils[50] throughout history that
have sought to interpret and understand Christian teaching, experience
and practice. Children's Outreach Projects must ask themselves what truth
looks like for the children who live in this place at this time.[51]

However, many authors would present a more apocalyptic view of
the emergence of consumerism. Withers writes:

> Even the youngest children are dressed as miniature adults with
> the consequent expectation that they will behave accordingly...
> An image-obsessed culture is having a negative effect on some
> children's sense of self-worth. As well as demanding special
> clothes and hairstyles to look like their sporting or pop idols, an
> increasing number of young children are thinking that they are
> 'fat' or 'ugly' and thus developing eating disorders or even wanting
> plastic surgery to change their bodies.[52]

Although agreeing that this generation of children is extraordinarily
image-conscious, this one-dimensional view of childhood presented by
Withers owes more to media projections than rigorous research.[53] For
example, the BBC, commenting on the research undertaken by the National
Consumer Council in 2005, reported on 13 June 2006 that 'By the age of ten,
many children in this country had become brand-aware shoppers – and
were feeling the pressures and stresses of adult consumers'. Subsequent
reports that featured in national newspapers carried similar and often far
more emotive comments along this same theme. However, the research
itself carried out by the National Consumer Council concluded in far
less pejorative language that 'Children see themselves as enthusiastic
consumers'.[54]

It may seem unnecessary to highlight this misreporting, but it
highlights the basic misconception that underpins this style of writing.
Children at the start of the twenty-first century do not see themselves as
victims, but this doesn't stop writers projecting on to them the victim status

that characterized previous generations. Although Withers' comments may have been true of a previous generation, they seem outdated when applied to this one.

Alongside consumerism, there has been a significant growth in electronic media. Lyon observes:

> The growth of communication and information technologies is one of the most striking and transformative changes of the twentieth century. They do not in themselves transform anything, but they contribute to the establishment of novel contexts of social interaction... They help to alter the significance of face-to-face relationships while simultaneously bringing all of us into daily contact with cultures once remote or strange.[55]

This twenty-four-hour information world has been one reason for the increasing pluralism of the twentieth and twenty-first centuries. Technology allows access to vast amounts of information. Previous generations knew only one world view, one construct for religious belief; this generation has access to a wide range of information on religious communities near and far and open access to their systems of belief – systems of belief that consumerism has taught them they can select at will. However, the situation for children at the start of the twenty-first century is more subtle. Not only do they have access to information on the culture or religious group, but technology has made it possible for them to have access to the actual group. It is possible for postmodern children to communicate with practically anyone, in any place, from the comfort of their own home. According to the National Statistics Association, in 1985, 13 per cent of the population had a computer at home; by 2001 the figure was 66 per cent. By 2006 the Children's Society reported that 64 per cent of children have access to the internet at home. This must be kept in perspective. Despite alarmist reporting from time to time, technology is not careering out of control; on the contrary, it more accurately reflects the desires of the users and their day-to-day priorities.[56] Technology continues to be a slave to humanity's free will.[57]

Technology has made it possible for children to be part of a global community. The effects of globalization should not be minimized. It is restructuring the way people live in a profound manner.[58] The global perspective is seen by the way the Leeds project raised funds for street children in India, and the way the Liverpool project was supporting an orphanage in Thailand.

However, globalization has a dual function; it not only connects local children with a global context, but it also allows that global context to affect the local. Moreover, Rushkoff suggests that the system is self-regulating:

> Our long-standing ideologies, cultural icons, and systems of morality are all being re-evaluated in their new chaotic context. The ones that work well get spread further and better than before, while the ones that don't work just fade into oblivion.[59]

Postman contradicts this when he writes:

> The single most important fact about television is that people *watch it*, which is why it is called *television*. And what they watch, and like to watch, are moving pictures – millions of them, of short duration and dynamic variety. It is in the nature of the medium that it must suppress the content of ideas in order to accommodate the requirements of visual interest; that is to say, to accommodate the values of show business.[60]

However, the comments suggest that Postman has never observed a child watching television. The child, far from sitting passively, is interacting with the technology. The child may watch two or three programmes at once. The storyteller who isn't trusted is turned over in favour of a different channel; the child with the remote control can deconstruct the content of the story. It is an active experience in which they constantly make judgment calls on the visual experience. Children are not passive consumers; they regulate themselves, free from outside control or censorship, with a sophisticated understanding of communication technology. Children and young people interact directly with others in a virtual world that has few boundaries.[61] At the 2007 summer camp organized by the Slough and Windsor project there was discussion on the safe use of Facebook™. Nevertheless, it was discussion and not a warning not to use it. Children's Outreach Projects are helping children to analyze the world in which they live and the technology they use. This comes from an understanding that technology is neither right nor wrong, but the use or misuse of that technology has moral and ethical implications. Parents find it increasingly difficult to mediate this interaction[62] and are often concerned that their children spend too much time playing computer games and not enough time in social interaction.[63] Interestingly, Ogilvie-Whyte's[64] ethnography of a Scottish primary school concluded that, for the child, one of the most important features of a toy was not so much its digital interactivity as its capacity to give them access to a network of other children. Rather than abandon their playmates to isolate themselves with the toy, children take the techno-toy to the playground to try to reach the outside group of players. The toy is thus used as a way of being enrolled or enrolling others. Technology within the study was seen to be making the children more socially interactive. It is not the experience of media itself as much as the way that media can act as social currency for other interactions.[65]

Tomlinson comments, 'The key to [globalization's] cultural impact is the transformation of localities themselves.'[66] Children feel that they are part of the global village; therefore, the effects of a tsunami thousands of kilometres away will affect them in more profound ways. Technological advances such as AIM™, Messenger™, Twitter™, Facebook™, Bebo™ and Skype™ allow the average computer user to engage in face-to-face conversations with others in different continents. Abbott comments, 'Speaking online takes a written form and writing in cyberspace almost has an oral function.'[67] This is not just intellectual contact; this is emotional contact, and these are their friends.

They have inherited characteristics from their parents, live in a culture where there are no absolutes and where consumerism, globalization and technological advance are firmly embedded; the effect of these factors working together is to produce a child who sees things differently to previous generations. They have a unique world view, a unique construct of reality and a unique view of themselves. Postmodernism has created a changed experience of space and time, which are core matrices of the development of identity.[68] Lyon aligns himself to the same position when he writes, 'At a profound social level, time and space, the very matrix of human social life, is undergoing radical social restructuring.'[69] Postmodernity has rejected modernity's belief in a better future and refocused on the present.[70]

Nevertheless, the resultant child is not the consumer-driven, rationalist that is often portrayed. They are not anti-God, although they would not be quick to join organized religion.[71] Bruce argues that as technology begins to fill in the gaps previously filled by religion, there becomes less need for the divine.[72] He further argues that the church is suffering from the effects of secularization. However, Bruce's hypothesis is far from convincing. Children today do not seem to be the products of secularization; they are in fact very spiritual. Rushkoff observes:

> Far from yielding a society of cold-hearted rationalists, the
> ethereal, out of body experience of mediating technologies

appears to have spawned a generation of pagan spiritualists whose dedication to technology is only matched by their enthusiasm for elemental truth and a neoprimitive, magical worldview... It is becoming difficult for us to distinguish between the physical and the digital, the scientific and the spiritual, the mundane and the magical.[73]

This combining of technology and spirituality is so subtle it often goes unobserved, but it is not new. Davies writes:

The world of renaissance and reformation was also the world of divination, astrology, miracles, conjuration, witchcraft, necromancy, folk cures, ghosts, omens and fairies. Magic continued to compete, and to interact with religion and science.

This same intermingling of religion, science and magic/spirituality can be observed today. Technical advancement is not closing the door to spiritual things – the two are not exclusive opposites. However, what form the presentation of Christian spirituality[74] should take, against this background, poses a challenge. Nonetheless, it is a challenge with which the Children's Outreach Projects will need to engage.

Rushkoff makes one more noteworthy observation: 'For a spiritual practice to work in the culture of chaos, it must indeed be a practice and not a passive absorption of dogma or morality.'[75] Hamilton highlights, 'A Christian faith is not learned by heart. It is set down for us in the symbols of words, in the creeds and practices of worship in the church.'[76] There are resonances here to Bushnell's comments that Christianity is something that is lived out and exemplified, and not just a concept of theory to be taught. However, this involves more than godly example; there is also a link to sacramental practice – sacramental in the broadest sense of an external act or practice being used to communicate an internal experience. In the context of the Children's Outreach Project, it involves the ability to show physically something that has been experienced, possibly through raising a hand, standing or lighting a candle.

Unfortunately, the Children's Outreach Projects visited were primarily focused on imparting information while the children sat, listened and watched. There was some opportunity to *do* as well as to listen in the small-group settings of the Slough and Windsor project, but even in this the level of *doing* was limited. All of the projects seemed a long way from moving to the position where involvement becomes a way of life,[77] a move beyond the impartation of chunks of information to opportunity to outwork that information in real-life situations. This diversity is twenty-first-century childhood and is the cultural context that the Children's Outreach Project must understand before it can communicate.

THE STATE OF THE CHURCH

There is often an unstated, but nonetheless believed, assumption within the Church of England and some other denominations that although there are ever decreasing numbers of children and young people within churches, they will nevertheless come back when they are older. In previous generations, the assumption was well founded; many of those who left the church as young people returned in later years. Moreover, as figure 7.3 shows, even those who did not return were more inclined to see Christianity in favourable terms.

	Non-churchgoers as children (%)	Regular churchgoers as children (%)
I know *God* really exists	19	40
I don't believe in *God*	54	27
I don't believe in *God* now, and never have	40	6
I believe in *God* now and always have	11	39
The Bible is the word of *God*	13	32
I never pray	70	41
I pray at least once a fortnight	6	18
I believe in life after death	31	35
I believe in heaven	22	40
I believe in hell	12	16
I believe in the devil	10	17

Fig 7.3 Survey of non-churchgoers from Gill (1999)

However, the present reality is that children and young people have nothing to come back to because they have never had connection with the church.[78] Sunday School attendance in England has dropped from 14 per cent of children in 1970 to 4 per cent in 2000.[79] The two generations who grew to maturity in the last thirty years of the twentieth century have stopped going to Sunday School.[80] The *Mission-Shaped Church* report of 2004 described this situation as 'a time bomb'. It is suggested that the effects of this are now becoming obvious, In 2005:[81]

39% of churches had *no one* attending under 11;

49% of churches had *no one* attending aged 11 to 14; and

59% of churches had *no one* attending aged 15 to 19.

Positive contact with the church as a child has always been beneficial for the church in the long term – whether in increased adult attendance (as shown in the early years of the nineteenth century and beyond) or a more favourable response to elements of the Christian gospel as shown in figure 7.3) Where there is no contact, there is a less favourable response and the church cannot see a return of lapsed attendees. Using Brown's observations, this is now the third generation of children who do not attend church activities. The diagram below (figure 7.4) from *Mission-Shaped Church*[82] highlights the implications of this.

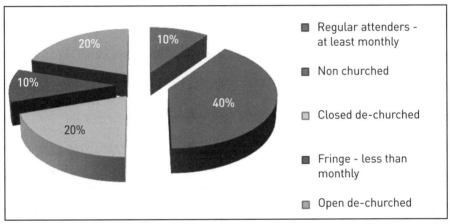

Fig 7.4 Adults in contact with church in 1998

There are areas that need to be included in this discussion. Firstly, the churches have implemented various strategies to deal with this decline. The majority are strategies implemented to try and engage with adults who have never been to church. To this extent a range of *fresh expressions of church*[83] have emerged and continue to emerge, although, in his summary of the findings of the 2005 English Church Census, Brierley comments that fresh expressions of church are statistically smaller than the average church congregation.[84] However, the understanding that a more adaptive church is necessary to engage with emerging generations is welcome.

Secondly, Withers observes that a third of the children in England are educated in church schools.[85] However, she contradicts this when she comments that 'Few children have any understanding of organized religion'[86] and has little confidence in the schools to which she alludes. The explanation for this may be that the schools themselves have not heeded (or not yet been able to implement) the comments of the Dearing Report that 'No church school can be considered part of the church's mission unless it is distinctively Christian'. The developing role of the church school must be seen as an important part in the equation for the development of Christianity over the coming decades.

Finally, there must be an acknowledgement that the model of trusting that children will make their way to church or Sunday School on a Sunday morning has not been effective for over half a century.[87] The changes in the makeup of the family, and the fact that children may spend one weekend with their father in one part of the country and the next weekend with their mother in another, only serve to increase the complexities of the situation. It is now universally agreed that the church operates in post-Christendom. Murray defines this as:

> The culture that emerges as the Christian faith loses coherence with a society that has been definitively shaped by the Christian story and as the institutions that have been developed to express Christian convictions decline in influence.[88]

Murray talks of the church having moved from 'the centre to the margins'. There is some debate around the nature of Christendom and post-Christendom,[89] but there is very little resistance to the belief that in post-Christendom the way church operates must change.[90] The demands of post-Christendom necessitate more novel ideas and adaptive initiatives to operate alongside traditional models of church.

Notes

1. Reitemeier (2006, p. 2).

2. 2006, p. 150.

3. The word *postmodern* was first popularised in the context of culture in 1979 by Jean-Francois Lyotard in his book *The Postmodern Condition: A Report on Knowledge.* The main thrust of his book being the breakdown of meta-narratives.

4. It is not the intention of this research to debate terminology. The terms *postmodernism, late modernity* and *the third phase of modernity* are all used by sociologists to refer to the present period (early twenty-first century) in which the tenets of modernity have been weakened or lost. The terms are used interchangeably.

5. 2006, p. 142.

6. 2001, p. 128.

7. Cray, Savage and Mayo (2006, p. 143).

8. 12 September 2006.

9. Lord Winston was responding directly to the Children's Society's (2006) report that 'Depression and anxiety have increased for both boys and girls aged 15–16 since the mid-1980s'.

10. 12 September 2006.

11. It is noteworthy that the 2006 launch of the Children's Society's *Good Childhood Inquiry*, with its aim to address levels of stress and depression in children, earned national media attention, whereas its conclusions, published in 2009, that there had been no increase in mental disorders in children in the past decade, went by practically without mention. The overall findings are a significant contribution to the conversation on the state of the twenty-first century child.

12. 1997, p. 173.

13. 1983, p. 14.

14. 2003, p. 25.

15. *Good Childhood Inquiry*, 2009.

16. 2006, p. 35.

17. 1977, p. 125.

18. McGrath 1993, p. 16.

19. Croucher (1998, p. 27). It is important to see that the shape of family has been evolving quite rapidly over the last 150 years. The earlier comments from Ariès (1962), Strauss (1978), Ozment (1983) and Pitkin (2001) show that the family has been evolving for at least five centuries. Giddens (2002, p. 58) points out that in *traditional family* (by which he refers to families before the twentieth century) 'The married couple was only one part, and often not the main part of the *family* system. Ties with children and with other relatives tended to be equally or even more important in day-to-day conduct of social life'. During the twentieth century, the couple became the core of who the family is. Giddens (2002, p. 59) continues, 'The couple came to the centre of family life as the economic role of the family dwindled and love, or love plus sexual attraction, became the basis of forming marriage ties.' Fukuyama (1999) suggests that from the 1950s the family went into long-term decline. Instead, it may be suggested that the shape

and form of family is changing, the number of couples who now bypass the wedding service and cohabit continues to rise (the percentage of single women co-habiting rose from 8 per cent in 1979 to 31 per cent in 2002). It is a matter of fact that the number of same sex couples is also increasing. Giddens (2002, p. 57) suggests this is the logical outcome of the severance of sexuality from reproduction.

20. National Statistics Commission (www.statistics.gov.uk).

21. Forty-three per cent of all children born in the UK in 2005 were born to unmarried parents, but it is not possible to know from the statistic whether these are lone parents or cohabiters.

22. *Good Childhood Inquiry*, 2009

23. Withers (2006, p. 2).

24. 2006, p. 4.

25. There is evidence that children who live in conflict situations – for example, situations of domestic violence – are negatively impacted by that experience (McGee, 2000, p. 93). There is also evidence to show that children suffer emotionally when parents initially split up, although Paris (2000) suggests that in some instances the eventual breakdown may come as a relief to the child/ren and therefore promote their emotional well-being.

26. Although it is likely that, given all other factors as equal, a case could be made that two people looking after a child would find it less stressful than one, in keeping with this, there is no measurable distinction in the child's well-being when brought up by two carers of the same sex or two carers who are of the opposite sex (Reder and Lucey, 1995, p. 209).

27. 2003, p. 25.

28. 2006, p. 154.

29. 1994, p. 17.

30. Cray, Savage and Mayo (2006, p. 154).

31. 1990, pp. 180f.

32. It is also too complex for there to be a single underlying post modernization process that underpins developments in all places leading inevitability to a single predetermined endpoint (Prout, 2005, p. 9).

33. Barna (1994, p. 17).

34. 1993, p. 17.

35. 1990, p. 186.

36. For example, in the debate as to whether withholding treatment was ethically correct in terms of terminally ill children, Dr Peter Saunders, general secretary of the Christian Medical Fellowship, stated that he agreed that 'in some cases withdrawing or withholding treatment would be appropriate' (*The Guardian*, 12 November 2006).

37. 1990, p. 188.

38. 1998, p. 27.

39. Toulmin (1990, p. 189). It is this assertion that gives validity to the ethnographic studies of the Children's Outreach Projects.

40. 1990, pp. 187–9.

41. 2000, p. 7.

42. 2006, p. 143.

43. 1998, p. 24.

44. 1994, p. 17.

45. 2000, p. 285.

46. Barna (1994, p. 17).

47. 1983, p. 120.

48. 1970, p. 435.

49. 2005, p. 87.

50. The Council of Nicea (ᴀᴅ 351) is the most famous, but the 2008 debates at General Synod regarding episcopacy are another example.

51. What is encouraging in keeping with this is that over half the projects surveyed (56 per cent) write their own curriculum material at some point.

52. 2006, p. 6. Croucher (1998) suggests this is because their parents were the first generation be raised completely by television.

53. American sociologist Neil Postman (1983, p. 14) allies himself to a similar position when he writes, 'Childhood is disappearing, mainly through the influence of television, but also by the use of child models in the advertising of children's clothes and adult products, the tendency of children's clothes to resemble adult fashion.'

54. The report summarized:

> They enjoy shopping and care about their possessions. They also feel pressure to have the latest 'in vogue' items. They do not think of themselves as naïve, but see methods of selling to young people as often intrusive and inappropriate. Girls, in particular, experience feelings of inadequacy as a result of 'images of perfection' promoted by advertising. Many young people feel they are being 'ripped off' by companies. They feel they get treated very differently to adults by shops and companies. The scrapbooks and photos taken by the children in the research highlight the volume of marketing activity that young people are exposed to on a daily basis. They accepted this as normal and their response to the commercial world around was characterized by cynicism. When it came to what they would want to see in relation to marketing and consumer life, they want more honesty and respect, and tighter curbs and controls.

55. 2000, p. 13.

56. Rushkoff (1996, p. 246).

57. When Youth with a Mission ran their child evangelism event Wildfire 2007, they allowed the children they contacted through the event to stay in contact with the team through a public forum on Facebook™ with the leaders instructed to ensure that all conversations with the children take place in the public areas of Facebook™.

58. Giddens (1999, p. 4).

59. 1996, p. 265.

60. 1987, p. 94.

61. Valerie and Holloway (2002, p. 316) cited in Prout (2005, p. 120) make the

interesting observation that 'On-line and off-line identities are not oppositional or unconnected but are mutually constituted'. That is to say that they may project different characteristics of their personality into the different settings, but they are still characteristics of the one personality. The virtual world may allow the child the opportunity to manifest the bold and confident side of their personality while they work through a difficult situation that is causing them to become quiet and introverted within the real world.

62. Children's Society (2006, p. 2).

63. Concerns about the supposed effect of new technologies on children have a prominence within research that stretches back at least to the start of the twentieth century; since that point, radio, cinema, comics, music, computer games and videos have all been accused of corrupting the young (Prout, 2005, p. 118). Research concerning children's use of technology usually presents one of six main conclusions:

> Children are naturally adept users of technology.

> Information technology can transform ordinary children into exceptionally skilled children.

> Computer technology can make children adept at adult activities, running businesses, etc.

> Computer technology can produce deviant children who seek adult information on internet.

> Technology taints innocent children who are exposed to inappropriate material.

> Children need information technology to fit them for the information society.

There is a wide range of research in each of these groupings, but it would be fair to say that the research projects presenting children's interaction with technology as wholly negative are becoming less common.

64. Ethnography conducted by the Department of Applied Social Science at Stirling University.

65. Rushkoff (2002, p. 50). Cited from an article in *Disinformation* (2002).

66. 1999, p. 29.

67. 1998, p. 86.

68. Cray, Savage and Mayo (2006, p. 149).

69. 2000, p. 11.

70. Lyon (2000, pp. 12–13).

71. That would be to close down all other choices. As Bauman (1995, p. 89) points out, 'The hub of postmodern life strategy is not identity building but avoidance of fixation, *keep the options open*'.

72. 2002, p. 29.

73. 1996, pp. 109-110.

74. To use Fox's (2000) terminology.

75. 1996, p. 124.

76. 1946, p. 4.

77. Lewis and Lewis (1983, p. 10).

78. It is also noteworthy that the return to church was often prompted by the desire to be married there, or to baptize their children. However, the services of marriage and baptism that encouraged people to return to the church in previous generations are at a historical low. Only 20 per cent of babies in England are now baptized as infants (Brown, 2001, p. 3).

79. *UK Christian Handbook* 2001.

80. Brown (2001, p. 2).

81. *Quadrant*, December 2006.

82. Based on the original research of Richter and Francis (1998). The 40 per cent who have left the church is split into two lots of 20 per cent because *Mission-Shaped Church* (2004) suggests that 20 per cent of those who have left have indicated that they may return, whereas the other 20 per cent of those who have left have indicated that they never would.

83. *Mission-Shaped Church* (2004, pp. 43f.) suggests that a *fresh expression of church* is a community or congregation that is already (or has the potential to grow into) a church in its own right. Many of these fresh expressions exist to connect the gospel with fresh cultures and unreached people (p. 80).

84. In *Quadrant* (October 2006), however, he also states that their congregations tend to be younger than the average church.

85. 2006, p. 11. Twenty per cent in Church of England schools and 10 per cent in Roman Catholic schools.

86. 2006, p. 12.

87. Darch (2006) suggests that the high water mark was 1904.

88. 2004, p. 19.

89. Kreider (2001, p. 45) writes, 'The nature of Christendom is controversial... both historians and theologians have strong and differing views.'

90. Michael Moynagh (2004), Steven Croft (2001), Peter Ward (2002) and countless others have written on new ways of being church in a post-Christendom society.

Chapter 8

PRACTICE

When a comparison of the practices and conventions embedded within the early Raikes Sunday Schools and the Children's Outreach Projects of the twenty-first century was undertaken, the outcomes fell into two distinct categories:

- Those practices that continue to be important and are fundamentally unchanged from the early model.
- Those practices that, although not identical to the original model, are present in a different form.

There are no elements of the original Raikes paradigm that are not represented in some form in the emerging Children's Outreach Projects. However, there are characteristics of the Children's Outreach Projects that were not present in the early Sunday Schools. These characteristics can be summarized in the following table (figure 8.1) and form the basis for the continuing interpretation of the Sunday School movement and the philosophies and practices that underpin the twenty-first-century Children's Outreach Projects.

Practices found in the original Raikes model that...	
... are present today and fundamentally unchanged	<ul><li>Professional teachers[1]</li><li>Hymn singing and prayer</li><li>Rewards, prizes and incentives</li><li>Connection between Children's Outreach Project and parents</li></ul>
... have changed in form but are still present	<ul><li>Meeting a clear social need/empowerment</li><li>Communication of a Christian message</li><li>Connections between Children's Outreach Project and church</li></ul>
Practices added to the original model...	
	<ul><li>Connections between Children's Outreach Project and local schools</li><li>Bus pick-up</li></ul>

Fig 8.1 Raikes Comparison Table

PROFESSIONAL TEACHERS

Professional teachers were one of the early casualties of the original Raikes model of Sunday School. Raikes employed gifted individuals who could both communicate a Christian message and keep order. The practice of employing teachers stopped in the early 1800s. The decline in the standard of teaching that followed has often been presented as the main reason the Sunday School institution was left waning.

This will prove a difficult area to interpret as the definition of *professional* in this context is ambiguous. In the early years of the Sunday School movement, professional meant paid teachers with ability to both control and educate the class. However, once the salary element is removed it is difficult to define professional. Watson comments on Mr Nisbet, one of the founder members of the Sunday School Union, who would rise at 4 a.m. to study the necessary chapters that had been appointed as the lessons for the next Sunday, aiding his study with reference to Matthew Henry's commentary.[2]

Although Mr Nisbet may be termed professional, the comments of Mr Graham White MP, speaking at the London Sunday School Union's Easter Convention of 1896, suggests he is not typical:

> The changes of the last thirty years or so have affected our school buildings considerably, and they have affected the scholars very largely; but I have grave doubts whether they have affected our teachers to the same extent.[3]

His words may have been heeded. The number of volunteer teachers increased, teacher training began to take on greater significance and many local unions began to organize training nights for its teachers. However, there was considerable variance in the uptake. New teachers were encouraged to attend a preparation class, but the unions had to admit that only 4 per cent of all new teachers attended and only 101 of the 209 unions had a class.[4]

The Times newspaper of 16 January 1911, commented in an editorial:

> Their general inefficiency, their lack of system and discipline, and the scanty qualifications of those who, with excellent intentions, undertake the teaching are well known. And if even in London, as we gather from the Bishop's recent manifesto, Sunday Schools are at present of very little use for real religious education, what

is likely to be the case in many country parishes?

The remedy for the situation, suggested *The Times*, was 'actual training for teachers'.

During the early twentieth century, many notable personalities influenced the Sunday School movement, but one man dominated: George Hamilton Archibald (figure 8.2).[5] In 1902, Archibald was invited to become the extension lecturer for the English Sunday School Union. His influence was primarily derived from his lecturing tours and his numerous publications of both principles and teaching. The main thrust of Archibald's message can be summarized as:

1. *All education begins not with lessons, not with the teacher, but with the child.*
2. *The child's love of nature must be recognized.*
3. *The appeal must be made principally through the child's imagination and his emotions rather than through his intellect.*
4. *The Sunday School of the future must be decentralized.*[6]

Fig 8.2 George Hamilton Archibald

However, as the twentieth century continued it was unfortunate that all that remained of Archibald's four-pronged philosophy was the decentralizing of the Sunday School,[7] and the outworking of this area alone led to greater decline in the standards of teaching. Within the pattern advocated by Raikes and used into the twenty-first century by the Children's Outreach Projects, the children are taught together as one large group. Within this structure, it is possible for those with a gifting to teach to do the teaching. It also allows for the development of people with abilities other than teaching. In my observation of the Leeds project, I recorded:

> The allocated jobs consisted of PowerPoint person, musicians, collection person, discipline, silent seat watchers, parent support, team captains, teaching people, walkers to keep control, bus watchers, corridor monitors and toilet monitors, to name a few.

In Archibald's model, factors such as the physical aspects of the Sunday School building and the number of available people became the main concerns in deciding the number of classes/age groups. Nevertheless, Archibald's general principle was clear: the more classes the better.

Although this seems a wholly sensible approach, the effect was the further deterioration of teaching. The weekly programme needed people who could sit in front of a group of children and deliver a lesson, and although most Sunday Schools had several good teachers, they rarely had enough teachers to cover all the groups, so substandard teachers were often appointed to fill teaching gaps. As a result, potential teachers did not have opportunity to learn from teachers that were more gifted. The demands on teachers meant that very few could afford the luxury of an apprentice, and numbers of Sunday School teachers continued to decline.

In 1943, *Christian World Magazine* ran an article entitled 'The Waning Sunday School'. It stated:

> The wane in Sunday School is due in large measure to the ineffective methods of recruiting and training teachers and inadequate support in interest, service and money by the Church.

The National Sunday School Union annual report of 1948/49 commented that 69 per cent of all teachers had no training or preparation class. In 1957, the National Sunday School Union issued 'A Leaflet to Encourage Sunday School Teachers to Examine their Programme of Work' (leaflet shown in Appendix 5). It drew Sunday School teachers' attention to the rapid decline in attendance and listed ten points under the heading 'Ten Point Policy'. One of these points reads, 'The members of the school staff… serve a period of probation and attend regular weekly teachers' fellowship where training and preparation is carried out…' However, there is little evidence that these suggestions were incorporated into the majority of Sunday Schools. Cliff suggests that the teachers in this period were, on the whole, untrained.[8] He cites that of all Sunday Schools in the 1960s, 64 per cent had no training or preparation classes. An examination of one Anglican diocese in 1980 recorded that 73 per cent of Sunday School teachers had no training.[9]

It has already been noted in the historical review that one of the reasons that many churches took the advice of the British Council of Churches and the Free Church Federal Council in the 1950s to move their Sunday Schools from the afternoon to the morning was a shortage of teachers.

It is not only the loss of teachers that should cause a revision of

Archibald's policy; the rationale itself needs exploring further. Archibald's basic argument, presented in *The Sunday School of Tomorrow*,[10] was that it would never be considered sensible to teach mathematics to a five-year-old and a nine-year-old in the same room at the same time. However, the logic is flawed, for Sunday Schools were not teaching mathematics;[11] instead they were to teach, using Archibald's own methodology, 'child-centred lessons drawing on a child's sense of awe of the natural world and based on imagination and emotion and not on intellect'. In fact, if a comparison had to be made with the educational system in England, the approach has more in common with the primary schools' required act of worship, which at primary level is often undertaken as a whole school,[12] than it has with actual school lessons. The observations of the last chapter may suggest that the intricate tasks of faith development are best accomplished in small groups, but there is no suggestion that they should be strict age groups. In a Slough and Windsor project small group, for example, boys and girls of eight or nine are perfectly comfortable in groups with eleven- and twelve-year-olds, and this small-group input is supplemented by regular teaching in the larger forum.

Before leaving the work of Archibald, one other aspect should be noted. Archibald was a pioneer in advocating the use of young people as helpers in the Sunday School. He recognized that often the best way to learn is to teach; he also recognized that the average age of the teachers was increasing. Cliff seems critical of the practice and suggests, 'Many were thrust into the work without any form of preparation.'[13] However, that same criticism could be applied to those young people who had just begun their apprenticeships with local tradesmen – they too had been thrust into the work without any form of preparation. David, the leader of the Fraserburgh project, advocates a similar practice with his young people. When I talked to Miriam, one of the leaders at the project who had come through the junior leader programme, she commented:

> I've been here since it started. I was 11 when it started [1996].
> I was one of the children. When I went to academy [secondary
> school] I became a junior leader. And you are a junior leader until
> you are 16. A junior leader's responsibility is to sit beside the kids;
> they are training for becoming a leader, they are showing their
> potential. I got to do the actions at the front, I got to help with the
> games, I got to do some teaching and I came early and set up and
> got to stay at the end.

The primary factor deciding the success of this sort of initiative is the talent and ability of those the young people were working with. If they were conducting a Sunday School class with an excellent teacher, then they had the ability to learn quickly; if they were placed with a substandard teacher, then Cliff's concerns are almost certainly warranted. The system in the Fraserburgh project worked because it was deliberate and the teaching model was a good one. This system of involving young people was demonstrated in most of the Children's Outreach Projects visited, the majority advocating a system of coloured T-shirts (figure 8.3) to show their apprentice status; at the Slough and Windsor and Leeds projects they were green.

T-shirt colour	Designation
Blue	The people make the project happen. They also are out and about every week visiting the children who come along.
Green	People who are learning the ropes.
Black	These people are the project security and 'techies', who create the sound, lights and work the computers.

Fig 8.3 T-shirt categorization at the Slough and Windsor project

At its best, this practice of apprenticeship works. On my first visit to the Slough and Windsor project I noted:

> Paul is not here today, but the morning will follow the same routine. Luke, the project's co-leader, calls the team together. He explains the theme of the day. Today they will be teaching the children that they should not follow others in doing wrong, and that if they stand for what is right, God will bless them.

On another visit to the Slough and Windsor project I was able to observe Natalie on her bus. I noted:

> To demonstrate how relationships are formed, Natalie was able to stand at the front of the bus and point to each of the children on the bus and call them by name. The connection is more than attendance at a project on a Saturday morning; she knows where

they live and has had conversations with their parents, she has met their younger and older siblings, and she will visit them every week for the 35 weeks that the children's club runs each year.

Both Luke and Natalie learned these skills as young leaders in the Slough and Windsor project. Luke joined in his mid-teens; Natalie was one of the children who attended the project as a child and graduated to become a leader.

By the year 2000, Brierley noted six key issues regarding Sunday Schools:[14]

1. *Fewer people willing to teach on a regular basis.*
2. *Adults attending less frequently, and when they do, they prefer to be part of the adult congregation.*
3. *Sunday School teachers are unsure how to communicate to today's children.*
4. *Many adults do not know their Christian faith well, but still teach children.*
5. *Those who do teach give up after short periods.*
6. *The volunteers teaching on a rota system and seeing the children infrequently are common.*

Many of these issues did not affect the Raikes model of Sunday School with their employed teaching staff, and neither were they characteristic of the Children's Outreach Projects. Workers in the Children's Outreach Project were typically members of local churches, but they never had to decide between attendance at the adult congregation or the Children's Outreach Project – of those surveyed, only one took place on a Sunday and even then it did not clash with the church congregation's timings. In many ways, the Children's Outreach Projects have reintroduced the old Sunday School practice of children's provision taking place at a separate time (and sometimes place) to the adult gathering.

	Full Time Staff	Part Time Staff	Volunteers
The Fraserburgh project	2	0	60+
The Slough and Windsor project	1	2	50
The Leeds project	1	6	67
The Hastings project	1	0	77
The Liverpool project	3	2	69

Fig 8.4 Staffing at the Children's Outreach Projects

The numbers in figure 8.4 suggest that Children's Outreach Projects have been successful in the recruitment of leaders. This may suggest that the reason the twentieth-century Sunday Schools struggled to recruit workers was not necessarily the time of day they met but had more to do with fact that Sunday School teachers and the institutions they represented were no longer clear of their purpose. If Sunday School existed to teach Christianity to the children of its members, then Sunday morning was a convenient time for doing this, without the need to run another service. This, of course, was not Raikes' purpose in recruiting Sunday School teachers. His target audience were those children who had never set foot in church. He was recruiting teachers who could prevent vice, teachers who would work with the unchurched child. In light of this, it is interesting to note that much of the worker recruitment strategy of the Children's Outreach Projects involved making the purpose of the project clear. The Liverpool project's website stated, 'This is all about sharing Jesus with some of the neediest and most vulnerable children in our city.' The Leeds project's website stated, 'Our vision is to reach children aged 4 to 11 with the gospel of Jesus Christ.' On both these websites there were numerous stories of families who had been added to church or experienced some form of transformation[15] as a result of the Children's Outreach Project. Leaders and workers were recruited to a clear vision. To this extent, the largest Children's Outreach Projects were all led by full-time children's workers who provided clear directional leadership to the team. When asked to describe his role, Paul, the leader of the Slough and Windsor project, stated:

> I am the holder of the vision and I try to instil that vision into the heart of my team of volunteers. I am a leader of volunteers and motivator of volunteers, trying to spur them on and keep them motivated, keeping them going on. The honeymoon period for many is long over and it's the weekly hard graft that is the key.

The very language used by the leaders of the Children's Outreach Projects was visionary and motivational in nature. Bernie, the leader of the Leeds project, stated, 'When I look for children's workers, I look for people who have a heart for the lost, a heart for the broken people and people who love God and that's all I need!' Bernie was recruiting people to work with the lost and the broken. Children's Outreach Projects place a high emphasis on training – 92 per cent of those surveyed had been to a training event in the last twelve months – but their recruitment was achieved by appealing to the heart, to the emotions and often to the conscience, but rarely to intellect alone.

These workers were generally employed by specific churches, but there were several examples of Children's Outreach Projects that ran ecumenically, and the salary of the lead person was shared between the partner churches. The statistics suggest that that to establish large children's programmes of this nature needs large teams of volunteers led by at least one salaried member who can give the project their full attention. This is another instance of the Children's Outreach Projects mirroring the practice of the Sunday Schools of 1780.

1. **Invite young people to become leaders**

2. **Recruit to a vision**

3. **Invest highly in training**

Fig 8.5 The Children's Outreach Projects' key to worker recruitment

HYMN-SINGING AND PRAYER

Singing and prayer are the components of the church's work with children that have remained constant. Cliff suggests that by the middle of the nineteenth century the basic form of the Sunday School lesson was fairly regimented and would include hymn-singing, prayer, a short biblical message, reading, writing and learning of the catechism.[16] By the middle of the nineteenth century, the Sunday School Union had taken over the work *The Gloucester Journal* had begun and was producing and selling its own hymnbooks.

With regard to prayer, other than the absolute statements in the commentaries and letters of the time that they prayed, there is little information as to the shape and form that this prayer took. From the practice of the churches at the time, an assumption can be made that the form of prayer employed in the Sunday Schools of the eighteenth century was twofold. The first form was of silent prayer; this is the form experienced when the children visited Gloucester Cathedral.[17] The second form was the reading together (or reciting together for those who had not yet learned to read) of written prayers. One of the best-known eighteenth-century prayers used for this purpose was:

Now I lay me down to sleep,
I pray thee, Lord, my soul to keep;
If I should die before I wake,
I pray thee, Lord, my soul to take.[18]

In the twenty-first-century Children's Outreach Projects, there were various examples of the leaders praying for the children; the prayers were always extemporary and took place before the event began, on the buses on the way to collect the children and at the end of the event. These prayers were shown at their most militant by the leaders of the Hastings project:

Let us see your reign and rule, Lord.
Show us your face.
Lord, do not just send us out, but also come with us.
You are the rock of ages who has come to save.
Reveal who you are to these children.
Your word says that all things are possible,
so move by your Holy Spirit today.

There were also examples of children being prayed for while they were present, from the front at the start of the event. The Fraserburgh project's opening prayer contained:

1. *Thanks to God for each child who is gathered.*
2. *Thanks for the time of fun that they will have.*
3. *A request that God will help them to learn more about him.*
4. *A request that God will help them know that he is interested in them, cares for them, and has chosen them.*

In some cases, children were prayed for, for healing and other needs, on a one-to-one basis. This was often demonstrated by the projects at Leeds and Hastings. However, in the Children's Outreach Projects the only prayers I heard from the children themselves were the prayers repeated after the leaders in response to the lesson of the day. The programme structure of the Children's Outreach Projects was not designed for children themselves to participate in times of prayer. In the case of the Slough and Windsor project, this was something that was visible in the small-group programme, and in the Fraserburgh project, I observed the young leaders praying in turn before the children arrived. The Leeds, Hastings and Liverpool projects do not seem to have a mechanism to facilitate the children themselves praying.

   With regard to music and singing, it is surprising how little research exists in this area. Some of the reason for this is technical. Weinberger[19] suggests that brain-imaging technology is necessary to evaluate the effects of music and singing, and equipment to obtain the necessary data has not been developed yet. However, without the need for technical data, there is one conclusion that all agree on: music and singing have the power to evoke emotions.[20] Beard, writing of nineteenth-century Sunday Schools, was able to observe that singing was in keeping with the natural tendencies and interests of the child.[21]

The songs sung in the twenty-first-century Children's Outreach Projects visited varied in style to the traditional hymns sung in eighteenth- and nineteenth-century Sunday Schools,[22] and many were written specifically for children, but it was clear in observation that they invoked strong emotions of joy and excitement. In my visit to the Liverpool project, I observed:

> The musicians play the introduction to the first song. Dave shouts, 'Boys, are we going to be the loudest?' Suzi shouts, 'Girls, are we going to be the loudest?' The song begins. They sing 'Stand up and shout it if you love my Jesus',[23] 'Swing low, sweet chariot',[24] 'What a mighty God we serve',[25] 'Whose side are you leaning on?',[26] 'He is the King of kings',[27] in a seamless medley. The words are displayed on the projector. The children are fully engaged and doing the actions and singing with extreme enthusiasm.

The More sisters in the nineteenth century were advocates of lively singing, but they were also aware, as Beard suggests, that 'Hymns sung in Sunday School perform an essential service, they are a means of instruction'.[28] Beard was highlighting the fact that hymns are a teaching tool – theology in song. So what theology was contained within these songs and has the theological emphasis changed since the inception of Sunday School? In terms of the subjects covered, there is no significant change. On first inspection, the hymns sung by the twenty-first-century Children's Outreach Projects may seem far removed from the hymns of the eighteenth century, but, putting the melodies aside, there are significant similarities. Songs that speak of God's creation are still present, but hymns such as:

> *O worship the Lord in the beauty of holiness!*
> *Bow down before him, his glory proclaim;*
> *with gold of obedience, and incense of lowliness,*
> *kneel and adore him: the Lord is his name!*[29]

have been replaced in the Children's Outreach Projects by songs such as:

God you're amazing, the heavens declare
glory and power, none can compare.
I look in wonder at all you have made,
oceans and mountains speak of your name.[30]

or:

He made dogs that point, pigs that oink.
He made dolphin smiles, crocodiles.
He made a zillion things, flies and wings.
He even gave us tongues so good for licking.
And it's lovely jubbly, all of God's creation.
Lovely jubbly, all of God's creation,
what a wonderful God we have.[31]

And hymns such as:

Fight the good fight with all thy might,
Christ is thy strength and Christ thy right;
lay hold on life, and it shall be
thy joy and crown eternally.[32]

are represented by hymns such as:

I'm gonna jump up and down,
gonna spin right around,
gonna praise your name for ever.
Gonna shout out loud,
gonna deafen the crowd,
gonna send my praise to heaven.

I will run this race and I will never stop.
I'll follow Jesus till the day I drop.
I can do all things through Christ who strengthens me.
When you've got such a lot.
When you've got not a lot.
What? Be happy![33]

Here are two hymns that appear very different on first examination, but at their core they both speak of persevering in the Christian faith. The style has changed radically but the theological sentiment has not. There are numerous songs that speak of Christ's sacrifice in both historical settings, but it is within these hymns that the subtle difference in theological emphasis can be seen. The difference is in the pronouns that populate the hymns. The eighteenth- and nineteenth-century hymns make use of the pronoun 'our', whereas the twenty-first-century hymns use the pronouns 'I', 'me' and 'my'. This is highlighted when comparisons are made with the hymns below. The first by John Ellerton from the early part of the nineteenth century:

> *Saviour, again to thy dear name we raise,*
> *with one accord, our parting hymn of praise.*
> *Once more we bless thee ere our worship cease:*
> *then, lowly bending, wait thy word of peace.*

has a different theological emphasis to this 2001 hymn from Hillsong:

> *You know that I love you, you know that I want to know you*
> *so much more, more than I have before,*
> *these words are from my heart, these words are not made up,*
> *I will live for you, I am devoted to you.*[34]

The Evangelical value system that gained momentum throughout the eighteenth and nineteenth centuries has embedded itself within the church's songs. Even within the context of the corporate worship experience, the emphasis of the songs is on individual faith and relationship with God. The songs of the Children's Outreach Projects are in complete agreement with their emphasis on the personal conversion experience and the outworking of a personal faith. Comment has already been made on this particular doctrinal position, but, as an additional comment, it is may be that this overemphasis on the individual is actually counterproductive to the Children's Outreach Projects' aims in terms of establishing a Christian community. Although it may be argued that the original model of Sunday School had an overemphasis on the corporate and therefore did not highlight individual faith, it is suggested that the pendulum has now swung too far in the opposite direction.

Comment is also needed with regard to the actions that accompanied the songs in the Children's Outreach Projects, ranging from simple movements to the more complicated choreographed songs of the Fraserburgh project. Codrington's research concluded that younger children viewed worship services primarily in terms of the physical experience – what they did.[35] However, although Codrington's work showed the benefits of these action songs, her definition of physical activity was far broader. She highlights how limited the Children's Outreach Projects' practice was in this regard, and how helpful the sacramental practices of lighting candles, using clay to represent an emotion or experience, and the use of paint or crayons for expression, utilized by the more Catholic denominations, could be. The strength of this was further highlighted in Codrington's work when her interviews with the children revealed that they would like to be more involved in the service and not just sing. Some of these elements were present in some of the small groups, but they are not present in the Children's Outreach Projects.

It is also necessary to be clear on the children's response to the singing time (Slough and Windsor, Hastings, Leeds and Liverpool call this *praise party* time). In most of the projects visited (other than the Liverpool project) there was a minority of children who disengaged from the programme during the singing. Many asked to go to the toilet and some became disruptive. They re-engaged when their favourite song was sung, which may be an indication that the children were enjoying lively songs and were not necessarily active in worship. Beard suggests that these songs should be *prayers being sung* in an atmosphere of reverence and spiritual feeling.[36] With the recognition that these are abstract terms and the interpretation of them is subjective, I would suggest that the majority of the Children's Outreach Projects are not achieving this. Paul, the leader of the Slough and Windsor project, has reached the same conclusion, indicated by his comment that he 'would like to move the children from singing to worship'. In addition, although the louder, action-based songs engaged most of the children, the quieter, more reverential songs caused the majority of children to disengage.

Beard suggested that reverence and worship are things that the children cannot learn by being taught from the front, but can only be learned by observing the leaders of the group. Beard further commented, 'Let the leaders create an atmosphere of reverence.'[37] It is undoubtedly for this reason that the best example of worship was at the Liverpool project, where leaders and children were fully engaged whether the songs were fast or slower and worshipful. Moreover, it is this understanding that led Paul of the Slough and Windsor project to state so strongly to his young leaders, 'You are here to be an example in the praise party. We need to be a good example; you are not here to try and look cool.'

The twenty-first century can learn much from the eighteenth century regarding corporate worship. Nevertheless, it is true to say that prayer and singing are two elements that have travelled through the centuries relatively unscathed and continue to be an important part of Children's Outreach Projects today.

REWARDS, PRIZES AND INCENTIVES

The giving of prizes, instituted by Raikes, continued until the Second World War when financial pressures ended the practice. The practice was renewed as soon after the war as the particular Sunday School was able to acquire the necessary funding to re-establish it. The pre-war conventions of star charts, outings and book prizes were reintegrated into Sunday School life.

In the Children's Outreach Projects visited, rewards and incentives were used in two ways. Firstly, they were used as a system of rewards to promote and reinforce good behaviour. The children at the Fraserburgh project were informed that the two best-behaved children in each of the three teams would be allowed to choose something from the prize table. Each of the Children's Outreach Projects visited had a prize table that acted as an incentive to the children in that they could see the rewards available if they behaved well. In my observation of the Fraserburgh project, I recorded:

> Three teenage girls have spread a golden tablecloth over a table at the front right hand side of the hall. It is the prize table. It is adorned with activity books, stationery sets, art equipment, sandals, skipping ropes, money boxes, Frisbees, sport bags, games, umbrellas, goalkeeper gloves, kites, children's jewellery – the items are arranged and rearranged as the girls debate the most attractive setup.

The prize tables at the other projects were all equally well equipped. It was noteworthy that the prizes and incentives were not usually given for intellectual accomplishment, but were instead given to reward positive character such as kindness and politeness, or for compliant behaviour such as sitting on their seat without talking or fidgeting, although children also received prizes for winning games. Other prizes were given for task-orientated accomplishment – for example, the Leeds project gave a certificate to the children wearing the most orange on Oompa-Loompa Day.

Into this category also falls the giving of incentives to promote attendance. This has often been criticized as bribing children to attend, but it is also the oldest form of incentive within Sunday School history; Raikes himself used this method to attract and keep children in Sunday School. However, the combs and other trinkets offered by Raikes are far removed from some of the more expensive prizes given away by the Children's Outreach Projects. The Slough and Windsor project announced:

> Everyone who comes on Saturday will get a glow-in-the-dark bracelet, but those who come for the next five weeks will be entered in a draw and you could win a DVD TV, a mountain bike or a PSP.

On a previous occasion the Slough and Windsor project gave away a holiday to Disneyland. Paul, the leader of the project, was clear in his motivation, 'We use incentives to draw the crowd.' The leaflets given out to the children advertised these prizes, and in the Slough and Windsor project the smaller prizes are shown to the children during home visits.

Often, practitioners and academics alike have difficulty with any reward-based system. Some oppose the system on financial grounds. The Family Church Movement of the mid 1900s, for example, felt that rewards were wasted money, and that the children would be better served by more equipment for common use.[38] Others attack the philosophy on a more fundamental basis. Maria Montessori, in her book *The Montessori Method*, spoke passionately against any form of prize-giving for achievement within the classroom as unnecessary and emotionally damaging.[39] In addition, if there are objections to this positive reinforcement of good or desirable behaviour, there are stronger objections to the second area of Children's Outreach Project practice: the removal of reward for negative behaviour. The practice was best explained in the words of Natalie at the Slough and Windsor project, speaking to the children at the start of the teaching time:

> Everybody needs to sit with their hands on their laps. If you are completely silent, then a leader will put a sweet in your hand. If you get a sweet, do not open it. If you talk, your balloon will be burst. If all three of your balloons are burst, then your sweets will go to the other team.

David of the Fraserburgh project used very similar words when he explains his system:

> You always have to create incentives for good behaviour. Johnny is going to look for the two best in the green team, Jasmine is

going to look for the two best in the red team and Matthew is going to look for the two best in the blue team. The kids know if they start jumping or messing, they will not get a chance to win a prize. Three balloons are at the front; if they mess about, a balloon is burst. If all the balloons are burst, then no sweets, but if the balloons are not burst, then everyone gets a sweet.

This form of control is a new addition to the methodology of child evangelism and owes much to the practice perfected by Bill Wilson in Brooklyn, New York. I never witnessed a project where all the balloons were burst, but the leaders assured me that it does happen.

All these methods of control exist to ensure the children listen, to ensure they do not disturb others and to ensure that adequate safety is maintained. Any control system that relies on prizes and rewards is open to criticism; however, to work with this many children without systems of control would be chaotic and potentially dangerous. I visited much smaller projects as part of the research where these systems of control were not in place, and where discipline and safety were very real issues.

Interestingly, several of the schools from which the Slough and Windsor project draws children also operated systems of reward for positive behaviour and removal of reward for negative behaviour. Several of the schools gave 'Star of the Week' certificates to the best child in each class and one school gave the children 'Star Time' at the end of each week – a thirty-minute slot where they were free to choose from a range of fun activities such as making toys, videos, chess and draughts, art and crafts. Children misbehaving during the week lost Star Time and, depending on how much they have misbehaved, waited in the school hall for a certain number of minutes. This account is included to suggest that the educational systems within the area that the Slough and Windsor project works have also felt it necessary to use various control mechanisms to modify the children's behaviour.

CONNECTION BETWEEN THE CHILDREN'S OUTREACH PROJECT AND PARENTS

The primary method for establishing and keeping a connection between the Children's Outreach Project and parents is the home visit. It is clear that Raikes took seriously the role of visiting the children who attended his Sunday Schools at their homes, but the records of the nineteenth century contain no reference to the practice continuing. This was despite the publication, in 1818, by the Sunday School Union of 'Hints On The

Establishment of Sunday Schools'[40] which stated that teachers are encouraged to 'Visit the parents and children at home, induce them to love and respect you as their best friend'. The breakdown of the link between Sunday School and parents is summed up by Cliff who, writing of the early nineteenth century, commented, 'There are no longer visits to the homes of the scholars.'[41]

Various attempts were made to regain this practice. An article called 'Steps to Better Teaching' in *News 1960* (No. 43), a production of the Birmingham Youth and Sunday School Union, pointed out:

> Caring implies visiting the homes from which they come at least once a quarter. By keeping accurate registers, the home should be visited in the week following any unexplained absence.

It was good advice, but coming in the 1960s it was too late to alleviate the decline in Sunday School attendance.[42]

The positive effect of involvement between Children's Outreach Project and the home should not be overlooked. In Klausmeier and Allen's study of cognitive development, they concluded:

> The cooperative relationship established between the home and the school and the better relationships between the parents and the child were judged to ameliorate some of the conditions associated with a slow rate of cognitive development.[43]

What is interesting in the Klausmeier and Allen study was the speed of development. The intervention period was seven weeks, and this was enough time to measure marked improvement in the child's self-esteem, motivation to learn and overall attitude. The key factor (and the factor most pertinent to the Children's Outreach Projects) is that the parents' attitude towards the school became positive and supportive when the school made the effort to make contact and involve the parents. Children's Outreach Projects that make contact with parents gained favour, and the Children's Outreach Project, and therefore the church, is viewed in a more positive light. This is evidenced by the comments of Dave of the Liverpool project who writes,

> Each week we make over 1,500 home visits. These visits enable us to practise what we preach – demonstrating the love of God with our words and our actions. As friendships are built and trust

is won, we get numerous opportunities to pray with people and
share testimony of God's goodness

Bill Wilson writes:

> These personal visits place people in someone else's world, and
> provide a person-to-person relationship. Personal visits prevent
> alienation, prepare young personalities for spiritual challenge,
> and promote productivity.[44]

All the Children's Outreach Projects with significantly high attendance
figures maintained a strict regime of visiting the children. In fact, the data
collected could legitimately be presented in a different form; those projects
who visit the children at home were more likely to have higher attendance.
The Leeds project, like many of the other larger projects, visited every
child every week. They went out in pairs and each pair has a designated
patch, so every bus pick-up area was made up of three to four patches.
Each patch contained anything from forty to 100 children and the patches
were allocated depending on the amount of time a volunteer could give to
visiting.

    Brierley showed that 89 per cent of children trust their parents
above everyone else and show a fervent faith in the family as a source of
unconditional support.[45] However, it is more than support and security
that children draw from their families; in the main, faith is organized
around the family.[46] To attempt to introduce a belief system to the child
that is alien to the household in which they live is at best problematic, at
worst abusive. Withers points out the reality:

> Adults who were ten years old in 1950, whether in churches or
> not, had brought up their children in 1970s, when religion in
> school and children's organizations was actively discouraged, and
> the traditional Sunday School had become tired and lacklustre.
> Children who grew up in a culture that marginalised religion in
> 1970s are the parents of today's children, and have, for most part,
> little if any experience of the basic knowledge that underpins the
> Christian faith to pass on to their children.[47]

The solution seems to be to visit the homes and engage with parents as
well as children. Earlier chapters showed that Raikes visited the homes of
people who were not church attendees; however, his accounts reflect no

antagonism towards Christianity from those he visited (although it is likely at this point in history that his social status guaranteed him respect). Visits from the Children's Outreach Projects were on the whole visits to non-churchgoers, but the response was generally positive. There are accounts of antagonism becoming acceptance over a period. Bernie, the leader of the Leeds project, commented, 'The more the kids get to know you, the more they want to chat. It's about consistency.' Dave, the leader of the Liverpool project, stated:

> The club is only effective because it is combined with home visits. Each week, every child who attends is visited. They befriend families, build relationship and by meeting the kids on their own territory, they demonstrate God's love in action... While many inner-city churches have given up on the hope of reaching the new generation of children around them, we have consistently demonstrated the light of God's love to literally thousands of children over the last ten years.

There was no antagonism towards Christianity in particular, more an attitude of indifference and a general distrust of authority and institutions. Nevertheless, to use the words of Dave from the Liverpool project:

> This two-pronged approach works [weekend children's club plus weekly visits]... whole families have been added to the church and we have over seventy teenagers who were introduced to the gospel through the Kidz Klub and have grown up with it, worshipping with us on Sunday mornings, their lives changed by the truth they heard as kids.

Most of the project websites contained stories of families who have been added to the church because someone visited them on a weekly basis. It is clear that the success of home visits came down to the consistency of the visits that allow relationships to develop. Bernie of the Leeds project stated:

> People are getting a lot of satisfaction from doing visits. Because it's their group of kids that they are visiting, that they are taking care of, they are making relationships with them. So to a child the visitor is the most important person, not who is on the stage on Saturday morning.

The home visit also gave the worker opportunity to address real issues. In a feedback session at the Slough and Windsor project one of the leaders spoke of a home they visited. The parents were not churchgoers, but the children had returned from the children's club and insisted on praying for their parents. The behaviour was clearly foreign to this family and may well have caused the family to rethink their decision to allow their children to attend the Children's Outreach Project. However, when the Slough and Windsor project worker visited, they were able to explain to the parents what prayer is and how the children wanted to pray for them because they cared for them. The result was that the parents described the experience as 'amazing and heart-warming'.

This practice of home visits marks a clear return to Raikes' practice of ensuring the Children's Outreach Project has a clear link to the community it serves and would appear to be as successful in the twenty-first century as it was in the eighteenth.

MEETING A CLEAR SOCIAL NEED AND EMPOWERMENT

It has already been noted that alongside religious instruction (and often as part of religious instruction) Raikes taught children to read and write. It is often suggested that Sunday Schools did not begin to focus on religious instruction until their original mandate of teaching literacy had diminished.[48] This fallacy has been addressed in a previous chapter, but it is also clear that these observations fail to understand the true versatility of the original Raikes model. Although the social need that Raikes' Sunday Schools met was educational, it was never limited to this. The Christian gospel has always had embedded within it the meeting of community and social needs, and the decline of Sunday School was due in part to the neglect of this basic principle. Hull, in impassioned words, writes:

> I want the Church of England to become a prophetic church, a church that refuses to accept the poverty that is still so widespread in our society. That refuses to accept the marginalisation of so many disabled men and women, seeks to eliminate from its language the long shadows of oppression... a church that perceives the Spirit of God at work in the world outside the church.[49]

It is possible to institute social reform without a religious element, but it is impossible to provide any form of religious education devoid of a social element. Nevertheless, the book *When I Was a Child*[50] illustrates that by the mid-nineteenth century there were signs that the Sunday School had lost sight of its origins. Shaw[51] writes:

> I was up betimes to be ready for the Sunday School, and no schoolboy with 'shining morning face' ever carried a brighter face or a cheerier heart than I did. But a cloud fell upon it, deep, dark, and chilling, and before that day was over I felt like 'a lost soul'... The scholars looked at me askance, and whispered to each other, they kept apart from me. In a very few minutes I was given to understand that I was not to sit near them. I returned to the Sunday School in the afternoon, no cry of leper in the old days of Israel could have put people more apart than I was apart from my schoolfellows. In the afternoon they had become bolder. My clothes were mockingly pointed at, I was laughed at, jeered at, and I saw that I was clothed with contempt in their eyes.[52]

However, Shaw continues to show that not all of the early Sunday Schools had forgotten their wider vocation. After several Sundays such as the one described above, Shaw left the Sunday School. However, he was not ready to give up on Sunday School altogether and several weeks later, accompanied by his younger brother, he described a visit to another Sunday School:

> At the top of our street there was a little chapel belonging to the Methodist New Connexion, where the Sunday School was held in the body of the chapel. Taking my younger brother by the hand... we crept up the street and stood against the wall of the little chapel, which fronted the market place.
>
> While standing there, a young man came to the door of the chapel, evidently on the lookout for scholars that might be loitering outside. When he saw my brother and myself, he came to us at once, bending down, asked me, as the eldest, if we went to any Sunday School. I told him in hesitating words we had gone to ---------[53] Sunday School. He then enquired why we had left, and when I told him his already gentle face became softened in a way I cannot express, and the tones of his voice, I should say now, from what I felt then, had tears in them. Taking each one of us by the hand, 'Come with me, my boys, and you shall be welcome in our school.'

The words of Raikes' summons – 'All that I required were clean faces, clean hands, and hair combed' – cannot help being recalled. It is unfortunate that the plight of the character mentioned above and the many like him who live in the UK today were not in the mind of Cliff when he concluded, 'Sunday School teachers cannot do for parents what they must do themselves. The classroom is no substitute for the family.'[54] He neglects to understand the intertwined strands of Christian education and social reform that so marked the strength of the original Raikes Sunday School. There clearly are many children who do not have parents able to do for them what Sunday Schools could do – some because their parents are not there (through death or through separation) and others because their parents are simply unable or unwilling to help them. It was for these children that Sunday Schools were birthed; it is an indictment on the Sunday School movement that it showed signs of losing its way within fifty years of Raikes' death.

However, within the framework of the Children's Outreach Projects there is a clear attempt to regain this aspect of Raikes' Sunday School model. All the projects visited have initiatives to help their communities, over and above the running of the Children's Outreach Project. The Leeds project gave hampers away every Christmas. They decided where the hampers should go based on the feedback from the Leeds project workers who had been doing home visits throughout the year. This project was also involved in helping children who had been expelled from school, and it had provided support and paid the funeral costs when the father of one of the children died and the family could not cope with their own grief, let alone organize a funeral.

There is also another dimension to the community work of these projects. The children who attend the Children's Outreach Projects, some of whom come from situations of poverty, are encouraged to give to others. On my visit to the Liverpool project I observed Dave introducing the offering:

> Dave announces the collection and a picture is projected on to the screen showing House of Grace, Thailand.[55] Dave informs the children that this is the place that the money they give each week has helped build. Now he wants to do more, he wants to be able to send all the children from House of Grace to the seaside. But he can't do it without the children's help. 'It's going to cost,' he announces, 'but everything worth doing costs. We have £18 so far and I'm going to empty my wallet in to the collection. How much do I have? £7.50, that's going in.' The offering is taken as the children sing a quiet song. They sing, and Dave says, 'God is proud of you when you help others.'

A similar thing took place in my observation of the Leeds project. I recorded:

> A presentation follows on a child the project is sponsoring through Compassion UK.[56] The Leeds project has raised £45.63 so far this term to help support the child they are sponsoring. A picture of the little girl is projected on the screen and underneath is the amount they have raised.

However, there is a third form of social and community work embedded in these projects. It is the form that lies at the core of Raikes' model of children's work in that it is to do with empowerment. When Raikes taught the children of the eighteenth century to read and write, he understood the culture he lived in; he understood the modernistic shift from the oral to the written. In teaching the children to read and write he empowered them for life in the late eighteenth century and gave them the capacity to rise out of their social settings. Raikes empowered the children with essential life skills. This final strand of empowerment was represented in many of the Children's Outreach Projects. Bernie of the Leeds project summed up the position when she stated:

> They are not surrounded by inspiration every day, so what motivates a kid to work if they see no jobs at the end of it? We teach them life skills; we teach them that they have choices.

Dave of the Liverpool project stated a similar position when he spoke at the Conservative Party Conference in 2007:

> Conference, we need to stop looking at our inner cities as if they are a problem; we need to start looking at the potential in our inner cities. The kids that I know and the families that I know who have been broken by crime, who have been broken by drugs, are just waiting for an opportunity, for someone to say, 'Come on, let me give you a hand up.' To say, 'Yes, you can go to university, yes, you can make something of your life.' We need to believe in the kids of our inner cities.

His conclusion captured well the Sunday School that Raikes formed in 1780 and should be the maxim for all Children's Outreach Projects into the twenty-first century:

> We need to begin to empower local people who are passionate
> about their local communities. You can have the best policies
> in the world and all the money you want to spend, but if you do
> not empower local people who have a passion for their local
> communities, you are not going to make any difference at all.

Empowerment releases the true potential of the Children's Outreach
Projects from the buildings in which they meet to permeate the communities
that they have set out to influence. Wes Richards, the leader of the church
of which the Slough and Windsor project is a part, summed up the goal for
Children's Outreach Projects that he felt represented the fullest teaching of
Christian values:

> The potential of reaching the child, who is secure in who they are
> in God, and have their own faith, and teaching them how to live,
> and how to die, and how to relate and how to act, how to react,
> how to cope with life's storms. If we can put that into children,
> then we have done the job well.

COMMUNICATION

As early as 1818 the Sunday School Union published materials that
highlighted the need for clear communication:

> In hearing children read or repeat what they have learned, much
> care should be taken to make them acquainted with the meaning;
> that they may understand the sense as well as retain the sound of
> what they read or repeat.[57]

Here was a clear directive that was beyond reading and memorization. The
need for understanding had been identified.[58] It is unclear to what extent
this advice was taken on board, but it should have been an important
building block for the establishment of teaching materials to come.

By 1840 Groser stated that the Sunday School Union had published
'The List of Lessons' – passages of Scripture considered suitable for Sunday
School children; by 1870, 'Notes on Scripture Lessons' – a book of notes on
these lessons – followed.[59] Cliff suggests, 'These are the forerunners of all
the lesson guides produced ever since.'[60] Although Christian education/
evangelism in Sunday Schools went through various evolutions in the last
two centuries, and Christian education became more elaborate, the essence
of the method of teaching has changed very little. The communication of

the Christian message can be clearly seen as parts of the original Raikes paradigm, but it has progressed little over the following two centuries and is in need of improvement for twenty-first century children.

Among Christian communicators, there is recognition of narrative as one of the most important developments in modern theology. With the widespread rejection of the Enlightenment idea *of universal rationality*, there is new interest in returning to the story-based world of Scripture.[61] There is no doubt that communication of the Christian message in a clear and relevant way lies at the very heart of child evangelism. However, the church's recent history would suggest that it has not been effective in doing this. Eighty-seven per cent of the teenagers who left church did so because they thought it boring.[62] The figures speak for themselves: of the 940,000 children (aged 0–9) in church in 1979, 210,000 left in the next decade; a further 400,000 left a decade later (figure 8.6).[63]

Age	1979	1989	1998	2005
0-9	940,000	780,000	480,000	383,000
10-19	960,000	730,000	450,000	394,300
20-29	600,000	480,000	330,000	230,600
30-39	580,000	540,000	430,000	330,800

Fig 8.6 Numbers attending church (Brierley, 2000, 2006)

The church is attracting fewer children and finding it difficult to retain those it attracts. The challenge this raises for ministry with children is significant. It is not about forcing children into adult modes of learning or into modes that demand cognitive processes beyond their abilities; instead, the task is to translate the truths of Christian faith into terms that can be both understood and experienced by boys and girls.[64] The 1980 Lausanne statement on Child Evangelism restates this position when it acknowledges that 'It is vital to understand their language, beliefs and ideology in order to penetrate the different world in which children live.' The Liverpool project has understood this and it was no coincidence that two of their illustrations involved football, in a city that is renowned for being passionate about football:

> A leader explains about the nature of celebrity using three pictures,
> one of Paris Hilton, one of Robbie Williams and one of a footballer

from Real Madrid, Kaka. The children are asked, 'Who is the biggest winner? Some people will give different answers, but if you ask God, he would say Kaka. Because Kaka lives for God. God makes him a winner.' A picture of Kaka wearing a 'I belong to Jesus' T-shirt is displayed.

The message was further reinforced by Dave who showed the children a football and explained:

> If we use this correctly, if we play with it on the grass where it's supposed to be used, then it will be fine. If we misuse it by playing with it in the street, it will become wrecked – like this one.

Fig 8.7 Kaka of Real Madrid

Dave holds up a flat and very damaged ball. He then draws attention to the memory verse Joshua 1:7, which speaks of obeying God's commands so that we can be successful.

Lewis and Lewis write:

> If we cling too tightly to five hundred years of homiletic tradition, we may soon find an unbridgeable gulf between the daily involvement, discovery and creativity our listeners experience during the week and the comparatively dull, ho-hum routine sermonic decrees.[65]

The church has often failed to understand how to communicate to this changing culture. Barna hints at this when he comments, 'They are the first generation among whom a majority exhibit a non-linear style of thinking – a mosaic, connect-the-dots-however-you-choose approach.'[66] The effect of this cultural shift can be seen in primary school education, particularly the teaching of history. Previous generations were taught history in a linear sequential pattern; for today's children, the picture of history is built like a jigsaw rather than a continuous story.[67] The average eight-year-old may be able to explain the details and events of the fire of London, produce artwork depicting the fire and put together their own version of Samuel

Pepys' diary, but they may not know whether it came before or after the Wars of the Roses, Battle of Hastings or the First World War.

This is particularly pertinent when the final point in Toulmin's hypothesis is considered: the shift within postmodernism from the written to the oral.[68] The renewal of concern with oral language, communication, rhetoric and discourse among the scholars of language and literature over the last twenty years is clear enough.[69] It is suggested that this generation of children learns differently – they take in information at a faster rate than previous generations. Children tune out after six to eight minutes unless a transition catches their interest.[70] Rushkoff observes:

> The skills we need to develop in order to become adept at surfing channels, computer networks, online services and the World Wide Web are the very opposite of what we traditionally valued in a good television viewer. We are coming to understand that what we valued as an attention span is something entirely different from what we thought.[71]

Moreover, children with the ability to pull themselves out of a linear argument while it is in progress, re-evaluate its content and relevance, and then either recommit or move on, are the children more suited to their twenty-first-century environment. They refuse to be the passive, receive-only audience members. They have developed a form of critical processing to cope with the vast amount of information they may have to process. The other key skill that may be linked to the so-called shortened attention span is the ability to process visual information very rapidly. A television image that takes an adult ten seconds to absorb might be processed by the child in a second.[72] Therefore, the very condition that some health professionals are terming a disorder may in fact be a necessary adaptation. Rushkoff[73] concludes:

> The child may have a much 'shorter' attention span as defined by the behavioural psychologists. Nevertheless, the same child also has a much broader range. The skill to be valued in the twenty-first century is not length of attention span, but the ability to multi task – to do many things at once, well.[74]

Lewis and Lewis continue this idea:

> Cognitive science's split-brain analysis would categorize

traditional sermons, both the preaching of them and the listening
to them, as left-brain activities. Homiletics leans hard on analysis,
logic and language. Sermons often stress intellectual concepts
more than imaginative or inventive ingredients, a sequential
instead of a holistic view, facts over feelings, rational rather
than relational orientations. Yet the cultural communications
revolution is aiming people in another direction. Today's visual
communications are retraining our minds. For the first time in
half a millennium the right side of the brain is clamouring for
prominence and insisting on involvement in life and learning.[75]

This change in the way children learn and process information requires
a different approach to Christian communication.[76] In some ways, it
necessitates a return to the storytelling traditions of pre-Enlightenment
times. Hull writes:

As the stories of what happened during the day, the highlights
of the day, are commented upon, laughed about, or made the
subject of reproach, the child emerges into a narrative world. As
the social horizon expands, the stories of family life, of previous
family holidays, and finally the stories from the lives of father and
mother before the child was born, and the doings of aunts and
uncles, grandfathers and mothers who have never been met will
be added to the story of the self.[77]

It is within the context of the story of the child's everyday life that the
stories of the Christian tradition are introduced. Great stories are those
that address us, draw us in as part of larger stories beyond our own selves,
act as a corrective to the distorted stories that seek to claim us, and give
new meaning to our own stories. The biblical stories of the Christian faith
traditions are such great stories.[78]

Bell makes an interesting observation when he asks, 'Is the
greatest truth that the bible happened or that it keeps on happening?'[79]
He uses the example of Adam and Eve and asks: is the greatest truth
that Adam and Eve took from a literal tree, in a literal garden, or that
humanity continues to disobey God today? As in all good storytelling,
we recognize ourselves in the depiction. Not the concept of liberation,
but the journey of Egyptian bondage;[80] not an essay on the teleological
suspension of the ethical, but Isaac and Abraham on Mount Mariah; not
the penal substitutionary theory of the atonement, but the blood of Jesus

on Golgotha; not an exposition of the motif of agape, but the open arms of the running father.[81] Buechner writes:

> Biblical narrative has one crucial difference to all other fairy tales, which is that the claim for it is that it is true, that it not only happened once upon a time but has kept on happening ever since and is happening still.[82]

This school of thinking is in keeping with correlation theology presented by Tillich.[83] Correlation theology suggests that the Bible answers a question that the theologian poses in the midst of the present situation. Further to this, theology undergoes constant reformation under changing needs and new questions.[84]

The power of biblical narrative is that the child becomes part of the story; their own personal stories are integrated into the stories of ultimate meaning and reality. The story is answering the questions they have there and then. The stories, when interwoven with the stories of their own lives and environment, allow them to develop their own understanding of themselves and their environment, to form their construct of self. However, there is a very real burden on the communicator, the storyteller, the evangelist, to trust the story and avoid the temptation to present linear logical explanations of words such as fall, redemption, repentance, reconciliation, substitution and atonement. Lengthy explanations of the story must be avoided, but the exceptionally rich and diverse biblical narratives that fill the Old and New Testaments, and other stories from further afield, from which these concepts are drawn, should not be. An example from Bettelheim may illustrate the point:

> Encouraged by discussion about the importance that fairy tales have for children a mother overcame her hesitation about telling such 'gory and threatening' stories to her son. From her conversation with him, she knew that her son already had fantasies about eating people, or people getting eaten. So she told him the tale of 'Jack the Giant Killer'. His response at the end of the story was 'There aren't any such things as giants are there?' Before the mother could give her son the reassuring reply which was on her tongue – and which would have destroyed the value of the story for him – he continued, 'But there are such things as grownups, and they are like giants.'[85]

At the age of five, the boy had demonstrated the hallmarks of faith stage 2, where the intuitive-projective child fuses fantasy, fact and feeling; the mythic-literal child works effectively at sorting out the real from the make-believe.[86] The boy understood the encouraging message of the story: Although adults can be experienced as frightening giants, a little boy with cunning can get the better of them.[87]

The same principle holds true concerning the alluring pieces of storytelling within the Gospels of Matthew, Mark, Luke and John that together form the Jesus story. Jesus is rarely listed in the books of great preachers, yet the Gospels record instances of people of varying ages travelling large distances to hear him speak. However, he does not use the deductive styles (figure 8.8) that define preachers from the eighteenth century onwards. He rarely preached without a story, and most of those were parables. The New Testament records thirty-three, or seventy-seven, parables of Jesus.[88] He does not use them merely as teasers, light introductions to get his hearers listening for what he really wants to say; they are often the primary expression of his message.[89] The story of the good Samaritan forms a sermon on compassion; the prodigal son teaches forgiveness. When Jesus preached, narrative carried much of the weight of his message. Lewis and Lewis' analysis of Jesus' eighteen-minute sermon on the Sermon on the Mount revealed:

- Jesus uses direct discourse – 221 times he says 'you' or 'your'
- He asks nineteen different questions
- He uses simple one-syllable words
- He uses 404 verbs for energy (in this 2,300-word message)
- He includes 320 pronouns
- He uses humour
- He cites twenty clear contrasts and many comparisons and illustrations[90]

The majority of Sunday School teachers, children's workers and Christian educators have rarely experienced difficulty when telling Bible stories. The difficulty begins when they use the words 'And this means, boys and girls…' This was illustrated at the Hastings project when a leader talked on 2 Samuel 6 and concluded the talk with the comment, 'God put Uzzah to death because he wasn't respectful'. Whatever the narrative is about, the children have been given one conclusion: God kills people who disrespect him! The strength of the example listed by Bettelheim is in that the parent resisted the desire to explain – she trusted the narrative to make its point. This style of communication is in keeping with Søren Kierkegaard's notion of indirect communication. Indirect communication is a matter of saying something to someone in passing, but not stopping to discuss it – instead leaving them to respond in their own way on their continuing journey.[91] This technique was employed by Jesus on various occasions.[92]

Bettelheim states strongly that:

> The fairy story communicates to the child an intuitive, subconscious understanding of his own nature and of what his future may hold if he develops his positive potentials... one must never *explain* to the child the meanings of fairy tales.[93]

Tolkein not only resisted the explaining of a story but also resisted the use of illustrations. He commented:

> ... illustrations do little good to fairy stories... If a story says, he *climbed a hill and saw a river in the valley below*, the illustrator may catch, or nearly catch, his own vision of such a scene, but every hearer of the words will have his own picture, and it will be made out of all the hills and rivers and dales he has ever seen.[94]

Polyani reinforces this point when he writes:

> The act of knowing includes an appraisal, a personal coefficient which shapes all factual knowledge. If the greatest scientist has to rely to a considerable degree on *personal knowledge*, it seems obvious that children cannot acquire knowledge truly meaningful to them unless they have first shaped it by introducing their personal coefficients.[95]

Many of the Children's Outreach Projects visited have a certain dependency on visual illustrations[96] that accompany their stories. They tended to sacrifice good storytelling for an over-dependency on the visual representation, or to prop up badly written stories and narrative by use of pictures. For example, David at the Fraserburgh project, when telling the story of Tori and Kiora, commanded the children's attention when he used power tools, hammer and nails to illustrate his point, in a way that he did not when he used the pictures of Tori and Kiora for the latter part of the story. In many ways, the pictures detracted from the storytelling. This was in contrast to my visit to the Slough and Windsor project in November 2007 where I was able to observe:

CONTRAST CHART	
Inductive	*Deductive*
Accumulative	Assertive
Achieve authority	Assumes authority
Asks questions	Asserts answers
Assemble facts	Asserts concepts as facts
Builds on facts to find causes	Binds facts into categories
Constructive	Constrictive
Creative	Cognitive
Defers assertions	Declares answers
Diagnoses reasons	Defends reason
Discovers causes	Declares conclusion
Expanding	Contracting
Explores, exposes	Explains, exhorts
Flexible, elastic	Firm, set
Intuitive	Intellectual
Invites participation	Imposes principles
Involves listeners in questions	Imparts answers
Open	Closed
Prophetic	Priestly
Practical	Perspective
Progressive	Protective
Reasonable	Reasoning
Relates	Restricts
Relational accent	Rational accent
Seeks causes, concepts, conclusions	States effects, conclusions
Seeks reasons, evidence, principles	States results, proofs

Fig 8.8 Inductive and deductive (Lewis and Lewis, 1983)

The verse for the day was a paraphrase of 2 Chronicles 13:12, 'God is with us all the time, he's your leader yours and mine.' The Bible lesson looked at 1 Samuel 16 and 17 and the account of David and Goliath, the principle being that David would lead David and guide David. The Bible lesson is told by one of the junior leaders and

is told without pictures. Nevertheless the narrative is presented
with such enthusiasm, the children are engrossed.

The true strength of narrative comes when it is allowed to be woven into
the experiences and current realities of the children; to allow the children to
learn the lessons of the story for themselves, to allow the morals of the story
to slowly merge with their own reality and become relevant specifically
to them. This is completely in keeping with what is understood by faith
development as presented by Hull and Fowler. Fowler asserts, when
considering pre-school children, it is unlikely that they have progressed
beyond faith stage 1. Evangelism for this age group involves contributing
to the rich tapestry of images and symbols from which they will construct
their image of *God*. At this stage it is all about 'construction' – they rely on
an absolute belief that the way they perceive *God* is the only way *God* can
be perceived. It is when new symbols and new stories are added that allow
them to rethink their image of *God* that *construction* becomes *reconstruction*
and the move to faith stage 2 has begun. Fowler writes:

> At the heart of the transition is the child's growing concern to
> know how things are and to clarify for him- or herself the bases
> of distinction between what is real and what only seems to be.[97]

Brierley observes, 'They have far less Bible background knowledge so there
is a need to be given much more detail.'[98] lack of knowledge is confirmed
by Voas who writes, 'The creators of Alpha and similar programmes are
correct in supposing that knowledge of Christian principles cannot be
taken for granted.'[99] The fact that the stories of the Bible are now unfamiliar
to children is an advantage to the Christian communicator. The stories
are fresh; they are without the preconceptions that previous generations
had of them, and they are free to do their work without being sieved
through the constructs of others. This is why the most appropriate form
of communication to children at faith stages 1 and 2 is narrative without
explanation – giving them the building blocks from which they are able to
construct their image and understanding of *God*.

Stage 2 is the point where children begin to understand the concept
of *journey* and it is at this stage that missionary stories and stories of those
who perform heroic deeds can be added to the narrative diet. Children are
beginning to understand concepts of purpose and destiny, of their lives
going somewhere. They are also becoming aware of community, of others
involved in their journey. It is at this point that the God *who was with*

David when he faced Goliath, or Aaron *coming alongside* Moses, become the most potent – they are both examples of others becoming part of the individual's journey.

Again there is fluidity between stages and some children who are emerging from stage 2 can understand and apply critical thought to the more guided learning of stage 3. Unfortunately, Children's Outreach Projects use predominantly stage 3 communication; they try to tell the children what to believe. Communication may seem difficult given the age spread, but the criticism is because there is predominantly only one form of communication being used and that form is aimed at the eldest age groups. There is no reason why multiple forms of communication cannot be implemented that give the construction material of stage 1 and 2 for the younger children and those in the older age groups who are still at these faith stages, and the more guided learning system of stage 3 for older children. The alternative, of course, is to split the children into two age groups, such as the pattern used in the Leeds project (unfortunately, even there the predominant form of communication for both age groups is still stage 3).

Lewis and Lewis suggest a list of nine key points to asses whether a piece of communication is in keeping with good inductive narrative communication. The points are:

1. *Use precisely the right word. Say it was oval, not it was sort of round.*
2. *Use specific, not generic words. Say pinto pony – not just horse. Say shack, mansion, lean-to, not just building.*
3. *Use descriptive words. Say the wind whined and clawed at the corner of the house, not the wind blew hard.*
4. *Use action verbs. Say he tore out, breezed out, strolled out – not went out.*
5. *Use short, forceful Anglo-Saxon words. Say he died – not he passed away, next to – not contiguous.*
6. *Use words found in your listeners' speaking vocabulary. Say swollen, not distended; I like you and not I hold you in high esteem.*
7. *Use imitative words that imitate natural sounds. Say soothe, lull, smooth, bang.*
8. *Use words with significant contemporary meaning, say home, not residence, meal not repast.*
9. *Avoid clichés, pastoral patter, trade talk, and stale fancy phrases.*[100]

It was Dave at the Liverpool project who demonstrated most of these elements in his communication style, but I also recorded in my field notes:

> This could be a revival meeting in the middle of the American Bible
> Belt, such is the passion of Dave's communication. The intensity
> is such that when a girl disrupts the teaching by talking, Dave
> asks her to leave the room.

Some may find this level of discipline disturbing, but what is clear in the observation is that over 200 children are listening intently to his words. In this context, passion communicates.

A return to the storytelling traditions is part of the equation. It has been observed that this generation of children has experienced the move from the written to the oral. However, Cray, Savage and Mayo suggest that it is more complicated:

> We have entered a 'second orality' – a move from book culture
> to screen culture. This move has caused significant changes in
> the way people learn, changes which the Church has not always
> adapted to well. Adults who were shaped by a limited-choice,
> terrestrial TV culture, are raising children shaped by a digital and
> interactive one.[101]

This is something that must be considered, but not to the extreme presented by Barna who writes, 'There is a constant need to use more technology, if only because children very often attribute greater truth to a technological source of information than they do a person.'[102] There is a basic misconception here. If people are converted by people and not by technology,[103] then it is the personal credibility of the storyteller that validates the story. Technology communicates information, but it is viewed with scepticism. The credible messenger, using technology as their tool, will be the most effective communicator to this generation. The credibility of the messenger is of fundamental importance, and the significance of that messenger has changed as society has moved from modernism. This was further evidenced in the research of Holland and Thompson who observed that 'Young people articulated an "ethic of reciprocity" arguing that their respect could be won by anyone who respected them... They tended to be very wary of claims to authority and respect on the basis of tradition, custom or force'.[104] Authority and tradition are no longer factors that allow the church to be heard and, as Holland and Thompson observed, credibility and the right to be heard are things that are earned.

The active programme of visiting every home evident in most of the projects achieves some of this; it gives the children contact with a leader and therefore an opportunity for the leader to earn credibility. This is necessary because the weekly children's clubs tend to allow very little time for this. The children arrive, they sit in their various teams, sing songs, watch or play games at the front, listen to the illustrations and stories and then return home. There is no opportunity within this structure for face-to-face contact with individual children. The Fraserburgh project had recognized this weakness and had introduced a Saturday morning activity-based programme that complements the teaching-based Friday evening. The Saturday morning event involved bouncy castles, table football, table tennis and uni-hoc. It also involved a café-style area where leaders sat and got to know the children better. Relationships were formed and children had opportunity to talk about their lives and often about their concerns. It was within the environment of the Saturday event that the leaders gained the credibility to be heard at the Friday event. The children saw what their leaders were like; the postmodern child wants to see people who live out their beliefs in wholesome, authentic and healing relationships.[105]

Both the positive and negative impact of credibility formed through relationship was shown at the Liverpool project. Whenever Dave, the project's leader, was the primary communicator, the children listened. When another leader spoke and Dave sat on the edge of the stage validating her words with 'Yes, that's right', the children listened. For the last element in the Liverpool project's presentation, however, I recorded:

> The teaching time concludes with a story about a boy who wanted to be in the sports team for his college and he got there because he worked hard and someone believed in him. The story was told in both words and projected pictures. The theme of being a winner because someone believes in you is embedded in the story, but the children are not interested in the story. They listen best when Dave is at the front, and he's not the one telling the story. As a result two balloons are burst,[106] both on the boys' side.

There are, of course, approaches that can be learned. Many of the narrative approaches have already been stated, but Lewis and Lewis point to the form of delivery and observe:

> Many objective studies have tested listener reactions to reading from a manuscript versus speaking extemporaneously with no more than notes for reference. Early tests revealed listeners retain approximately 36% more of the content when the message

is delivered via extemporaneous speech. Additional tests have found audience reactions more sympathetic and more attentive when speakers use extemporaneous delivery rather than manuscript reading.[107]

Bettlelheim is advocating a similar practice when he suggests:

> To attain in full its consoling propensities, its symbolic meanings, and, most of all, its interpersonal meanings, a fairy tale should be told rather than read. Extemporaneous speech makes the speaker seem more vulnerable and accessible and therefore more credible.[108]

All the large Children's Outreach Projects visited used extemporaneous communication, but the quality of that communication varied considerably. Some of the communicators were clearly nervous[109] and this affected their communication. Others took wonderfully graphic pieces of biblical narrative and reduced them to a two-dimensional sketch, such as the Hastings project's telling of the healing of the beggar at the Gate Beautiful (Acts 3).

Of course, the subject matter itself is also of great importance. The principles for telling, interpreting and understanding fairy tales are useful, and it is clear that these principles can be applied to a wide range of narrative. What is exclusive to the teaching of Christianity is that it is narrative *theology* that is being presented. Within the narrative are the elements from which the child draws and constructs what they understand of the nature and character of God. It is within this area that narrative theology has particular strength. It is the narrative itself that communicates, but because it is the retelling of theological stories, it does not allow for the sterilization of Christian belief that happens when the narrative is interpreted. Rushkoff presents Christianity as something that is restrictive and disempowering, and history bears witness to the fact that Christianity has often been used as a system of control, rather than the system of liberation.[110] Narrative theology allows for the exploration of a mature theology. It allows for movement past the tacit belief systems that epitomize many modern churches. Narrative theology is not sterile. The 'bad bits' and difficult passages have not been removed as is so often the case in modern preaching. Sometimes the innocent suffer as in the case of Job; sometimes God appears to act unfairly, as in the case of Cain and Abel. Stories of God ordering genocide are not always easy to reconcile with the concept of a God of love. However, these are the elements essential to the development of a mature theology, and although this form of theology may seem uncomfortable, its honesty and integrity are attractive to a postmodern world and specifically to postmodern children.

The concepts of Godly play[111] are also in keeping with this style of learning, a learning style that is focused around discovery and guided learning, and built on an understanding that children learn best when they learn for themselves. Although many of the principles of Godly play are used within the Children's Outreach Projects, particularly within the small groups of some Children's Outreach Projects, the more interactive elements makes it difficult to implement in the larger Children's Outreach Projects.

The context in which communication took place and the format of that communication need consideration. Although the physical environments of the largest Children's Outreach Projects were vibrant and lively, the format and layout of the large event was unchanged from week to week – with the exception of the backdrop that changes according to the theme.

Many of the curriculum materials used by the Children's Outreach Projects followed the same format every week. Even when the projects wrote their own materials, they tended to stay within that established format. There is an important reason for this. Maslow presents what he terms the *hierarchy of needs* (figure 8.9). The first needs that must be met are physiological needs; children will not listen if they are hungry,[112] cold or unwell. The secondary needs of both adults and children are needs for safety and security. The Children's Outreach Projects that maintained their layout and format from week to week encouraged this sense of security. Children who experience a warm welcome and then walk into familiar surroundings are children who are most likely to listen and to learn – they are able to relax and feel secure because their basic needs have been met. This agrees with the nest metaphor advocated by the Fraserburgh project, and is another reason why the Slough and Windsor project encourages the children to become part of the small-group programme. This further engaged with the child's need for security and allowed context for hermeneutic phenomenology.

CONNECTION BETWEEN THE CHILDREN'S OUTREACH PROJECT AND CHURCH

In 1941 an influential individual in the development of church-based children's work, Herbert Alfred Hamilton,[113] wrote:

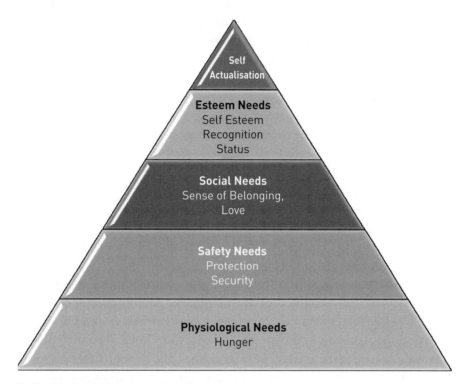

Fig 8.9 Maslow's hierarchy of needs

> The church is neither a building, nor a service, it is a community
> of Christian people. One of the great tasks of Christian Education
> is to discover how to develop the sense of Christian family life
> between the 80% of children who come to us from homes which
> have no connection with the Church and the members of the
> Christian community we want them to enter.[114]

The key component of the Raikes paradigm had been identified – the need to make the link between the church and the community. What is also interesting is the acknowledgement that 80 per cent of the children in attendance on an average week were not from churchgoing families. These were not the children who attended the eucharistic service with their parents. Under Hamilton's influence, many churches were to advocate corporate worship services where adult and child could worship together, and to actively work towards a common curriculum where the subjects taught in Sunday School would also be covered in the adult congregation. Hamilton pushed for shared worship opportunities where worship could be felt and experienced, not just talked about. He advocated a system of church parents or sponsors who would help the children from non-churchgoing homes be assimilated into the faith community. Nevertheless, over the following decades a major shift would take place. Cliff writes:

> When Hamilton began his work in 1933, 80% of the children in the Sunday School came from non-churchgoing homes. When he died in 1977, about 80% of the children came from churchgoing homes.[115]

Hamilton had highlighted what he saw as the need to make the link between unchurched children and the faith community. He advocated a mechanism of church parents – not actual parents but a kind of spiritual foster parent who would help with the child's spiritual nurture, who would mentor and provide support on the journey. Nevertheless, despite his pleas the church did not implement the philosophy.

The earlier observations from 1780 showed clearly that there was no regular contact between the church and much of the community other than on certain special days in the church calendar (Christmas and Easter) and for weddings, funerals and baptisms. The focus of Raikes' Sunday Schools was not only to make contact with children who would otherwise have no contact with church or church groups, but also to connect once more an emerging generation with traditional church.[116] However, the Sunday Schools of the early 1800s, although advocating attendance at the local church, often operated outside of church control through its own elected committee. The friction that this relationship caused is shown by Ward when recording the views of a Salford Methodist minister, commenting on the work of the Sunday School teachers:

> They are doing more evil than good. The children are trained up without any regard to God's public worship; and reverence for the sanctity of the Sabbath, or any respect for the ministers of the Gospel. Ask nineteen out of every twenty of the boys and girls you find running around in the streets of a Sunday evening in this populous town, whether they did not belong to some Sunday School, and they would answer, 'yes'.[117]

As the nineteenth century progressed, the link between Sunday School and church in many areas became closer. This is particularly true of the Methodist churches where new churches were built to incorporate an upper level for adult worship and a lower level for Sunday Schools.[118]

Interestingly, even in these newer buildings the government of the Sunday School was through a distinct Sunday School committee rather than by Methodist church leaders, although as the century drew to a close there was a much greater overlap between church leadership and Sunday School committee.

The choice of the phrase *traditional church* is deliberate; although *fresh expressions of church* are a viable and helpful innovation, the value of traditional church, defined as adherents with a unified system of beliefs and practices that unite them into a single and moral community,[119] is helpful. Traditional church should be intergenerational, but although the cultural sharing group may be intergenerational, there is no reason why the sub-cultures that form that group should not be generational. The children of the Children's Outreach Project may never meet at the same time or in the same place as the adult congregation (although members of the congregation may well form part of the leadership of the Children's Outreach Project), but both Children's Outreach Project and adult congregation are part of the local church in that area. The reason for advocating this view is straightforward. In an intergenerational model, there are always areas that the children can move on to: when they are children they may be part of the Children's Outreach Project, when they are teenagers they may form part of the youth programme, and as adults they may be part of the adult congregation. From the surveys returned, there were clearly many Children's Outreach Projects who existed in isolation from the local church (many, using the *fresh expressions* definitions, saw themselves as church), but within the projects visited there were also some clear distinctions in this respect. The Fraserburgh project was a traditional church model. Many of the workers came from the adult church, the senior minister of the church was present on the evenings the Children's Outreach Project met to demonstrate that this was a church activity, and there was a clear philosophy of children graduating from the children's programme to the youth programme and ultimately to the adult church. It was an intergenerational model of Children's Outreach Project as part of traditional church. The Leeds project, in contrast, was run by eighteen different churches. Provoked by the question 'What do you do with the older ones who are too old for kids' club?', Bernie. the leader of the Leeds project, responded, 'Lots of people are critical when they ask this question, but I really felt God say work with the kids, and the rest is God's responsibility.' The Leeds project fell into the pattern of *fresh expressions* of church, but also highlighted the issues of projects that are not connected to *traditional church*; there is no long-term thinking in terms of children becoming a regular part of a faith community. The strength of the Children's Outreach Project as part of traditional church was highlighted by Wes Richards, the leader of the church of which the Slough and Windsor project is a part:

> It has institutionalized the value of children's ministry right at the core of the church, it is growing from strength to strength. We are seeing now not just the immediate response of children, but they are growing up and staying. It has to come out of the vision and the values of the church. The senior leader and the senior leadership have to own it and then reproduce it in the people that they lead. If you want a ministry so you can say we are doing something for the kids, but your heart is not in it, then it will not have dynamism and life. It must come out of the heart of the leader. You cannot hire professionals just to do a job and say that's our kids sorted. The church has to have a heart and vision for kids.

Churches like this have the capacity to be involved with people from the cradle to the grave. These churches also run children's works on Sundays for the children of church members. They have recognized that while the Children's Outreach Projects have an important part to play, the Sunday morning teaching programme for the children of Christian parents is also important. To communicate a Christian message and to evangelize unchurched children while at the same time continuing to haemorrhage the children who are already part of the church is counter-productive. The Slough and Windsor project (a similar pattern was mirrored by Fraserburgh, Hastings and Leeds) shows that the two can and should work together.

As well as there being more than two philosophies at work within these projects, there was also an interesting dichotomy in the ecclesiology of the churches of which the projects were part. The Hastings project was clearly trying to bring families into Sunday church. There was a clear paradigm being outworked that suggested that the gathered community on Sunday mornings was *proper* church and the other activities of the church were stepping stones or bridges to that event. Chris, the leader of the Hastings project, commented, 'So, ultimately we want to see people coming up here on Sunday morning and hearing the word of God preached and getting saved and added to the church.'

In contrast, the church of which the Slough and Windsor project is a part saw the Saturday children's club as one of its weekend church congregations. It is given the same weight and credibility as the Sunday gatherings. I commented in my field notes:

By 12 noon the children are gathered back on to their buses for the journey home. While the buses are out, people who have not been part of the children's programme, but who are part of the church, will arrive and start cleaning up. This is not where the church meets, but it is clear that the whole church own this event. The clear-up operation is intensive; there are lighting rigs, sound cables and projection screens to clear away as well as the seating and general litter generated by the children.

Further to this, the leaders of this church are also involved in speaking to the children. Wes Richards concludes:

We've got a saying, 'Team work makes the dream work.' The value of team is that we need lots of different people: people to do backdrops, to help pack up; we need big burly blokes, we need grandparents, all involved. This is win/win.

Richards had concluded that people stay part of church for a range of reasons, but one of the primary reasons is involvement. They are part of it, not just consumers of it. The Children's Outreach Project gives opportunity for the whole church to be involved, to outwork their gifts for a common goal. Brierley writes:

Growing churches do have an effective children's ministry... because they deliberately see the children's ministry which they exercise as being very much part of the mainstream activity of the church. This integration mechanism of the children's ministry with the totality of the church activity is as important as the quality of the actual ministry itself if growth is to take place.

It may be true to say that Western society is sailing away faster than the church can build bridges,[120] but the Children's Outreach Project should not be seen as an attempt to build a bridge. It is the place where children who are part of a wider church sub-culture, made up of a variety of ages, gather for the purpose of Christian teaching, prayer, singing, games, arts and crafts, and a wide range of other activities. The churches that are growing see the Children's Outreach Project as a vital part of their engagement with the community *and* as a significant part of the church. However, what was also interesting to see alongside this was the flow of unchurched children, who were contacted initially through the Children's Outreach Project, becoming part of the Sunday morning programme or more usually the Sunday morning youth programme.[121]

Before leaving this section, it is necessary to make a further comment on the denominational affiliations of the projects. In general, the largest Children's Outreach Projects were run by free churches which described themselves as *network* churches. These network churches gather from large areas and while most of them gather their congregations from the city in which they are based, some people travel from much further afield to be part of that church. They do not see their area of work as a particular parish and tend not to work within geographical boundaries. It is for this reason that the largest Children's Outreach Projects in the UK are not Anglican projects. Anglican projects tend to confine themselves to working within a fixed geographical area, and although some of their members may come from outside of that area, they would not tend to evangelize in another parish.

The larger projects were gathering hundreds of children, but they were covering areas where tens of thousands of children live in order to gather their hundreds. For example, the Liverpool project sent six buses distances of up to ten kilometres from its meeting point to bring children to the Children's Outreach Project. This is not to criticize the work that they do; they were collecting children from areas where children would otherwise have no contact with church or church groups. But this geographical factor is an important one.

CONNECTION BETWEEN THE CHILDREN'S OUTREACH PROJECT AND LOCAL SCHOOLS

The elements considered within this chapter so far are all part of the original Raikes model, but there is an additional characteristic of the Children's Outreach Projects that was not part of the original Sunday School pattern. It is the link with local schools.

In 1942 the then Archbishop of Canterbury, William Temple, wrote:

> [Christian education in schools] means much more than the inclusion of Christian doctrine in the curriculum, though without this the goal could not be reached. There must be regular corporate worship,[122] and the atmosphere of the school must be as far as possible Christian.[123]

He refuted the idea that these were only church school distinctives, and suggested that they should be the hallmark of all British schools. He identified three key areas:

1. *Corporate worship*
2. *Religious instruction*
3. *Christian atmosphere/ethos*

The then Minister for Education, R. A. Butler, was influenced by Archbishop Temple to the extent that he wrote a White Paper in 1943 that would form a significant part of the 1944 Education Act. This act required both state schools and church schools to provide a daily act of worship and religious instruction. These dual characteristics were to be the defining features of Christian education.

Key changes took place in the 1960s when Goldman published his research on religious thinking. There was a general feeling that knowledge and acceptance of other world religions would make Britain a more tolerant society. The most significant factor, however, was that fewer teachers held firm religious views themselves and therefore were not comfortable leading acts of worship.

However, the 1988 Education Act was to reinforce the earlier principle: 'The overall pattern of worship in every school must be wholly or mainly of a broadly Christian character.'[124] The first major overhaul of church schools came in 2001 with the publication of the Dearing Report.[125] This report was to challenge more forcibly the way church schools functioned. Dearing commented:

> With the state being a willing provider of education, the justification for the Church's presence in education must be to offer an approach to education which is distinctively Christian.

In basic terms, if the church schools are not distinctively Christian, then their very existence is unjustifiable. The Dearing Report went further to state, 'Church schools stand at the centre of the Church's mission to the nation.'[126] The government put its strength behind the report; David Blunkett, the then Home Secretary, stated:

> The vision of schools developing their own distinct ethos does not mean individual schools becoming isolated. Far from it. The best schools spread their successful ideas to others, just as specialist schools are expected to develop partnerships with nearby schools to help them lift standards.[127]

Dearing is both significant and timely. The role of Church of England schools in the overall mission of the church is more important today than ever before. In 2001 the church had 900,000 young people attending its schools.[128] This is in comparison to 229,000 young people who attended Anglican churches in the same period.[129] This is certainly a significant figure and cause for some hope.[130]

In many ways, the fact that teachers are not comfortable with leading acts of worship in school has worked to the advantage of the Children's Outreach Projects. Many schools have been pleased to accept the offer of Children's Outreach Projects offer to take a school assembly because they felt that they could not lead an act of primarily Christian worship themselves.[131] The Liverpool project is not unique when it stated:

> We currently do assemblies in twelve local primary schools. By going in each term and presenting a brief message on the love of God, we're making sure that 4,000 children regularly get a taste of his goodness.

The Leeds project had a member of the team whose main focus was school assemblies; they took twenty-six school assemblies each term. Luke at the Slough and Windsor project stated:

> I think we are very privileged in this country to be able to go into schools and speak to children. In this country, all children are supposed to have an act of worship that is Christian in nature. Therefore, we are there to present an act of Christian worship and we allow time to reflect and think about God. And although there are more and more children of other faiths, we still have freedom to talk about Jesus.

Topics covered in schools by the Slough and Windsor project from 2006 to 2008 included:

- Choose your friends carefully
- Stop lying and tell the truth
- God always helps us in times of trouble
- True meaning of Easter
- True meaning of Christmas
- What you say can mean life or death
- Use every chance you have for doing good

- Forgive one another
- I am precious to God
- People look on the outside but God looks at the heart
- Show respect to everyone
- Don't get angry too quickly
- If you want to be great, you have to serve

The Slough and Windsor, Leeds, Hastings and Liverpool projects all speak about the privilege of being able to present an act of worship in schools (the Fraserburgh project didn't have a regular programme of school visits). However, they also used the opportunity to advertise their projects and to give out leaflets. Most allow the school to distribute the leaflets to every child, but the Leeds project did the distribution differently. Bernie from the Leeds project explained:

> We do an assembly and then we'll leaflet at the school gate at the end of the day. It's much easier when we can make contact with parents and explain what we do. It's good when the parents can put a face to what's going on. Putting a face to a project rather than a child going home with a leaflet and the parent says, 'I have no idea who these people are.' The kids are doing the selling for you, they say, 'Mum, it's someone from Kidz Klub. Can I go?' Often other mums will say, 'Oh yes, my kids go, they look after them really well.'

Although the input of the Children's Outreach Projects into local schools was substantial, what they were outworking was an attempt to use the school as a halfway house, a bridge to the church. It is not suggested, however, that if the Children's Outreach Projects were not able to hand out their leaflets, they would no longer take the assemblies. All the projects were clear that being able to take the school assembly had value in itself.

The Dearing Report is bolder than this. Dearing makes the school the place of mission on the same level as the church. Not only is it bolder, but it may have a stronger integrity. It is not advocating a model that uses the school to attract people to the church; instead, it is a model that recognizes the significance of the school as a place of mission in its own right.[132]

Dearing offers a model to clarify the hypothesis (figure 8.10). This link between Children's Outreach Project and local schools, alongside the implications of the Dearing Report for Church of England schools, makes this an interesting point in history. However, few Church of England

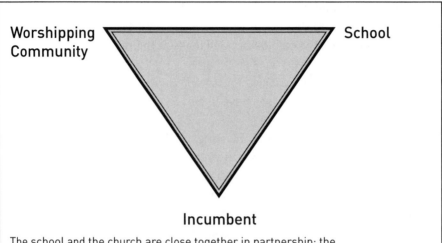

Worshipping Community — **School**

Incumbent

The school and the church are close together in partnership: the school and parish church see themselves as an active association – as an extended community – together at the heart of the church's mission to the community.

Fig 8.10 The Dearing Mission

schools seem to have taken up the challenge of Dearing. There are only three reasons to explain why:

1. *They have not understood the implications of the report.*
2. *They are unable to implement the report.*
3. *They are unwilling to implement the report.*

However, where the schools have engaged with Dearing, the effect has been positive. The last inspect report of Bradfield Primary School in Reading stated:

> In conversations with learners it is evident that the school has given them an understanding of themselves as being precious in the sight of God. They speak naturally and confidently about how God cares about each one of them, valuing what each can give to enrich the lives of others... Collective worship is at the heart of school life. A parent said she always looks forward to Friday's assemblies and stated, 'Coming here helps me to feel close to God'... Staff are present at worship and speak of the inspiration they gain from it... The headteacher, chair of governors and parish priest have a distinctive relationship in regularly meeting together for prayer.[133]

NOTES

1. In the largest projects, there were employed staff to run the activities. A commitment to training was evidenced in the majority of the Children's Outreach Projects that returned their questionnaires.

2. 1833, p. 76.

3. West London Auxiliary Annual Report (1896, p. 68).

4. Cliff (1986, p. 182).

5. George Hamilton Archibald (1858–1938). Most of the information on Archibald is from Johnston (1945).

6. 1902, p. 10.

7. The first half of the twentieth century saw Archibald's practice of grading gather considerable momentum, the curriculum adapted accordingly. Archibald himself was to write *Bible Lessons for Beginners*; his wife would contribute *The Primary Department*; Archibald added *The Junior Department*. The Anglican Church produced their own materials, but gradually they to were to become age-specific. Initially, in 1911, curriculum was simply offered for Beginners and Primary, but by 1950 materials were generally available in beginners (three and four), primary (five to eight), Junior (eight to eleven) and seniors (eleven to fourteen). By 1950, a new category called *Youth* had been introduced covering those who were fourteen plus. It is worth mentioning that even in 1950 the practice of grading was still not wholeheartedly embraced and was criticised by many, some even attributing the continued decline to the practice; however, it was close to becoming a universal practice. The vast majority of this graded material came from the Scripture Union (founded in 1867 by Josiah Spiers) which by 1950 had established itself as the main provider of Sunday School materials.

8. 1986, p. 280.

9. Cliff, 1986, p. 303.

10. 1909.

11. Ironically, it was St Augustine who first stated, 'The Holy Spirit wants to make us Christians not mathematicians.' However, it is freely acknowledged that he did so in a very different context!

12. A Lutheran Study (1998b) into corporate worship in schools concluded that:
    Children participating in the study from years one, four and seven benefited from attending the same whole school chapel services. Each year level group was able to learn something of the nature of Christian worship at their own level... This implies that educators can design school worship so that it is beneficial to all primary school aged children.

13. 1986, p. 235.

14. 2000, p. 109.

15. The Liverpool project's website features accounts of drug addicts and alcoholics who have become Christians as a direct result of the work of the Children's Outreach Project.

16. 1986, p. 96.

17. Mentioned in Raikes' letter to Townley of 1783.

18. Various editions of this prayer exist. This version is taken from *The English Primer* (1784 edition).

19. Norman M. Weinberger (1996, 1998) is Professor of Psychobiology at the University of California.

20. North and Hargreaves, 1997.

21. 1900, p. 18.

22. Initially, the hymns sung by the children were adult hymns from adult hymnbooks. As the Sunday Schools grew, they developed their own Sunday School hymnal, but many of the songs in these hymnals were songs written for adults but felt appropriate for children. *The Primitive Methodist Sunday School Hymnal* of the late nineteenth century contained hymns such as 'O worship the Lord in the beauty of holiness' and 'Fight the good fight with all thy might', both taken directly from the adult Methodist hymnal.

23. Traditional, author unknown.

24. Spiritual folk song.

25. Author unknown.

26. Author unknown.

27. Scripture in Song, 1980.

28. 1900, p. 18.

29. John Samuel Bewley Monsell, 1863.

30. 'Super Strong God' by Julia A'Bell and David Wakerley. Copyright (c) 2005 David Wakerley and Julia A'Bell/Hillsong Publishing/kingswaysongs.com for the UK and Eire (www.kingsway.co.uk).

31. 'Lovely Jubbly' by Doug Horley. Copyright (c) 2001 Thankyou Music.*

32. Words by John Monsell (1863) and music by William Boyd (1864).

33. 'I'm gonna jump up and down' by Doug Horley. Copyright (c) 2001 Thankyou Music.*

34. 'King of majesty' by Marty Sampson. Copyright (c) 2001 Marty Sampson/Hillsong Publishing/kingswaysongs.com. Copyright (c) 2005 David Wakerley and Julia A'Bell/Hillsong Publishing/kingswaysongs.com for the UK and Eire (www.kingsway.co.uk).

35. Finding some agreement with Goldman's (1964) research into religious instruction in school.

36. 1900, pp. 19–20.

37. 1900, p. 19.

38. Cliff (1986), p. 270.

39. 1912, p. 101.

40. Reprinted in *Sunday School Chronicle and Times*, 1927.

41. 1986, p. 225.

42. The Anglican Church, in its 1949 report *Children Adrift*, advocated the greater working between church and community and suggested that the work begin at baptism, with greater emphasis given to preparation and community relations.

43. 1978, pp. 275f.

44. 2000, p. 30.

45. 2002, p. 22,

46. Cray, Savage and Mayo (2006, pp. 44, 51).

47. 2006, p. 22.

48. Orchard (2007, p. i), Cliff (1986, p. 2).

49. 2006, p. 36.

50. An autobiography by Charles Shaw (1903).

51. Shaw's (1903, pp. 134–135) accounts are set in the 1830s. A slight indulgence is taken here with regard to the length of the quotation, primarily because it draws out the point being made so effectively.

52. Shaw's (1903) account indicates that his treatment by the other children is because he spent some time in the workhouse as a result of his family's extreme poverty.

53. Shaw (1903) does not provide the name.

54. 1986, p. 322.

55. An orphanage located in the mountains of northern Thailand, House of Grace was founded in 1987 to protect and care for tribal girls who are at risk of being sold into prostitution in Bangkok. (www.houseofgracethailand.com)

56. Compassion UK is a Christian organisation that allows individuals and groups to support children in poverty in other countries through a child sponsorship programme. (www.compassionuk.org)

57. Hints on the Establishment of Sunday Schools.

58. Religious education from earliest times has always come to this conclusion eventually. In rabbinic schools the rabbis had no interest in students producing a memorized answer; they wanted to know if the child understood it, if he had wrestled with it. In rabbinic education, the emphasis was on questions, which demonstrated that the student not only understood the information but could take the subject a step further (Bell, 2006, p. 128).

59. 1903, p. 41.

60. 1986, p. 153.

61. McGrath, 1993, p. 18.

62. Brierley (2002, p. 105) also shows that the majority of those who left as teenagers made their decision to do so between the ages of eight and ten.

63. Interestingly, there is no decline (or enough additions to balance out those that leave) after this point – possibly suggesting that if people are still in church in their thirties, they are likely to stay.

64. Richards (1993, p. 123).

65. 1983, p. 10.

66. 1994, p. 17.

67. Brierley (2006, p. 37).

68. Gadamer (1975) reinforces this point when he writes of a philosophical shift back towards a concern with the rhetorical contexts of speech and thought.

69. Toulmin (1990, p. 186).

70. Brierley (2000b, p. 110).

71. 1996, pp. 49–52.

72. Rushkoff (1996, p. 50).

73. 1996, p. 51.

74. Some balance needs to be maintained in this argument. Although believing that the way children assimilate information is different and therefore the form and style of communication must reflect that, Grafman (chief of the cognitive neuroscience section at the National Institute of Neurological Disorders), writing in *Time Magazine* (19 March 2006, pp. 4–6), comments:

Although many aspects of the networked life remain scientifically uncharted, there's substantial literature on how the brain handles multitasking. And basically, it doesn't. It may seem that a teenage girl is writing an instant message, burning a CD and telling her mother she's doing her homework – all at the same time – but what's really going on is a rapid toggling among tasks rather than simultaneous processing. You're doing more than one thing, but you're ordering them and deciding which one to do at any one time... The ability to multiprocess has its limits, even among young adults. When people try to perform two or more related tasks either at the same time or alternating rapidly between them, errors go way up, and it takes far longer – often double the time or more than it would to get the jobs done than if they were done sequentially.

75. 1983, p. 10.

76. This is not as straightforward as it sounds because the majority of Sunday School teachers are from older generations (Brierley, 2000, p. 110). They tend to teach in the way that they learned.

77. 1985, p. 182.

78. Birch, 1991, p. 54.

79. 2005, p. 58. Rushkoff (1996) uses almost the identical sentence.

80. This is particularly poignant because this was one of the stories that Goldman (1965) relied upon for his research that contributed to the reduction of religious teaching in schools. Goldman (1965) insisted that children didn't understand abstract concepts. It was this aspect that defined Goldman's research, research

specifically into the effectiveness of religious instruction (1965, p. xi). Goldman considered several popular Bible stories and evaluated the children's ability to understand them, but the inherent difficulty in Goldman's research is highlighted in his evaluation of the crossing of the Red Sea:

> As an adventure-action story younger pupils may enjoy the narrative, but as a story told to reveal religious truths it appears to fail due to the limits of experience and undeveloped concepts of love, justice and historical purpose. The significance of the Exodus as a whole, and this part of the story included, is dependent on the historical continuity of the Old Testament. (p. 221)

Goldman's criticism is that children do not understand abstract concepts of love and justice, leading him to conclude that 'the Bible is the major source book of Christianity for adults, it is plainly not a children's book' (p. 71), and 'very little biblical material is suitable before Secondary schooling' (p. 225). Fackre's (1993, p. 346) point is that it is about presenting the story and allowing the story to communicate, not about trying to present the abstract truth. Hull (1991) concludes that although the child cannot understand everything about God, they will understand at their level. To use Goldman's (p. 221) example, it could be said that understanding that the narrative is about action and adventure and about a God who rescues people is perfectly acceptable level of understanding for the small child. The fact that younger children cannot understand the further complexities of the narrative do not in any way undermine the value of that narrative.

Goldman's second research question connected with the Red Sea narrative, asked the child:

> Does God love everyone in the world?
> Did he love the men in the Egyptian army?
> Why was it that he allowed the men in the Egyptian army to be drowned?

It is based on this question that he concludes that children of a younger age group do not understand the concepts of love and justice. However, as presented by Fowler, many adults would struggle with the concepts of justice, love, innocent suffering and free will embedded within this account. It is clear that Goldman has a fixed idea himself of what is taking place in the narrative, a position that may not go unchallenged by contemporary theologians. These factors led Hyde (1968, p. 429) and others to ask whether Goldman's research was adequate to carry the weight of his conclusions.

Further to this, to say that children do not understand abstract concepts is not specific enough. If an abstract idea is an idea about something which you cannot touch or such as love or justice, then consider also abstract words like tomorrow, darkness, big and heaven. Children can certainly use the word *tomorrow* at quite an early age. So in the first sense of abstract idea, children seem able to work quite well (Hull, 1991, p. 7). Children can understand abstract ideas and concepts, but there is a different area of development needed to be able to think abstractly. The Piagetian term *concrete thinking* is often applied to the child who can understand basic abstraction, but who cannot think abstractly. Hull (1991, pp. 8–9) suggests, 'The child between the ages of about six and ten years tend to think within the limits of the objects, people, and situation which have been encountered. The older child tends to think in terms of sentences and is no longer confined to the actual situation or object.' Abstract thinking is therefore about sentences, whereas concrete thinking is about places, objects and people. Further clarification is needed, as the word *concrete* implies thought processes that are rigid and inflexible. This could not be further from the truth. The concrete thinker can deal with abstract words and with the spontaneous people and situations around us, and is able to deal with stories of God speaking to Jeremiah or the child Samuel.

81. Fackre (1983, p. 346).

82. 1977, p. 94.

83. Paul Tillich (1886–1965).

84. In contrast to Barth who is non-correlational. In essence, Barth believes that the word of God gives a specific unchanging answer that is not affected by time or location. The debate is recorded in Tillich's *Systematic Theology* (1973, vol. 1).

85. 1977, p. 27.

86. Fowler (1981, p. 135).

87. Bettelheim (1977, p. 27).

88. Depending on which definition of parable is used.

89. Lewis and Lewis (1983, p. 69).

90. 1983, p. 147.

91. Kierkegaard (1941, p. 247).

92. Tinsley (1996, p. 26).

93. 1977, p. 155.

94. 1965, p. 95. For example, asking children to draw the monster they have heard about in a story will produce considerable variation from child to child. Showing the children an illustration of the monster in the story and then asking them to draw the monster will produce only variations on a theme. Bettelheim (1977, p. 60) concludes that the idea of the monster produced will 'leave us entirely cold, or may scare us without evoking any deeper meaning beyond anxiety'.

95. 1958, p. 15.

96. Usually projected using overhead projectors or, more usually, video projectors.

97. 1981, p. 134.

98. 2000, p. 110.

99. 2005, p. 1.

100. 1983, p. 142.

101. 2006, p. 147.

102. 1998, p. 58.

103. Ullman (1989).

104. 1993, p. 3.

105. Grenz (1996, p. 169).

106. As has been mentioned previously, balloons are one of the control systems in the Liverpool project. The children lose a balloon for breaking various rules. If they lose all their balloons, their team does not get a prize.

107. 1983, p. 149.

108. 1977, p. 150.

109. My presence as an observer may have contributed to this.

110. 1996, pp. 260f.

111. Godly play is a learning style that owes much to Ignatian spirituality in that it is based on imagination and discovery. A full account of Godly play can be found in the *Godly Play* series by Jerome W. Berryman.

112. Although none of the UK projects mentioned food, international projects of this nature – for example, a project in Sydney Australia, working with indigenous children – found that these children were unable to listen until they had been fed. Many of the children had not eaten a proper meal for several days. (This project was the Impact Kids project run by Hillsong City Church, Sydney.)

113. Herbert Alfred Hamilton (1897–1977).

114. 1941, p. 19.

115. 1986, p. 246.

116. In Raikes' case, Gloucester Cathedral and St Mary de Crypt Church.

117. 1972, p. 137.

118. However, as Orchard (2007, p. xv) points out, 'Moves towards assigning Sunday Schools to particular churches did not end the ecclesiological ambiguity. Sunday School leaders still saw themselves as answerable to the community they served rather than to church authorities.'

119. Durkheim (1912, p. xxi).

120. Lings (2006).

121. Young people are of an age where they can make the journey to church for themselves; children are still dependent on the goodwill of parents to get them there. Many unchurched parents are not prepared to make that journey on a Sunday morning.

122. Temple defined worship as 'Opening of the heart to receive the love of God'.

123. Kay and Francis (1997).

124. Kay and Francis (1997, p. 212).

125. This report is titled *The Way Ahead* and is properly cited in the bibliography; however, it is most commonly referred to as the Dearing Report after the chair of the committee, Lord Dearing.

126. 2001, p. 1.

127. *The Times*, 12 February 2001.

128. 2001, p. 9.

129. Research and Statistics Department, Church of England, 2001.

130. As Copley (2005, p. 136) writes:

> The support for Christianity may be more passive than active, but it is in inclination not disinclination. 'We' – in this case the intellectuals among 'us' – must stop pretending to be 'post Christian', without at the same time reintroducing the undemonstratable claim that Britain is a Christian country. This is our Alice in Wonderland situation. We were never a Christian country in the first place, but we can hardly be a post-Christian country when 71.6% of the population claims to support Christianity. ... The statistics of church attendance remind us that 'we' are by no means as supportive of institutional Christianity. For the mission alone, trying to march people up the old church path would be a non-starter. But so would turning our collective back on Christianity altogether.

131. Although it is often suggested that teachers do not want to take school assemblies because they feel hypocritical presenting a Christian world view that they do not believe, in my discussions with the teachers at many of the schools that the Slough and Windsor project visit this wasn't given as the primary reason. Many teachers were happy to talk about Bible stories and Christian morality in their own classrooms. What they did not want to do was stand in front of their peers and speak to large crowds of children. In general, it seems that taking school assemblies is not something taught in teacher training colleges.

132. An incarnational model involves a clear link between school, church and community. A model is outlined in *Mission-Shaped Church* (2004, p. 69):

> The guiding principle behind what we are trying to achieve at All Saints (church and school) is that of liturgical formation. We have begun to establish a pattern of worship which links church and school together. Every Thursday at 9.15 the school meets in the adjacent church for a midweek service, which follows the Common Worship pattern. After this the children return to school and any adults who wish to stay for Holy Communion remain in church.

In this example, the model is one of church and school linked, both working in an interdependent way towards a common goal. Dearing (2001, p. 11) clarifies:

> We take this to mean that they stand alongside the parish churches, which lead the missionary work of the Church, as an integral part of the Church community, offering Christ to the young and through them, to varying degrees, offering parents the opportunity to learn from children and to engage in the life of a Christian institution.

133. March 2008.

* Adm. by worshiptogether.com songs excl. UK & Europe, adm. by kingswaysongs.com (www.kingsway.co.uk).

Chapter 9

CONCLUSIONS AND RECOMMENDATIONS

This exploration of the comparisons between Raikes' initial Sunday School and the Children's Outreach Projects of the early twenty-first century addressed two primary questions. The first is whether the twenty-first-century projects are indeed the legacy of Robert Raikes. The second is the consideration of whether there are suggestions/implications that can be advanced as a methodology for child evangelism today.

The success of Raikes' model of child evangelism and its impact on the last two centuries has been considerable. The pattern modelled by Raikes, although more visceral than conceptual in design, was nonetheless an effective form of child evangelism (effectiveness defined by Raikes' ability to reach large numbers of children and see many of them incorporated into Christian churches). The sudden increase of child evangelism implemented by Robert Raikes in the late eighteenth century arrested a prolonged period of decline in the church. The effect of the first decades of the Raikes Sunday Schools rippled through history, ensuring high church attendance for over a century afterwards. The combination of professional teachers, hymn-singing and prayer, rewards, prizes and incentives, clear connection between Children's Outreach Project, parents and church, the meeting of social needs, the empowerment of children and the clear communication of the Christian message have helped connect unchurched children with church.

Nevertheless, it is suggested by way of conclusion that the greatest asset in the development of child evangelism is not the structure or pattern that developed, but Raikes himself. He developed the work of child evangelism in the microcosm of his Gloucester parish. He then promoted it throughout the country, through constant representations in his newspaper and through the articles and editorials he distributed to other newspapers and journals. Raikes had developed a pattern for communicating Christianity to unchurched boys and girls and then propagated that model. This ability to propagate the pattern is as important as the pattern itself and greatly increases its influence and effectiveness.

This ability to propagate the pattern is shown more recently in the work of the Liverpool project. Dave, the project leader, has not only established a Children's Outreach Project, he has established a network of children's clubs. The Liverpool project website features over a hundred projects as part of its network. It has been instrumental in encouraging others to start Children's Outreach Projects and resourcing them in the process. The Liverpool project also propagates the Children's Outreach Project by providing a range of branded clothing for sale to those in its network. At the 2007 Conservative Party Conference, Dave stated that the network makes over a million home visits every year. The size of the network is questionable, as is the number of visits stated, but there is no debate that the Liverpool project has helped spread Children's Outreach Projects throughout the UK. The Fraserburgh, Slough and Windsor, Hastings and Leeds projects all visited the Liverpool project before launching their projects. The Liverpool project itself was launched through the input and resourcing of Bill Wilson from Metro Ministries New York.

The Slough and Windsor project fulfils a similar function to the Liverpool project but focuses primarily on the South of England. During the period of my field research at the Slough and Windsor project, there was a constant stream of groups and potential groups visiting to see what they could learn. This was taken a stage further in 2008 when the Slough and Windsor project launched a similar project in South Africa, a project they now resource and help to develop. Technology and globalization have further helped to facilitate this. On most Monday mornings, the project's leader, Paul, has face-to-face conversations (via his computer) with his leaders in South Africa. They discuss how the project is progressing and how the Slough and Windsor project can further help in its development. The South African project will in turn help to start other African projects.

The leader of the Fraserburgh project is the national children's director for the Elim stream of churches and is now replicating the Fraserburgh project throughout the Elim movement. The Leeds project and Hastings project have similar opportunities to propagate their projects, but on a smaller scale.

The leaders of the five Children's Outreach Projects analyzed in depth shared characteristics with Raikes. They were all entrepreneurial in the establishing of their projects, they were all, to varying degrees, passionately committed to their goals, and they all show the tenacity and perseverance necessary to keep the Children's Outreach Project running.

This understanding of how these projects began enables us to answer two of the questions posed in the Introduction.

1. *Are there similar patterns and 'cultural norms' embedded within the projects?*
2. *If so, then:*

i) *Have they independently and exclusively developed similar patterns of practice?*

ii) *Have these groups learned from each other or from a common outside source, possibly Raikes?*

There are clearly embedded norms within the projects. Some of these are obvious: they all tend to have a common structure with regard to their activities and programme format; they tend to use the same mechanisms for keeping control; all the teams are dressed in project T-shirts. However, there are more subtle cultural norms. For example, they tend to use a common vocabulary in terms of *visitation, preaching time, silent seats* and *memory verse sheets,* and tend to promote their project with passionate emotive statements such as 'This is life or death to these children' or 'This is the most important hour of this child's week'. There is no possibility that each of these projects has developed these practices exclusively and independently. Fraserburgh, Slough and Windsor, Leeds and Hastings all claim to have taken their inspiration, at least in part, from the Liverpool project, with the Liverpool project in turn taking its lead and direction from the Metro Sunday School, New York, established by Bill Wilson. The findings of the Children's Outreach Project survey revealed that 39 per cent of the Children's Outreach Projects in the UK pointed to Bill Wilson of Metro Sunday School New York as a direct influence. A further 34 per cent cited the Liverpool project. It is therefore possible to conclude from this that over 70 per cent of the Children's Outreach Projects in the UK can be traced back to the primary or secondary influence of Bill Wilson and the Metro Sunday School pattern.

Nevertheless, before it is concluded that these twenty-first century Children's Outreach Projects are not the legacy of Robert Raikes, consideration of a further historical factor is necessary. In his *History of Christian Education,*[1] Eavey writes that the first American Sunday School opened in Virginia in 1785. It was established on the same pattern that had been witnessed at one of Raikes' projects in England. The Sunday School movement in America grew and followed a similar path to the Sunday Schools of the UK, in terms of both growth and decline (with a caveat that the American decline has been less pronounced).[2] Although Bill Wilson's projects take place from Monday to Saturday, he still calls them Sunday School, an open recognition that he understands the roots of what he has developed. In many ways, Wilson has recaptured Raikes' original intention and repackaged it for twenty-first-century children. Wilson writes, 'Why is Sunday School attendance dropping? Because our people are not really concerned with outreach any more... and our teaching is not relevant.'[3] Wilson has taken the Raikes pattern that had become primarily focused on teaching church children and once again emphasized Raikes' passion for reaching the unchurched child. However, not only has Wilson adopted the Raikes pattern, he has adapted and developed it to communicate to the postmodern child. His writings show an astute understanding of today's child, and his programme shows the results of many years of experimentation in learning how to communicate to them.

It is an intriguing journey, but the pattern of the majority of Children's Outreach Projects in the UK is not a straightforward inheritance of the pattern developed by Raikes. Instead, it is Raikes' pattern, exported to America in the late eighteenth century and now, two centuries later, returning in an updated and repackaged format. Nevertheless, it is still very much the legacy of Robert Raikes.

Where the twenty-first-century Children's Outreach Projects can be criticized is in the area of theological reflection, particularly their ability, or lack of it, to review the theological position they hold. The church has often prided itself on being counter-cultural; by this it means that it does not readily embrace the patterns of the emerged culture but evaluates and critiques them. However, history shows that this is rarely true. The church often fights to hold on to its traditions,[4] but these are often traditions that simply reflect the previous culture. This is also true for patterns of child evangelism, evidenced in relation to its models of conversion, that owe more to an eighteenth-century construct than to orthodox Christian doctrine. When the Evangelicals began running Sunday Schools they added their personal conversion doctrine to the model. This was not part of the original pattern of child evangelism, but it has been embraced and propagated by many of the Children's Outreach Projects, advocating paradigms of modernity and not understanding the twenty-first century audience. This is further illustrated by talk of moral absolutes that owes more to the Enlightenment than to biblical exegesis. The methodology of child evangelism has needed to develop throughout history; the pattern needed to adapt to reach new generations of children. The current move to a postmodern culture presents an opportunity to explore afresh what child evangelism should look like today.

This adaptation, while staying true to the patterns modelled by Raikes, is essential if the current child evangelism projects are to be sustainable. However, the conclusion of this research highlights a concern that the large projects that have emerged in the last ten years may not be sustainable. Although the Liverpool project lists over 100 projects as part of its network, when I attempted to contact these projects, many of them had closed after operating for only a few years (in some cases they lasted less than twelve months). The Liverpool project itself is now 80 per cent smaller than it was at its height (average weekend attendance has reduced from 1,000 children at the start of the century to 200 by 2008). These projects are labour-intensive, and the issues faced by the Liverpool project are not unique. The Hastings project closed for three months in 2007 because of a shortage of workers willing to commit to Saturday mornings.

The Slough and Windsor project changed its format in September 2008 from a weekly gathering to a monthly event. In their own press release to the other projects, they stated:

> Following the success of Kidz Cells [the Slough and Windsor project's small-groups programme] we have decided to put a lot more effort into developing and building these groups going forward. Therefore in order to advance the children's ministry and take it to the next level we will be launching more weekly cells and will move the Kidz Klub from being every Saturday to a brand new look and feel monthly event.

There is a distinction between the stated reason of the Slough and Windsor project and the accounts of the Hastings and Liverpool projects. The Slough and Windsor project is making a strategic, adaptive change in the way it runs, rather than trying to respond to a crisis in the number of leaders. The change is necessary because, to paraphrase the words of Paul, its leader, although the weekly children's club is an effective way to reach children, it has not proven to be an effective way to keep children. There may be hundreds of children in the Slough and Windsor project small groups, but the Slough and Windsor project records that over 5,000 different children have attended since 2001.[5] The Slough and Windsor project has recognized that adding more unchurched children to the church will involve an increasing emphasis on their small group programme. The move to a monthly Children's Outreach Project will also mean that the Slough and Windsor project is able to reduce its bill for bussing the children to the project, which currently runs to tens of thousands of pounds annually.

The Leeds project has solved much of the difficulty of staffing and funding the Children's Outreach Project by the ecumenical nature of the project. Nevertheless, the consequences of that philosophy have already been highlighted in analysis; the Leeds project does not have the necessary design to facilitate input into the lives of children/young people in the long term. When a child becomes a teenager, they are disconnected from the project which is focused only on children. For this reason, the Leeds project may well be sustainable but, in terms of effectiveness, it is flawed.

The only other project (of those analyzed) that seemed immune to staffing issues and yet still managed to see children and families incorporated into their church was the Fraserburgh project. Several factors contribute to the Fraserburgh project's ability to do this. The first factor is a return to one of the keys of Raikes pattern. The Fraserburgh project is not trying to draw children from a large geographic area, as is the case with all the other projects examined. Fraserburgh is working within a fixed geographic area, similar in size to a typical Anglican parish. Some of the other projects send their buses out as far as ten kilometres from the base. They may draw in hundreds of children, but they are gathering children from an area of over 100 square kilometres. Is the goal to achieve high attendance, but achieve this attendance by drawing children from a wide geographical area and at the same time using huge expenditure to achieve it? (Between them the five projects visited hire twenty-three buses of varying sizes every week. It costs the Hastings project alone £50,000 a year to run its project.) Would this expenditure be better spent on employing more workers who could establish localized projects of the 150–200 size? Certainly, the early Sunday Schools benefited from being parish-based, and although this is not a plea to use the parish system, there is strength embedded within the system that should not be overlooked. Working within a fixed geographical area enables greater community impact.

When the Fraserburgh project decided to reach the children in a nearby village, instead of sending buses to bring the children in, they established a new project in the village, trained the new leaders, including leaders from the village itself, and allowed the project to develop. This is the style of propagation advocated by Raikes. The survey results made it clear that it was possible to establish projects of up to 200 children without the need to bus those children into a central venue. However, there are no projects in the UK that consistently reach more than 200 children without transporting the children to the venue.

The second factor is the way the Fraserburgh project is integrated into the local church, evidenced by the presence of the senior minister at each of the Fraserburgh project events. The project is clearly an integral part of the church and not an add-on, although this comment could also be made of several of the other projects. The fact that the Fraserburgh project has now been working in this parish for over a decade means it is beginning to see the children of children who first attended the project.

They have permeated a community and become an intrinsic part of its activities. This is why sustainability is so important: to influence a community takes time.

As a general conclusion, it can be seen that Raikes was a leader who developed and propagated a sustainable system, within a fixed geographical area, for communicating a Christian value system to primarily unchurched children. Similarly, the twenty-first-century leaders analyzed also demonstrate this ability to develop and propagate effective models of child evangelism. However, there is concern about the sustainability of the twenty-first-century Children's Outreach Projects, due primarily to their wide reach in most cases and, in one case, to the difficulties of working in an ecumenical context with no strategic programme for those over the age of twelve.

It is for this reason that the first factor in the establishment of a Children's Outreach Project must be *finding (or being) the right leader*, a person with the ability to develop and promote a Children's Outreach Project. However, this must be a sustainable project and, to that extent, it is suggested that working within a parish or fixed geographical area is preferable to sending buses out several miles from the project to collect children. This may mean that part of the Children's Outreach Project leader's job is to train and equip churches in nearby areas to run their own Children's Outreach Projects (such as the pattern advocated by the Fraserburgh project), or at least to make known the format of their Children's Outreach Project and encourage others to replicate it (as was Raikes' practice). The established project must also be seen as long-term. It is about the establishment of a Children's Outreach Project that may well adapt and evolve (as seen in the changes in the Slough and Windsor project in 2008) but should be seen as existing for generations to come, noting again Cliff's observation that there is a thirty-year time-lag between cause and effect.

With regard to the format of the Children's Outreach Project, the pattern developed by Raikes continues to be an effective model for child evangelism today. Raikes employed professional teachers and he employed them on the basis that they could keep control and communicate. There is a common misconception that a children's worker is employed because the church has children who need teaching; the whole basis of child evangelism emphasizes the need to employ a children's worker because there are no children. The need, therefore, is for children's workers who have the ability to develop Children's Outreach Projects and to attract boys and girls using the promotional and entrepreneurial skills so evident in

Raikes. Furthermore, they need *the ability not only to attract children, but also to attract and develop new leaders.* The leader must have the capacity to equip others and recognize in them the varying gifts that are necessary for child evangelism – gifts that vary from the ability to look after a sound or video system, to the ability to teach, to sit and listen to the children or to visit them in their homes. Because one of the main reasons cited for the decline of the Sunday School was ineffective methods of training and inadequate support, the leader must also ensure that the children's workers have *regular opportunity for training and development*; whether by bringing someone in to complement the in-house training or by taking the workers to regular training events.

It is also suggested that the practice advocated by Archibald and embraced by many of the Children's Outreach Projects analyzed, of *using young people as helpers*, is fundamentally important. It works on two levels: young people will continue to belong to a church they feel part of and involved in, and it is important to take a long-term view of the project and invest the time, energy and resource into training the next generation of leaders. The development of new projects from the Fraserburgh project was only possible because of a prolonged programme of training and developing young leaders.

This is, of course, about child evangelism, so the format of the project is significant. One of the significant consistencies from Raikes forward has been *the practice of prayer* and the singing of Christian songs/hymns in the projects. Most of the examples of children praying took place in the small groups, but there were many examples of the children being prayed for by the group leaders, often in general terms – 'God, give these children a good time today.' Sometimes there were cases that were more specific, where the leaders prayed for individual children, usually for a general blessing, but there were also occasions when the children with very specific needs were prayed for – for healing or God's intervention into a particular situation. Overall, many of these prayers were not handled well, primarily because the children were rarely given opportunity to give feedback on the prayers being prayed. The consistent exception to this was the Leeds project where the children were given opportunity for personal prayer in a calm reflective environment at the end of each Children's Outreach Project programme. If nothing else, the opportunities for prayer reminded the children that God was active and wanted to be involved in their lives, accomplishing a similar purpose to the Old Testament festivals and memorials.

Singing should be an important part of any Children's Outreach Project and was clearly an important part of the projects analyzed, not only because the songs invoke strong feelings of joy and excitement, but also because songs are an effective way of teaching theology – certainly the memorization of it. Lyrics that speak of God's work in creation, God's protection in times of trouble, about staying close to God through difficult times, and about commitment to God, are all contained in the songs of the Children's Outreach Projects. However, it is important that the lyrics of the songs are critiqued and not just sung because they have a good tune. There is an emphasis on personal conversion in the songs, and an overemphasis on individual responsibility at the expense of the corporate. An overemphasis on the individual may prove counterproductive to the task of establishing a Christian community.

It is further suggested that while the actions that accompany the songs are helpful, this should be expanded to incorporate more of Codrington's findings (alluded to in Chapter 8). Many children learn by doing, and *worship* is more than the singing of songs. Codrington suggests the use of candles as a way of making a promise, the moulding of clay as part of expressing something to God or the use of art and craft materials to express a prayer. And, of course, the best way to teach worship is to allow the children to see examples of leaders worshipping, so the leaders need to be completely engaged in the singing/worship experience.

It is the practice of prayer and the more complex implications of a greater understanding of faith development that lead to the conclusion that the Children's Outreach Project needs to meet in both a large-group context and in smaller groups. It is clear that there is no real opportunity for children to learn the practice of prayer within the large group environment, and, if it were possible, it may well be intimidating to ask a child to pray aloud in large groups. There were many examples of children repeating a prayer prayed from the front in the Children's Outreach Projects and fewer examples of children *reading* prayers in front of the larger crowd, but the only examples of children praying extemporary prayers took place in small groups.

This dual arena of large gathering and small group is also important for communication. Communication in the Children's Outreach Projects is vital; *the communication of the Christian message* lies at the heart of why the Children's Outreach Project exists. Nevertheless, it was clear in visiting the Children's Outreach Projects that there was a vast discrepancy in the projects' ability in this area. There has been a significant shift in the way children learn; therefore, there must be a significant shift in the way the Children's Outreach Projects communicate. It is evident that not all the projects visited have understood this. This inability to communicate effectively, particularly in understanding the power of narrative, will ultimately lead to further decline. It is imperative that those who speak in Children's Outreach Projects or lead the associated small groups become students of public speaking, giving time to understanding the subtleties of communication today. Communicating to both large and small groups of children in this context should involve a technical understanding of faith development as well as competent presentation skills. Those working in small-group settings will also benefit from an understanding of hermeneutic phenomenology. These are the background skills – the *how* we communicate before consideration of *what* we communicate. The *what* involves an understanding of theology. Many of the Children's Outreach Projects were presenting theology that they had heard elsewhere or had taken verbatim from a curriculum book, without a proper grasp of the implications of the theological position being advocated. To this extent, the communicator should also be prepared to undertake some *theological reflection* on what they are communicating, particularly with regard to critiquing the creation/fall/redemption model of salvation advocated by all the Children's Outreach Projects visited.

The *context* in which the communication takes place should also be considered, with due regard to the children's physiological needs, in terms of whether they are warm and well-fed, their safety needs, in terms of whether they feel secure and protected, their social needs, in terms of whether they feel they belong. Much of this has to do with *the quality of the welcome and the physical environment* of the Children's Outreach Project. However, an opportunity for the children to be part of free-play activities such as those run in Fraserburgh also helps to facilitate needs for belonging, and ensures leaders have opportunity to form relationship and earn credibility before the more structured programme takes place.

Certainly, the most controversial area continues to be the giving of rewards and incentives for appropriate behaviour and the removal of reward for inappropriate behaviour. It was clearly shown in Raikes' initial experiment and is present in all the Children's Outreach Projects visited. An argument has been made that the majority of the schools from which the children are drawn operate a similar system of rewards and incentives and their own version of removal of reward for inappropriate behaviour. Further to this, it is suggested that the social fabric of most of the world works on a similar pattern; whether it is in the world of work and employment or the penal system, there operates a system of reward for particular actions and the removal of that reward for inappropriate actions. The only provision should be that although society may reward intelligence or sporting prowess, the Children's Outreach Project should also reward good character. There should be *rewards for kindness, patience, good manners* as well as for excellent colouring or winning a game.

Although the points made with regard to the format and structure of the project themselves are important, the connections that the Children's Outreach Project makes outside the large gathering and small groups are vital. The primary method of connecting with the wider community is through *home visits*. This was a practice initiated by Raikes, neglected through most of the last two centuries in spite of periodic calls for its reinstatement, which has now regained its prominence in the activities of the large Children's Outreach Projects. The Liverpool project makes over 1,500 home visits every week, but that is primarily because it works within a geographical area of more than 100 square kilometres, and although this level of community involvement must be commended, it has already been suggested that greater influence is possible if projects restrict themselves to smaller, more manageable areas. The Liverpool project visits 1,500 children but in a geographical area of 90,000 children (2001 census). How much greater the impact of the Fraserburgh project which works in a geographical area of 1,200 children (by the summer of 2008 the Fraserburgh and Liverpool projects were seeing similar numbers of children at their weekly events). It is clearly not about one-off visits. The Leeds project stated that their success was all about consistency. In this postmodern culture, it takes several months to get past the universal antagonism and distrust of institutions before relationships can be formed. Certainly, some of the home visits involved dropping off a leaflet to a child and no contact with parents; other visits were primarily about conversations with parents and very little contact with the child. Nevertheless, positive favour with the community is won through an ongoing programme of consistent visiting.

Although not available to Raikes, there is one additional factor of significance – the opportunity to have *input into local schools*. The Children's Outreach Projects' primary involvement in local schools has been by way of school assemblies, assemblies in which they are able to help the school fulfil its statutory responsibility to hold an act of worship (every day, where possible) of a broadly Christian nature. But as well as presenting an exciting, lively and informative assembly, the Children's Outreach Projects also take advantage of the visit to promote the Children's Outreach Project and to hand out literature advertising the event and bus pick-up times (the Slough and Windsor project's handout is shown in Appendix 8). The areas in which the larger Children's Outreach Projects operate have large numbers of primary schools, with the result that the Children's Outreach Project can only visit the school once or twice a year. Again this is unfortunate; relationships cannot be established with either staff or children over that period, and this is another reason for advocating that Children's Outreach Projects focus on smaller areas. There is one more point that should be made with regard to schools. When the contact point is a Church of England school, there may exist the opportunity to do more than school assemblies. Some projects are running their Children's Outreach Projects in the schools themselves – some after school, some during the lunch break. Others are running church services as part of the school day. There is still ambiguity among Church of England primary schools as to what General Synod meant when it suggested that they should be centres of mission, despite Lord Dearing's clarification. What is clear is that there is room for more than simply taking an assembly once or twice a year, and it is an area in which Children's Outreach Projects could gain significantly by being more creative in their approach.

It was also noted that Raikes made a point of ensuring that the Children's Outreach Project was an *intrinsic part of the local church*. The difficulties facing projects that are not attached to a single local church (both historically and today) or are parachurch (whether in design or practice) have already been highlighted. However, the need to provide mechanisms to incorporate children from the Children's Outreach Project into the wider adult church is vital. When the children graduate from the Children's Outreach Project, it is important that a suitable youth programme is available for them to join, and at some point an adult congregation as well. This is the strength in having a Children's Outreach Project as part of a traditional church. The traditional church thinks children through to old people (with varying degrees of success from church to church).

It is easy for churches and Children's Outreach Projects to become insular and forget that the primary focus is to *enhance the communities in which they are based*. All of the projects studied do this, but there are also direct intervention activities that Children's Outreach Projects should instigate/support to meet clear social needs. The Leeds project gives food hampers to those in need; the Fraserburgh project runs a charity shop to provide affordable clothing; other projects have provided bereavement support, paid for funerals, organized community clean-ups and run countless coffee shops. The primary purpose is to help the community, but the effect is always to win favour and respect for the Children's Outreach Project and the church that runs it. However, there is more than this. It has been emphasized that Raikes was not only meeting a social need, he was *empowering* boys and girls and giving them the skills necessary to thrive in their modernistic world. Today Children's Outreach Projects run homework clubs, provide skills training events for parents, help with the filling-in of forms for childcare credits and run parenting courses. The emphasis is not just on meeting a need but helping people to meet their own needs – empowering local people.

The issues may not be as complicated as they seem, but they are complicated enough for one of the recommendations of this study to be that our theological colleges take seriously the subject of communication and that consideration be given to whether courses can be offered which, at least in part, focus specifically on child evangelism.

This book is limited. Although the field of ethnography is evolving, traditional ethnography as part of the discipline of anthropology was conducted over several years, sometimes decades. Some of the purists still struggle with the notion of an ethnography being possible in a twelve-month period. Reflecting on the developments of the five Children's Outreach Projects I examined, the purists' concerns are justified. Many of the Children's Outreach Projects at the end of 2008 have undergone major transition since this research began. The Slough and Windsor project has become a monthly event with a firm network of small groups; the Liverpool project has continued to decline in numbers; and the Fraserburgh project has introduced another Children's Outreach Project in a nearby village. The opportunity to track these projects over a longer period might have proven a valuable exercise. Given several more years, I suspect that one or two of these projects will no longer exist, and some of the others will be unrecognizable as they adapt and change to ensure their sustainability.

NOTES

1. Written in 1964

2. Only a very sketchy overview is possible with regard to this area because it is not the primary focus of this book. For a more detailed account, refer to Boylan, A. M., *Sunday School: The Formation of an American Institution, 1790–1880*, New Haven, Connecticut: Yale University Press, 1988.

3. 1992, p. 159.

4. Cray's (2005) definition of tradition is useful here: 'Principles followed for a relatively short period of time within a set culture.'

5. As of May 2008.

APPENDICES

Appendix 1
METHODOLOGY AND LITERATURE REVIEW

This details the method for investigating the comparisons between Raikes' historical model of child evangelism and the current practice.

The research was conducted using a four-phase approach:

Phase 1:   Interpretive biography
Phase 2:   Quantitative research using a self-completion survey
Phase 3:   Qualitative research using ethnographic methodology
Phase 4:   Implications, recommendations and action research

PHASE 1

The first phase of the research involved developing a portrait of Robert Raikes and the original model of Sunday School. From this phase came an understanding of what Raikes initially developed as distinct from what the Sunday School movement became. Through careful analysis of the movement's formation, it was possible to identify the practice of the earliest Sunday Schools – the regular repeated pattern with gradually emerging and built-in norms and sanctions.[1] The pattern of working identified for the first decades was then used as a template to evaluate what came after it.

The analysis of Robert Raikes and the early Sunday School was primarily a classical biography in which the researcher is concerned with validity and criticism of documents and materials.[2] The biographical study used original documentation such as articles and letters in the eighteenth-century newspapers *The Gloucester Journal* and *The Manchester Mercury* and the minutes, advertisements, letters, accounts and photographs held by Birmingham University Library, Manchester University Library and Gloucester Library regarding Robert Raikes and the Sunday School movement. Consideration was given to early writings such as those of Bailey,[3] Watson,[4] Grosser,[5] Stratford,[6] Harris,[7] and Kendall.[8] These early writers made no attempt at rigorous academic study, but instead provided biographical information pertaining to Raikes and general information regarding Sunday Schools. Often this was presented in the form of conversations with those who were present. However, their primary intention was to record the achievements of the Sunday School movement and to celebrate its founder Robert Raikes, not to provide an objective study. It is probable that the audiences they wrote for were expecting a positive report of the institution's founder, and they wrote to fulfil those expectations. Besides the occasional comment on the need for reforming the Sunday Schools that existed at their time of writing, there are no overtly negative comments regarding Robert Raikes or his family in the literature written during the century after his death. It was therefore necessary to read between the lines on occasion to understand more fully the characters involved.

This research built on earlier research, particularly the research of Frank Booth.[9] Booth is a historian, and as such presents a book that is widely researched and balanced in its findings. His primary subject is Raikes the individual, and from that position he contributes a useful discussion on whether Raikes can truly be identified as the founder of the Sunday School. Phillip B. Cliff's initial research and eventual PhD thesis,[10] looking at the Sunday School movement, laid the foundations on which the early chapters of this research were built. Cliff has compiled a large number of original documents from 1800 onwards, looking at all aspects of Sunday School, including buildings, rules, materials, finance, committees and government, and has traced the movement's unprecedented growth and eventual decline over two centuries. This book owes a debt to Cliff's seminal work; however, while his ability to collect and present raw data is not in question, there were numerous occasions when I disagreed with his conclusions.

It is important to stress that this is more than the portrait of a man; the aim of the first phase was to form a portrait of the man *and* the institution he founded and promoted. This task was not straightforward. As Cliff comments:

> Writers in the time of the centenary tended to see the history in light of the task of 1880, which was that of a Bible-teaching institution in a mainly evangelical milieu, playing down, if not altogether hiding the genuine attempt at the popular education of the masses that was the original Raikes' idea.[11]

Careful deconstruction was necessary to understand what Raikes developed.

PHASE 2

Having identified the defining characteristics of this portrait, the study then moved on to the second phase. This involved the development and distribution of a basic self-completion questionnaire (Appendix 2) with the aim of gaining an overview of churches involved in church-based Children's Outreach Projects and identifying churches that have Children's Outreach Projects with particularly high attendance.

The two distinctive elements of church-based Children's Outreach Projects need defining. Firstly, the projects were church-based. Durkheim[12] defines religion as 'A unified system of beliefs and practices relative to sacred things, which unite adherents into a single moral community'. This definition of religion today is controversial; there are many who believe that religion can be a private and individual experience. Nevertheless, it is a useful definition for church since a church is a bounded system with unified beliefs. Children's Outreach Projects are based in churches whose theology and practice are broadly in keeping with biblical orthodoxy as outlined by the Nicene Creed. The projects under consideration were staffed by a sub-group of the church, rather than the whole church – in effect, a sub-culture within the cultural sharing group.

Secondly, church-based Children's Outreach Projects deal with children's outreach. Children's Outreach Projects, in the context of this research, are defined as those projects that exist for the evangelism of children who would not otherwise attend church. The word *evangelism* is deliberately used. The projects were concerned with communicating Christianity to children who have little or no knowledge of it. These projects include nurture, but they acknowledge that this is not their primary concern.

Furthermore, although the terminology *church-based Christian Outreach Project* has been developed for this particular research, one of the earliest forms of Children's Outreach Project should be credited to Robert Raikes and the formation of the Sunday School Institution. The latter part of the twentieth century and the early years of the twenty-first century have seen the development of hundreds of Children's Outreach Projects in the UK. However, only a minority of these projects have reached the attendance figures that the early Sunday Schools achieved.

The survey was distributed to the following groups/denominations who agreed to be involved:

- Anglican National Children's Advisor
- The Methodist Children's Advisor
- Pentecostal National Children's Directors (Elim and Assemblies of God)
- Baptist National Children's Director
- Scripture Union
- New Wine[13]

This phase was repeated for Australia and New Zealand and those findings recorded in Appendix 3. A decision was made not to conduct a similar survey for North America because of the vast diversity from state to state.

PHASE 3

The next phase of the research necessitated the recognition of a significant minority from the questionnaires received. While there were many Children's Outreach Projects with up to 150 children in average weekly attendance, there were very few above this number. After giving due consideration to the responses, it became clear that there was a significant minority (five) that had extraordinary weekly attendance and also had high indicators for all other areas – for example, number of leaders, social involvement, contact outside the Children's Outreach Project, families joining the church. It was evident that these projects should form the basis of the third research phase.

The selection of a methodology for analysis of the significant minority was not straightforward. With an understanding that each style of research has a purpose for which it is particularly well suited,[14] it was clear that a questionnaire would not allow for the complexities and diversity of analysis that the Children's Outreach Projects require. It was also felt that the leaders of these projects were by nature pragmatists and would not give sufficient time to accurately completing complex questionnaires. A case-study approach was considered, but case studies tend to focus on a particular event[15] and this study looks at a whole series of events and the cultural sub-group that makes the events possible. Therefore, a process of primarily ethnographic data collection was selected to form the cultural portrait(s).[16]

Ethnography is a description and interpretation of a cultural or social group or system. The researcher examines the group's observable and learned patterns of behaviour, customs and ways of life.[17] As a process, ethnography involves observation of the naturally occurring, ordinary events of a cultural group, over time, in the group's natural setting. This is primarily but not exclusively ethnographic, because the research also necessitated a close analysis of the leader of these projects and this involved further biographical research.[18]

The first visit involved interviews only; the second visit involved informal interviews, but was primarily concerned with observation and analysis; and the third visit remained unchanged. It was also clear that two to three visits would not present the depth of analysis necessary. To this extent, after the initial interviews, one of the five projects was selected for a prolonged ethnography (six to twelve months), which took place after the visits to the other four projects were complete. The analysis of the initial four projects was then used to inform and add clarity to the final investigation.

The revised framework was as follows:

Data Collection 1: Initial visit to each of the significant minority, primarily to interview leader and key informants.

Evaluation: A decision made on which Children's Outreach Project to set aside for future, more detailed analysis.

Data Collection 2: Revisit having reflected on initial visits, primarily to observe and to analyze programme and relational interaction – identifying, where possible, recognizable institutional norms.

Data Collection 3: Revisit, this time to show the key informants and the leader the observations made and include their comments in the final research.

The visit to these significant minorities involved a combination of observation and interview. The respondent was encouraged to tell their story in detail rather than answer lots of questions.[19] It is suggested that listening to their accounts was a legitimate and meaningful way to generate data, data that was then analyzed and coded using the conventions of narrative analysis[20] and open coding. The interviews of the leaders and key informants of the significant minority were much more fluid on the first meeting, allowing a design to emerge so that more focused questions could be asked as the research developed. This was dynamic research, in the sense that it was flexible and constantly developing. For this reason, the research was conducted inductively, with the patterns learned from Phase 1 providing the initial areas of investigation, but observation and comments from key informants within the group produced further areas for exploration.

1. Tell me a little about yourself and your family background.
2. Tell me about the project.
3. Why do you run the project?
4. Talk me through a typical day in the life of the project.
5. Talk to me about your contact with children outside of the project.
6. Tell me some of the exciting things you've seen in, or because of, the project.
7. Tell me about the impact of this club on your community?
8. How do you recruit your leaders?
9. How do you fund the project?

It was the interviews and the written-up field notes derived from visiting these projects that became the backbone of this qualitative research. It was by scanning these notes and attaching preliminary codes and then extracting coded segments and drawing conclusions that the process moved from description to analysis and then eventually to interpretation.

From July 2007, one the significant minority became the subject of a more prolonged study, forming the next phase of the research (Phase 3b). This phase necessitated spending six months immersed within this particular culture-sharing group. This phase of research was interested in understanding and describing a social and cultural scene from the insider's perspective.[21]

Using a more traditional form of ethnography,[22] the previous research phases were built on to analyze further the group's observable patterns of behaviour, customs, beliefs and ways of life. The main analytical tasks were to uncover and explicate ways in which people in a Children's Outreach Project come to understand, account for, take action and otherwise manage their day-to-day situation; to move beyond the snapshots achieved by the intense contacts of Phase 3a, and to explore just how and why things happen as they do – and even assess causality, as it actually plays out in a particular setting; to attempt to understand the meanings people place on events, processes and structures in their everyday lives.[23]

> **Data Collection 4:** Six months spent with one Children's Outreach Project. A prolonged period of scheduled and informal interviews and observation, contributing to ongoing description and analysis. With occasional visits for the six months following.

Whereas Phase 3a looked at the basic workings of the Children's Outreach Projects and the personalities involved, Phase 3b looked at the wider role of the Children's Outreach Project. Time was spent with some of the members of the Children's Outreach Project as they visited the children at home and comments from parents regarding how they see the role, function and purpose of the Children's Outreach Project were recorded. In addition, at this level, comments from the children who attend the Children's Outreach Project were recorded.

The research took ever-deepening analysis levels from the overview that the questionnaires gave, to the more detailed ethnographic study of the significant minority to the intense ethnographic study of the largest Children's Outreach Project.

PHASE 4

The final phase involved conclusions and recommendations as to whether there are suggestions/implications within this study that can be advanced as a methodology of child evangelism today.

The research also incorporated a review of the current literature. The historical analysis of the books and documents relating to Raikes and his work have already been mentioned, but a theological and philosophical analysis was also necessary to explore the apparent lack of child conversion in the initial Raikes model and the issues related to this. To consider this issue required engagement with the social sciences, specifically the development theorists and particularly James Fowler's *Stages of Faith*. Building on the contributions from Piaget, Erikson and Kohlberg, Fowler draws on a wide range of literature and first-hand research with nearly 600 people to build a comprehensive picture of faith development. I will argue that Fowler's conclusions are incomplete and that his construct of faith stages breaks down after stage 3. However, Fowler presents a useful contribution to development theory, laying foundations on which this research further builds.

The context in which Raikes developed the Sunday School movement and a consideration of the context in which the twenty-first-century Children's Outreach Projects function required a study of sociology, particularly with regard to:

- Social environment and influences on the child
- The state of the church

Fukyama, Bauman, Giddens, Huntington and Rushkoff[24] and other leading sociologists were considered in relation to social conditions and influences on the child. These observations were used to underpin the more specialist books of Brierley, based on the church census of 1998 and 2005, and Cray, Savage and Mayo. The work of Cray, Savage and Mayo is of particular relevance as it looks at the sociology of young people and children.[25] The Children's Society's report *The Good Childhood Inquiry* was also consulted and its conclusions considered.

Having formed the portrait of Raikes and the cultural portrait of the Children's Outreach Projects, it was then possible to begin to answer the question:

- Are the emerging child evangelism projects of the early twenty-first century providing an effective method for child evangelism today?

This research addressed this by means of a conclusion that asked two sub-questions:

- Are there similar patterns and 'cultural norms' embedded within the projects?
- If so, have they independently and exclusively developed similar patterns of practice?[26] And have these groups learned from each other or from a common outside source, possibly Raikes?[27]

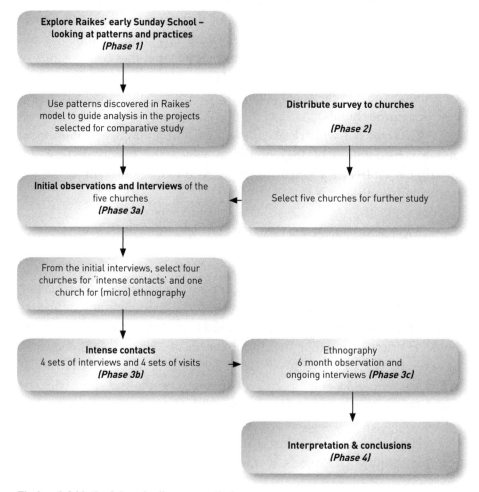

Fig App 1.1 Methodology in diagrammatic form

Notes

1. Cliff (1986, p.51).

2. Denzin, 1989.

3. 1815.

4. 1833.

5. 1869.

6. 1880.

7. 1885, 1890.

8. 1939.

9. 1989.

10. Initial research 1981 and PhD 1986.

11. 1986, p. 2.

12. 1912, p. xxi.

13. A network of mainly Anglican Evangelical Charismatic Churches.

14. Brewer and Hunter (1989, p. 77).

15. Compare Creswell (1998, p. 61). Although a linguistic debate is not necessary, it is clear that until relatively recently, that which is now termed *ethnography* was freely termed *case study* by most anthropologists. In Keiser's (1967) research with street gangs, he lived with them for a significant period and gathered information through observation and interview, but still refers to his research as a case study. Wolcott (2005) would prefer to use the term micro-ethnography to describe any study that involves less than twelve months in the field.

16. The plural is suggested because there is no guarantee or assumption that the cultural sharing groups will be the same or even similar. It may have been that we were left with 6–10 dissimilar cultural portraits.

17. Harris (1968, p. 16).

18. The biographical information was gleaned through interviews with both the leader and their team. It is possible that the life history of the leader will not be verifiable or even factually accurate. In these cases, the life history was still invaluable because the record captured an individual's perception of the past, providing a unique look at how the key actor thinks and how personal and cultural values shape his or her perception of the past. (Fetterman, 1989, p. 61.)

19. However, there are some direct questions used at the end of the interviews.

20. Although there are elements of discourse analysis within the study – that is, *how* things are said – this is much more about narrative analysis – that is, *what* is said.

21. In Fetterman's (1989, p. 12) ethnology, he suggests that 'The ethnographer is both storyteller and scientist'. However, Wolcott (2005, p. 22) introduces a further dimension when he suggests that the ethnographer is 'both scientist and

artist'. Wolcott's (2005, p. 5, p. 24) comments are helpful as they introduce a more intuitive element to the ethnography:

> Whatever constitutes that elusive 'more' makes all the difference. That needs to be stated emphatically, for a crucial aspect of fieldwork lies in recognizing when to be unmethodical, when to resist the potentially endless task of accumulating data and to begin searching for underlying patterns, relationships, and meanings... You need a capacity for observing and reporting, but you need as well to trust your instincts, value your experience, and have a clear sense, both of what you know, and what you don't know.

22. Such as Keiser's (1969), *The Vice Lords: Warriors of the Streets*.

23. Miles and Huberman (1994, p. 10).

24. Douglas Rushkoff is deliberately included in this list of prominent sociologists because of the unique contribution he brings to the debate. Rushkoff is professor of Media Culture at New York University and advisor to the United Nations Commission on world culture. Rushkoff is an accomplished academic and sociologist and he is included because his method of immersing himself in the culture he writes on brings some important and necessary insights. Because of this, his books represent an ethnography of twenty-first century culture.

25. There are questions as to the validity of the research of Cray, Savage and Mayo (2006) given the relatively small size of the sample group, but their observations, although in need of critique, are perceptive and prepared to challenge some of the ingrained assumptions about this age group.

26. Outworking the hypothesis of the ethnologist Lewis Henry Morgan (1818–1881) that similarities mean that different groups had passed through the same stages of cultural evolution.

27. Ethnologist Grafton Elliot Smith (1871–1937) argued that different groups with similar cultural norms must somehow have learned from one another or from a common source, however indirectly.

Appendix 2

THE SELF-COMPLETION QUESTIONNAIRE

E-MAIL INTRODUCTION

Good Morning,

Why am I emailing?

I am writing a doctoral research thesis on child evangelism with the University of Nottingham and I need your help. I am looking for at least 50 churches that have children's outreach programmes – in keeping with the definitions below – who will be willing to answer 25 questions. All you need to do is click the reply button, fill in the answers in the questionnaire below (it'll take no more than 10–15 minutes), and then hit send (if you prefer, I have enclosed the questionnaire as a file attachment, so you can open it and answer in your word processing package). If someone has forwarded this to you, the reply address is markgriff@lineone.net. It would help considerably if you could e-mail it to other children's leaders before completing it. The research, among other things, will allow us to form an overview of what works in child evangelism – in effect, what are the characteristics of the most successful projects.

Thank you for your time.

Mark Griffiths
Tel. 0115 922 4805

THE QUESTIONNAIRE

This questionnaire is deliberately straightforward, the 25 questions should take no more than 10-15 minutes to complete. Please write your answers under the question, or simply underline your response where appropriate.

Definitions:
Church based children's outreach projects (CBCOP) are those projects that exist *primarily* for the evangelism of children who would not otherwise attend church.
Child evangelism within the context of this questionnaire is seen as the communication of the Christian gospel to children primarily, but not exclusively, through proclamation.

1. **Information:**   What is your name?
2. **Information:**   Describe your denominational affiliation (and the affiliation of the *CBCOP* if different):
3. **Information:**   How did you receive this questionnaire?
    - i.   Anglican Children's Advisors Network
    - ii.   The Methodist Children's Advisor
    - iii.   Pentecostal National Children's Directors (Elim or AoG)
    - iv.   Baptist National Children's Director
    - v.   Children Matter
    - vi.   Scripture Union
    - vii.   New Wine Network
    - viii. Kidz Klub Network
    - ix.   Directly from Mark Griffiths
    - x.   Other
4. **Information:**   Do you run a CBCOP? (if no then go to question 25)
5. **Information:**   What is the name of your *CBCOP*?
6. **Information:**   How long has the *CBCOP* been running?
7. **Information:**   What is the name of the leader of the *CBCOP*?
8. **Information:**   Do you charge an admission fee?
9. **Role:**   What is your position within the *CBCOP*?
10. **Numbers:**   How many children attend your project when the *CBCOP* takes place?
11. **Numbers:**   How many children do you have on the register?
12. **Transport:**   Do you use buses to transport the children to the venue? If yes, how many?
13. **Influences:**   Has any outside organization been instrumental in the formation of your *CBCOP*? (If yes, please state)
14. **Leaders:**   How many leaders work within the *CBCOP*?
15. **Leaders:**   Do the leaders attend training events? (if yes, please list up to 3 they attend – state 'internal' if you do your own training)
    - i.
    - ii.
    - iii.
16. **Programme:**   How often does the *CBCOP* take place and for how long?
17. **Programme:**   Which of the following are parts of your programme? (or if you think it easier, please write two or three sentences to describe your project):
    - i.   Prayer
    - ii. Singing
    - iii. Christian Teaching

18. **Community:** Is there contact with the children outside of the *CBCOP*? (if yes, please state how, tick all relevant boxes)
    - i. Small Group Meetings   If yes, how often?
    - ii. E-mail   If yes, how often?
    - iii. Visit at home   If yes, how often?
    - iv. Postal Contact   If yes, how often?
    - v. Contact through school assembly   If yes, how often?
    - vi. Other (please state)

19. **Context:**   How would you describe your community?
    - i. Rural
    - ii. Semi-rural
    - iii. Country Town
    - iv. Industrial
    - v. Suburban
    - vi. Urban
    - vii. City Centre
    - viii. Inner City
    - ix. Outer Housing Estate

20. **Curriculum:** What teaching materials do you use? (list up to three)
    - i.
    - ii.
    - iii.

21. **Social Action:** Do you run any social action projects alongside, or as part of the *CBCOP*? (if so, please state the nature of the project – the definition of 'social action project' can be as broad as you feel necessary)

22. **Church Link:** In the last 12 months, have members of your *CBCOP* or their families become members of a local church because of your project?

23. **Church Link:** In the last 12 months, have members of your *CBCOP* been added to a Christian youth programme because of your project?

24. **Uniqueness:** Is there anything that marks your project as particularly unique?

25. **Others:** What are the largest *CBCOPs* that you know of? And how many children attend (approximately)? List up to 3.

Appendix 3

SURVEY AND QUANTITATIVE RESEARCH (PHASE 2): NEW ZEALAND AND AUSTRALIA

The questionnaires for Australia and New Zealand were distributed through the following conferences for children's workers between 2007 and 2008:

- Kidshaper, Melbourne, Australia
- Kidsreach, Sydney, Australia
- Kidsreach, Hamilton, New Zealand
- MTC, Melbourne, Australia

And also by e-mail in early 2009 to:

- New Wine Networks, New Zealand
- Kidsreach e-mail distribution list

Approximately 300 questionnaires were distributed, of which eighty-five were returned. There were several duplicates (members of the same organizations completing the form); only one form was kept for each organization, bringing the total of separate projects to seventy-eight. Of those, 82.3 per cent were involved in running Children's Outreach Projects. This 82.3 per cent represented 953 children's workers who had contact with 6,927 boys and girls, primarily from unchurched homes.

The Children's Outreach Projects were from a wide geographical area and there was no statistical distinction in their location. (See Fig App 3.1 diagram on page 320.)

The projects analyzed were primarily weekly children's clubs, but there were also special events and holiday play schemes represented. The chart (Fig App 3.2) shows the wide diversity in the number of denominations represented. This probably highlights the vast interdenominational nature of the conferences and organizations that agreed to collect the data.

Interestingly, while the Assemblies of God/Australian Christian Churches[1] have the largest number of respondents, the Salvation Army, although having fewer projects, is more likely to have larger attendance.

Fifty-one per cent of the projects charge an admission fee. As with the UK figures, there is no discernable pattern as to which projects charge: some city projects charge, others do not; some rural projects charge, others

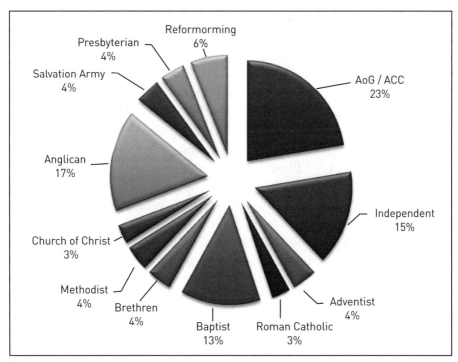

Fig App 3.1 Denominations of respondents

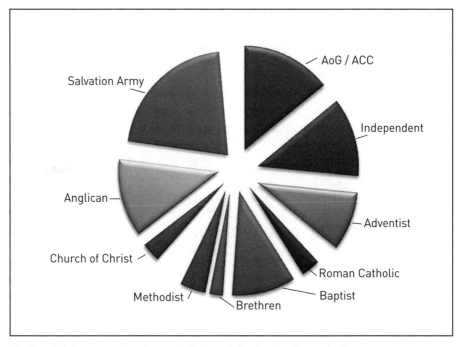

Fig App 3.2 Average attendance at Outreach Project by denomination

do not. The decision to charge also has no correlation with the number of full- or part-time leaders or the church's denomination. The decision to charge and the amount to charge appears to be completely random; the largest admission fee was $7.

Leaders in 44 per cent of the projects attended training courses organized by their denomination (although it has an increasingly interdenominational pull, the Kidshaper Conference is still recorded here because it is still seen as the training conference of Australian Christian Churches). Of those who attended training organized by non-denominational organizations, the largest number attended the Kidsreach Conferences taking place in Australia and New Zealand (50 per cent of the overall). However, what is of great concern is the fact that 15 per cent of those involved in Children's Outreach Projects had not attended or received any form of training in the last twenty-four months.

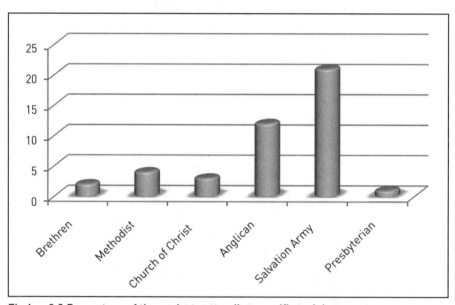

Fig App 3.3 Percentage of the projects attending specific training events

While similar to the UK in terms of the diverse nature of the programme – with sports of various kinds, drama/theatre skills, café-style events and craft activities – there were some consistencies: large numbers of the projects featured prayer (84 per cent), singing (81 per cent) and Christian teaching (96 per cent).

A far higher percentage of the Southern Hemisphere projects (87 per cent) write their own curriculum material than do the UK projects, but they tend to subsidize this with purchased materials. Of the materials purchased, Scripture Union materials were the most popular followed by Kidsreach materials and the *Fusion/Impact/Detonate* series that has made its way across from the UK. Also mentioned were curriculum materials produced by Tammy Tolman and Rangers Curriculum. Again, the Scripture Union material was split between several Scripture Union products.

Responses to the question 'Do you run any social action projects alongside, or as part of, the Chidren's Outreach Project?' were surprisingly sparse. Southern Hemisphere churches don't as yet seem to have taken advantage of the opportunities that the Children's Outreach Project gives them to further integrate into their community. It appears on occasion as if the church projects are a separate and distinct thing to the local community's projects; there is no easily visible integration into the community. And because of the lack of basic integration projects, it was difficult to find any of the empowerment type modelled by Raikes. Certainly, the Planetshakers church in Melbourne has a wide and expanding network of after-schools clubs, breakfast clubs and holiday activity weeks, but there is clearly room for expansion in this area.

In terms of attendance figures, the majority of the projects had attendance between ten and fifty, but there were a significant number of projects with over 200. The statistics for attendance becomes even more interesting when compared with the length of time the projects have been running. Nearly half (46 per cent) of the respondent projects had been running for less than five years; 19 per cent had been running for between five and ten years; and nearly a third (31 per cent) had been running for over ten years. However, there were several projects that had been running for over forty years. Interestingly, most of the longest-running projects were Ranger projects. It is also interesting that the Southern Hemisphere statistics reveal a distinct relationship between the length of time a project has been running and the attendance, to the extent that the longer a project has been running, the higher the attendance is likely to be. It was impossible to draw this same conclusion from the UK statistics as there were not enough projects that had been running for more than ten years.

There was a low response to the question regarding outside influences, and the few that mentioned anyone mentioned Scripture Union and Rangers (although the mentions of these two groups combined only amounted to 2 per cent of the returns), suggesting that the Southern Hemisphere projects have been formed with little outside input, or that the influences on the projects are so subtle that the project leaders are unaware of their effect.

Contact outside the project fell into the categories of small groups, e-mail, home visits, postal contact and school visits. The highest form of contact was postal (35 per cent) followed by home visits (19 per cent). It is also encouraging to see the large numbers engaging with their local schools (13 per cent).

Unlike the UK projects, there is no significant difference in the form of contact used by the small and the large projects, with the one exception

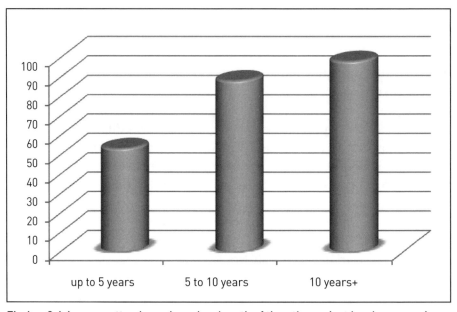

Fig App 3.4 Average attendance based on length of time the project has been running

that nearly all the projects with over 150 children in attendance maintain close links with their local schools.

The most surprising statistic was in relation to the number of children who have graduated to a youth programme from the Children's Outreach Project in the last twelve months and the number of adults who have joined the church as a result of the Children's Outreach Project in the last twelve months. The figures for this in the UK were 57 per cent and 56 per cent respectively, climbing to 100 per cent and 81 per cent for projects over 150. In the Southern Hemisphere returns the number of children graduating to a youth programme was 32 per cent and the number of families joining the church as a result of the Children's Outreach Project was 29 per cent. These figures are surprisingly low and are possibly areas that require attention.

The five highest-attended projects are split between Adventist, Anglican, Assemblies of God/Australian Christian Churches, Baptist and Church of Christ. There is clearly no denominational advantage in children's ministry in the Southern Hemisphere. And if this had been the area of my primary research, it would have been be a worthwhile piece of research to look at these five projects and make the necessary contrasts in terms of their methodology and doctrinal stance, and at the same time draw out the similarities that make these particular projects so effective in reaching large numbers of boys and girls.

NOTES

1. The Assemblies of God in Australia have recently changed their name to Australian Christian Churches.

BIBLIOGRAPHY

BOOKS

Abbott, C., *Making Connections, Young People and the Internet*, London: University College London, 1998.

Abraham, W.J., *The Logic of Evangelism*, London: Hodder and Stoughton, 1989.

Archibald, H., *The Sunday School of Tomorrow*, London: Sunday School Union, 1909.

Ariès, P., *Centuries of Childhood*, London: Jonathan Cape, 1962.

Avis, P., *An Anglican Understanding of the Church*, London: SPCK, 2000.

Bailey, T., *A Eulogium on the Character of Mr Robert Raikes*, London: Sunday School Union, 1815.

Bamford, S., *Passages from the Life of a Radical*, London: Unwin, 1843.

Barna, G., *User Friendly Churches*, California: Regal Books, 1994.

Barna, G., *The Second Coming of the Church*, Nashville: Word Publishing, 1998.

Barna, G., *Transforming Children into Spiritual Champions*, California, Regal Books, 2003.

Barrett, D., *World Christian Encyclopedia*, Oxford: Oxford University Press, 1982.

Barton, J., *Ethics and the Old Testament*, London: SCM, 1998.

Bateson, C. D. and Ventis, W. L., *The Religious Experience*, Oxford: Oxford University Press, 1982.

Bauman, Z., *Society Under Siege*, Oxford: Blackwell, 1995.

Bauman, Z., *Work, Consumerism and the New Poor*, Maidenhead: Open University Press, 1998.

Bauman, Z., *Liquid Modernity*, Cambridge: Polity Press, 2000.

Bauman, Z. and Tester, K., *Conversations with Zygmunt Bauman*, Cambridge: Polity Press, 2001.

Beasley-Murray, G.R., *Baptism in the New Testament*, Toronto: Paternoster, 1962.

Bell, R., *Velvet Elvis*, Grand Rapids: Zondervan, 2006.

Bendroth, M., *The Child in Luther's Theology (The Child in Christian Thought)*, Cambridge: Eerdmans Publishing Company, 2001.

Bettelheim, B., *The Uses of Enchantment: The Meaning and Importance of Fairy Tales*, New York: Vintage Books, 1977.

Bettenson, H., *The Later Christian Fathers*, Oxford: Oxford University Press, 1977.

Bosch, D., *Transforming Mission*, New York: Orbis Books, 2004.

Bradley, J., *Religion and Politics in Enlightenment Europe*, Notre Dame: Erasmus Institute Books, 1999.

Bradley, J., *Church History: An Introduction*, Grand Rapids: Eerdmans Publishing, 1993.

Bretherton, F.F., *Early Methodism in and around Chester*, Chester: Phillipson & Golder, 1902.

Brewer, J. and Hunter, A., *Multimethod Research Methods*, London: Sage Publications, 1989.

Brierley, P., *The Tide is Running Out*, London: Christian Research Organisation, 2000a.

Brierley, P., *Steps to the Future*, London: Christian Research Organisation, 2000b.

Brierley, P., *Reaching and Keeping Tweenagers*, London: Christian Research Organisation, 2002.

Brierley, P., *Pulling Out of the Nose Dive*, London: Christian Research Organisation, 2006.

Briggs, A., *Innovation and Adaptation: The C18th Setting*, London: SPCK. 1981.

Brown, A., *Primary School Worship*, London: National Society, 1992.

Brown, C., *The Death of Christian Britain – Understanding Secularisation 1800–2000*, London: Routeledge, 2001.

Brown, R., *Church and State in Modern Britain 1700–1850*, London: Routledge, 1991.

Bruce, S., *God is Dead: Secularization in the West*, Oxford: Blackwell Publishers, 2002.

Bryman, A., *Social Research Methods*, Oxford: Oxford University Press, 2004.

Booth, F., *The Founder of Sunday Schools*, London: National Christian Education Council, 1989.

Brueggemann, W., *The Bible and Postmodern Imagination*, London: Augsburg Fortress, 1993.

Brueggemann, W., *The Psalms & the Life of Faith*, Minnesota: Augsburg Fortress Publishers, 1995.

Buchanann, C., *Evangelical Essays on the Sacraments*, London: SPCK, 1972.

Buchanann, C., *Is the Church of England Biblical*, London: Darton, Longman and Todd, 1998.

Buckingham, D., *After the Death of Childhood*, Cambridge: Polity Press, 2000.

Buckland, R., *Children and the Gospel*, Milton Keynes: Scripture Union, 1975.

Buechner, F. *Telling the Truth*, San Francisco: HarperCollins, 1977.

Bushnell, H., *Views of Christian Nurture*, New York: Scribners, 1847.

Cameron, H., *Studying Local Churches*, London: SCM Press, 2005.

Calvin, J., *Commentary on Genesis*, Cambridge: Eerdmans Publishing Company, reprinted 1963.

Calvin, J., *Commentary on Psalms Vol. 1*, Cambridge: Eerdmans Publishing Company, reprinted 1963.

Caputo, J.D., *Philosophy and Theology*, Nashville: Abingdon Press, 2006.

Chadwick, O., *The Victorian Church – Vol. 2*, Oxford: Oxford University Press, 1970.

Chadwick H., *Augustine*, Oxford: Oxford University Press, 1986.

Chadwick, H., Augustine's *Confessions* (translated by Henry Chadwick), New York: Oxford University Press, 1991.

Cheney, M.B., *Life and Letters of Horace Bushnell*, New York: Harper and Brothers, 1880.

Collins, M. and Price, M.A., *2000 Years of Faith*, New York: Dorling Kindersley, 1999.

Cone, J., *The God of the Oppressed*, New York: Seabury Press, 1975.

Colwell, J.E., *An Exploration of Sacramental Theology*, Carlisle: Paternoster, 2005.

Copley, T., *Indoctrination, Education and God*, London: SPCK, 2005.

Cliff, P.B., *The Rise and Development of the Sunday School Movement 1780–1980*, Birmingham: National Christian Education Council, 1986.

Cliff, P.B., *Myths – Utilities and a Meaningful Existence*, Christianity, Society and Education, London: SPCK, 1981.

Cray, G., Savage, S., Collins-Mayo, S. and Mayo, B., *Generation Y*, London: Church House Publishing, 2006.

Creswell, J., *Qualitative Inquiry and Research Design*, London: Sage Publications, 1998.

Croft, S., *Ministry in Three Dimensions*, London: Darton, Longman and Todd, 1999.

Croft, S., *Transforming Communities*, London: Darton, Longman and Todd, 2001.

Currie, R., Gilbert, A. and Horsley, L., *Churches and Churchgoers*, Oxford: Oxford University Press, 1977.

Dallmayr, F.R., *Phenomenology and Social Science*, The Hague: Njhoff, 1973.

Dawkins, R., *The God Delusion*, Boston: Houghton Mifflin Company, 2006.

Davies, D., *Studying Local Churches*, London: SCM, 2005.

Davies, N., *Europe – A History*, Oxford: Oxford University Press, 1996.

De Vaux, D., *Surveys in Social Research*, Melbourne: Allen & Unwin, 2002.

Denzin, N.K., *Interpretive Biography*, London: Sage Publications, 1989.

Dey, I., *Qualitative Data Analysis*, London: Routledge, 1993.

Dix, G. (editor), *The Apostolic Tradition*, London: SPCK, 1937.

Donavan, V., *Christianity Rediscovered*, London: SCM Press, 1982.

Durkheim, E., *The Elementary Forms of the Religious Life*, Oxford: Oxford University Press, 1912.

Eavey, C.B., *History of Christian Education*, Chicago: Moody Press, 1964.

Egan, H., *Karl Rahner: Theologian of the Spiritual Exercises*, New York: Crossroad Books, 1992.

Elliott, S., *Raikes and Reform, Christianity, Society and Education*, London: SPCK, 1981.

Fetterman, D.M., *Ethnography: Step by Step*, London: Sage Publications, 1989.

Frank, P., *Too Little – Too Late! Children's Evangelism Beyond Crisis*, Cambridge: Grove Books, 1998.

Freud, S., *The History of the Psychoanalytic Movement*, Montana: Kessinger Publishing, 1914.

Finney, J., *Finding Faith Today*, Swindon: British and Foreign Bible Society, 1992.

Finney, G., *Revivals of Religion*, New Jersey: Old Tappan, 1847.

Fitzmyer, J.A., *Romans (The Anchor Bible)*, New York: Doubleday, 1993.

Fowler, J., *Stages of Faith*, San Francisco: Harper, 1981.

Fox, M., *Original Blessing*, Vermont: Bear and Company, 1983.

Francis, L.J. and Astley, J., *Children, Churches and Christian Learning*, London: SPCK, 2002.

Fukuyama, F., *The Great Disruption*, London: Profile Books, 1999.

Gadamer, H.G., *Truth and Method*, London: Sheed and Ward, 1975.

Gay, J.D., *The Geography of Religion in England*, London: Trinity Press, 1971.

Gergen, K., *An Invitation to Social Reconstruction*, London: Sage Publications, 1999.

George, M.D., *England in Transition: Life and Work in the 18th Century*, London: Routledge, 1953.

Gibson, W., *The Church of England – 1688–1832 – Unity and Accord*, London: Routledge, 2001.

Giddens, A., *Runaway World*, London: Profile Books, 2002.

Gill, R., *Churchgoing and Christian Ethics*, Cambridge: Cambridge University Press, 1999.

Goldman, A., *Epistemology and Cognition*, Harvard: Harvard University Press, 1986.

Goldman, R., *Religious Thinking from Childhood to Adolescence*, London: Routledge, 1964.

Goldman, R., *Readiness for Religion: A basis for developmental religious education*, New York: The Seabury Press, 1965.

Grenz, S., *A Primer on Postmodernism*, Cambridge: Eerdmans Publishing Company, 1996.

Grosser, W.H., *A Hundred Years Work for the Children*, London: Sunday School Union, 1869.

Gunkel, H., *Introduction to the Psalms*, Georgia: Mercer University Press, 1933.

Guroian, V., *The Ecclesial Family (The Child in Christian Thought)*, Cambridge: Eerdmans Publishing Company, 2001.

Hall, S.G., *Doctrine and Practice in the Early Church*, London: SPCK, 2000.

Hamilton, A., *The Family Church in Principle and Practice*, Surrey: Religious Education Press, 1941.

Hamilton, W., *A Compendia of Baptism*, New York: Funk & Wagnalls, 1882.

Hammond, M., Howart, J. and Keat, R., *Understanding Phenomenology*, Oxford: Blackwell, 1991.

Hargreaves, D.J. and North, A.C. (editors), *The Social Psychology of Music*, Oxford: Oxford University Press, 1997.

Harris, J.H. (editor), *Robert Raikes, the Man and his Work*, London: National Sunday School Union, 1885.

Harris, J.H., *Robert Raikes – The Man who Founded the Sunday School*, London: National Sunday School Union, 1890.

Harris, M., *The Rise of Anthropological Theory*, New York: Crowell, 1968.

Hay, D. and Hunt, K., *Understanding the Spirituality of People who Don't Go to Church*, Nottingham: University of Nottingham, 2000.

Hegel (1882), (trans. Sibree, J.), *The Philosophy of History*, New York: Prometheus Books, 1992.

Heidegger, M. (1927), (trans. Maquarrie, J. and Robinson, E.), *Being and Time*, New York: Harper and Row, 1962

Heinrich, R. (1893) (trans. Reisman, G.), *Science & History*, Princeton: Princeton University Press, 1962.

Helfaer, P., *The Psychology of Religious Doubt*, Boston: Beacon Press, 1972.

Hendrick, H., *Construction and Reconstructions of British Childhood* (ed. James, A. and Prout, A.), London: Routledge, 1997.

Hennell, M., *Evangelical Leaders of the Victorian Church*, London: SPCK, 1979.

Hinsdale, M. A., *Contribution to Modern Catholic Thought on the Child (The Child in Christian Thought)*, Cambridge: Eerdmans Publishing Company, 2001.

Holland, J. and Thompson, R., *Respect – Youth Values, Identity, Diversity and Social Change*, Swindon: ESRC, 1999.

Huberman, A. M. and Miles, M. B., *Qualitative Data Analysis*, London: Sage Publications, 1994.

Hull, J. M., *What Prevents Christian Adults from Learning*, London: SCM Press, 1985.

Hull, J. M., *God-Talk with Young Children*, Philadelphia: Trinity Press International, 1991.

Hull, J. M., *Mission-Shaped Church – a Theological Response*, London: SCM Press, 2006.

Hooker, R., *Of the Laws of Ecclesiastical Polity (in The Folger Library Edition of the Works of Richard Hooker)*, London: Belnapp Press, 1977.

Ihde, D., *Hermeneutic Phenomenology*, Illinois: Northwestern University Press, 1979.

Jackson, B., *Hope for the Church*, London: Church House Publishing, 2002.

Johnston E.A., *Crusader for Youth*, Surrey: Religious Education Press, 1945.

Katz, J., *Virtuous Reality*, New York: Random House, 1997.

Kay, W. and Francis, L., *Drift from the Churches*, Cardiff: University of Wales Press, 1996.

Kay, W. and Francis, L., *Religion in Education 1*, Leominster: Gracewing, 1997.

Keiser, R.L., *The Vice Lords: Warriors of the Streets*, New York: Holt, Rinehart and Winston, 1969.

Kendall, G., *Robert Raikes*, London: Purnell & Sons, 1939.

Kent, N., *Gentlemen of Landed Property*, London: J. Dodsely, 1775.

Kierkegaard, S., *Concluding unscientific Postscript*, Princeton: Princeton University Press, 1941.

Klausmeier, H. and Allen, P., *Cognitive development of Children and Youth*, New York: New York Academic Press, 1978.

Kraus, H.J., *Theology of The Psalms*, Minnesota: Augsburg Publishing Company, 1979.

Kraus, H.J., *Psalms 1-59*, Minnesota: Augsburg Publishing Company, 1988.

Lankshear, D., *Denominational Inspection Handbook*, London: National Society, 1992.

Latuorette, K., *A History of Christianity Volume 1*, Melbourne: Harper Collins, 1976.

Latourette, K., *A History of Christianity Volume 2*, Melbourne: Harper Collins, 1976.

Laqueur, T., *Religon & Respectability in England*, Yale: Yale University Press, 1987.

Layard, R. and Dunn, J., *A Good Childhood Inquiry*, Children's Society, Dublin: Penguin, 2009.

Leinenweber, J. (translator and compiler), 'Augustine's Letter to Jerome' in *Letters of Saint Augustine*, New York: Triumph Books, 1992.

Lewis, C.S., *Mere Christianity*, New York: Macmillan Publishing Company, 1943.

Lewis, R. and Lewis, G., *Inductive Preaching: Helping People Listen*, Illinois: Crossways Books, 1983.

Locke, J., *An Essay in Dialectical Theism (the study of Anglicanism)*, Oxford: Clarendon, 1984.

Lyotard, J.F., *The Postmodern Condition: A Report on Knowledge*, Minnesota: University of Minnesota Press, 1979.

Lyon, D., *Memory in the New Millennium, in Grace and Truth in the Secular Age*, Cambridge: Eerdmans, 1998.

Lyon, D., *Jesus in Disneyland*, Cambridge: Polity Press, 2000.

Lull, T., *Concerning Rebaptism*, Minnesota: Augsberg Fortress, 1989.

Mantoux, P., *The Industrial Revolution in the 18th Century*, London: Jonathan Cape, 1961.

Macaulay, T., *Macaulay's History of England*, Philadelphia: E.H. Butler & Company, 1847.

Marcel, P., *The Biblical Doctrine of Infant Baptism*, London: James Clarke & Co., 1951.

Marshall, M., *The Anglican Church Today and Tomorrow*, Melton: Mowbray, 1984.

Maslow, A., *Motivation and Personality*, New York: Harper & Row, 1970.

Matson, D.L., *Household Conversion Narratives in Acts*, Sheffield: Sheffield Academic Press, 1996.

McGee, C., *Childhood Experiences of Domestic Violence*, London: Jessica Kingsley Publishers, 2000.

McGrath, A., *The Renewal of Anglicanism*, London: SPCK, 1993.

McGrath, A., *Christian Theology – An Introduction,* Oxford: Blackwell Publishing, 2001.

McKenna, M., *Not Counting Women and Children*, Tunbridge Wells: Burns and Oats, 1994.

McLuhan, M., *Understanding Media: The Extensions of Man*, New York: McGraw Hill, 1964.

Meyers, C., *Families in Early Israel*, California: Westminster Press, 1997.

Montessori, M., *The Montessori Method*, New York: Schocken Books, 1964.

Moo, D., *The New International Commentary: Romans*, Cambridge: Eerdmans, 1986.

Moynagh, M., *Emergingchurch.intro*, Oxford: Monarch. 2004.

Murray, S., *Post-Christendom – Church and Mission in a Strange New World*, Carlisle: Paternoster Press, 2004.

Norman, E.R., *Church and Society in England 1770–1970*, Oxford: Oxford University Press, 1976.

Nye, R. and Hay, D., *The Spirit of the Child*, London: Jessica Kingsley Publishers, 2006.

Orchard, S., *The Sunday School Movement*, Milton Keynes: Paternoster, 2007.

Ozment, S., *When Fathers Ruled: Family Life in Reformation Europe*, Harvard: Harvard University Press, 1983.

Paris, J., *Myths of Childhood*, Philadelphia: Brunner and Mazel, 2000.

Parker, M., Hartas, D. and Irving, B., *In Good Faith,* London: Ashgate Publishing, 2005.

Parsons, R., *Bringing Home the Prodigals,* London: Hodder and Stoughton, 2003.

Percy, M., *Power and the Church*, London: Cassell, 1998.

Piaget, J. (1947), (trans. Piercy, M. and Berlyne, D.), *The Psychology of Intelligence*, Oxford: Routledge, 1950.

Piaget, J., *Science of Education and the Psychology of the Child*, New York: The Viking Press, 1970.

Pitkin, B., *Children in the Theology of John Calvin (The Child in Christian Thought)*, Michigan: Eerdmans Publishing Company, 2001.

Polanyi, M., *Personal Knowledge*, Chicago: University of Chicago Press, 1958.

Postman, N., *The Disappearance of Childhood*, London: W. H. Allen, 1983.

Postman, N., *Amusing Ourselves to Death*, London: Methuen London, 1987

Pratney, W., *Fire on the Horizon*, Canada: Gospel Light, 1999.

Prout, A., *The Future of Childhood*, New York: Routledge, 2005.

Rahner, K., *Faith in a Wintry Season*, New York: Crossroad Books, 1990.

Reardon, B., *Hegel's Philosophy of Religion*, New York: Macmillan Press, 1977.

Reder, P. and Lucey, C., *Assessment of Parenting: Psychiatric and Psychological Contributions*, New York: Routledge, 1995.

Richards, L.O., *A Theology of Children's Ministry*, Grand Rapids: Zondervan, 1983.

Ricouer, P., *The Symbolism of Evil*, Boston: Beacon Press, 1986.

Rizzuto, A.M., *The Birth of the Living God*, Chicago: University of Chicago, 1981.

De Mause, L., *The History of Childhood*, London: Souvenir Print, 1976.

Robinson, H.W., *The Christian Doctrine of Man*, Edinburgh: T&T Clark, 1926.

Rousseau, J.J., *Émile (Everyman)*, London: Phoenix Press, 1993.

Rushcoff, D., *Playing The Future*, New York: Harper Collins, 1996.

Satre, J.P. (1958), (trans. Barnes, H.), *Being and Nothingness*, London: Methuen, 1969

Sashkin, M., *Leadership that Matters*, San Francisco: Berrett-Koehler, 2003.

Schaff, P. *St. Augustine: Anti-Pelagian Writings*, Grand Rapids; New York: Christian Literature Publishing Company, 1886.

Shaw, C., *When I Was a Child*, Stafford: Churnet Valley Books, 1903.

Sherrill, L.J., *The Rise of Christian Education*, New York: Macmillan Publishing Company, 1944.

Shenk, W.R., *Henry Venn – Missionary Statesman*, New York: Orbis, 1983.

Smale, I., *The History of Ishmael*, Eastbourne: Kingsway, 1988.

Smale, I., *Angels with Dirty Faces*, Eastbourne: Kingsway, 1989.

Smith, F., *A History of English Elementary Education 1760–1902*, London: University of London Press, 1931.

Stevenson, M., (revised by Frend, W.H.C.), *A New Eusebius*, Cambridge: Cambridge University Press, 1987.

Stevenson, M., (revised by Frend, W.H.C.), *Creeds, Councils and Controversies*, Cambridge: Cambridge University Press, 1989.

Stortz, M.E., *Augustine on Childhood (The Child in Christian Thought)*, Cambridge: Eerdmans Publishing Company, 2001.

Stott, J., *Christian Mission in the Modern World*, London: Falcon, 1975.

Stratford, J., *The Founders of Sunday Schools*, London: Sunday School Union, 1880.

Straus, G., *Luther's House of Learning*, Baltimore: John Hopkins University Press, 1978.

Stonehouse, C., *Joining Children on the Spiritual Journey*, Grand Rapids: Baker, 1998.

Strohl, J.E., *The Child in Luther's Theology (The Child in Christian Thought)*, Cambridge: Eerdmans Publishing Company, 2001.

Sykes, N., *Church and State in England XVIII Century*, Cambridge: Cambridge University Press, 1934.

Sykes, S. and Booty, J., *The Study of Anglicanism*, London: SPCK, 1988.

Tappert, T. G. (trans.), *Confessions of the Evangelical Lutheran Church*, Philadelphia: Fortress Press, 1959.

Thompson, R., *Is there an Anglican Way? Scripture, Church and Reason*, London: Darton, Longman and Todd, 1997.

Thornton, D., *Leeds – The Story of a City*, Ayrshire: Fort Publishing, 2002.

Tillich, P., *Theology of Culture*, Oxford: Oxford University Press, 1964.

Tillich, P., *Systematic Theology – Volume 1*, Chicago: University of Chicago Press, 1973.

Tolkein, J.R.R., *Tree and Life*, Boston: Houghton Mifflin, 1965.

Tomlinson, J., *Globalization and Culture,* Cambridge: Polity Press, 1999.

Toulmin, S., *Cosmopolis – The Hidden Agenda of Modernity,* New York: The Free Press, 1990.

Traina, C.L.H., *Aquinas on Children and Childhood (The Child in Christian Thought),* Cambridge: Eerdmans Publishing Company, 2001.

Ullman, C., *The Transformed Self,* London: Plenum Press, 1989.

Vines, W.E., *Expository Dictionary of New Testament Words,* Virginia: MacDonald Publishing Company, 1989.

Virgin, P., *The Church in an Age of Negligence,* Cambridge: James Clarke and Co., 1989.

Waddington, R., *A Future in Partnership,* London: National Society, 1984.

Walker, A., *Telling the Story,* London: SPCK, 1996.

Ward, P., *Liquid Church,* Oxford: Monarch, 2002.

Ward, W.R., *Religion and Society in England 1790–1850,* London: Batsford, 1972.

Werpehowski, W., *Reading Karl Barth on Children (The Child in Christian Thought),* Cambridge: Eerdmans Publishing Company, 2001.

Westerhoff, J.H., *Kerygma v Didache: Christianity, Society and Education,* London: SPCK, 1981.

Wilcock, M., *Psalms 1–72,* Leicester: InterVarsity Press, 2001.

Withers, C., *Yorkshire Parish Registers,* Yorkshire: Yorkshire Wolds Publication, 1998.

Withers, M., *Mission-Shaped Children,* London: Church House Publishing, 2006.

White, G., *The Journal (1751–75),* edited by Greenoak, F., St Albans: Ebury Press, 1982.

Wilson, B., *Whose Child Is This?* Florida: Creation House, 1992.

Wolcott, H.F., *Writing up Qualitative Research,* London: Sage Publications, 1990.

Wolcott, H.F., *The Man in the Principal's Office,* London: Sage Publications, 1994.

Wolcott, H.F., *Sneaky Kid and its Aftermath,* Oxford: Altamira Press, 2002.

Wolcott, H.F., *The Art of Field Research,* California: Altamira Press, 2005.

Young, A.F. and Ashton, E.T., *British Social Work in the Nineteenth Century,* London: Routledge, 1956.

Young, A., *The Farmers Letters,* Edinburgh: Balfour, 1769.

REPORTS

1945 *Towards the Conversion of England,* Press and Publications Board of the Church Assembly, London.

1970 *The Fourth R,* London: Church House Publishing.

1988 *Children in the Way?,* London: Church House Publishing.

1991 *All God's Children?,* London: Church House Publishing.

1994 *The Gospel, the Poor and the Churches,* Christian Aid, Spencer, L. and Snape, D., London.

2001 *The Way Ahead: Church of England Schools in the New Millennium* (also referred to as the *Dearing Report),* London: Church House Publishing.

2004 *Mission-Shaped Church,* London: Church House Publishing.

2004 *Revised Ethical Guidelines for Educational Research,* London: British Educational Research Association.

2005 *Shopping Generation,* London: National Consumer Council.

2006 *The Good Childhood: A National Inquiry (launch report),* London: The Children's Society.

2006 *Excellence and Distinctiveness – Guidance on RE in Church of England schools,* York: Diocese of York

2008 Bradfield Church of England Voluntary Aided School Inspection Report, London: National Society.

DISSERTATIONS

Codrington, M., *An Investigation of Children's Understandings and Perceptions of Christian Worship,* University of Australia, 2000.

Pridmore, J., *The New Testament Theology of Childhood,* Nottingham University Library, 1967.

Spencer, N., *Beyond Belief,* London Institute for Contemporary Christianity, 2003.

Terry, I., *A Chance for My Spirit to Dance,* University of Surrey, 1999.

Weinberger, M., *Sing, Sing, Sing!* University of California, 1996.

Weinberger, M., *Understanding Music's Emotional Power,* University of California, 1998.

LECTURES

Kay, W., 'The History of Christian Education', Doncaster: Mattersey Hall, 1987.

Shemilt, L., 'Roses in Afghanistan, Nottingham': St John's College, 2004.

Darch, J., 'The Gregorian Church, Nottingham': St John's College, 2006.

Ling, G., 'New Models of Church', Nottingham: St John's College, 2006.

ARTICLES

Anderson, B. E., 'Who May Receive Communion in The United Methodist Church?' *Idaho: Methodist Quarterly Review*, 2001.

Astley, J., 'Evangelism in Education: Impossibility, Travesty or Necessity?' *International Journal of Education and Religion*, New York: Routledge, 2002.

Attfield, D.G., 'Child-evangelism and Religious Education', *British Journal of Religious Education*: 16.1, Oxford: Routledge, 1993.

Babcock, W.S., 'Augustine's Interpretation of Romans', *Augustinian Studies* 10: 55–74, Virginia: Philosophy Documentation Centre, 1979.

Beard, F., 'Religious Instruction by Sunday School Hymns', *The Biblical World*, Vol. 16. No.1: 18–23, Chicago: The University of Chicago Press, 1990.

Burns, J.P., 'The Interpretation of Romans in the Pelagian Controversy', *Augustinian Studies* 10: 43–54, Virginia: Philosophy Documentation Centre, 1979.

Coupe, R., 'The Fifties Freefall', *Quadrant*, Worthing: Christian Research Organisation, 2004.

Croucher, R., 'The Truth Is Out There', *Ministry Today*, Florida: Strang Communications, 1998.

Dawson, K., 'Education, Society and Industry in the 19th Century', *Journal of History*, Oxford: Blackwell Synergy, 1969.

Fackre, G., 'Narrative Theology: An Overview', *A Journal of Theology and Bible* No. 37: 340–352, Virginia: Interpretation, 1983.

Francis, L. and Brown, L.B., 'The Influence of Home, Church and School on Prayer among Sixteen-year-old Adolescents in England', *Review* of *Religious Research* No. 33, London: Sage, 1991.

Francis, L. and Jewell, A., 'Shaping Adolescent Attitudes towards the Church and County Secondary Schools', *Evaluation and Research in Education* No. 6: 13–21, London: Sage, 1992.

Francis, L. and Stone, E.A., 'School Governors and Religious Ethos of C of E Voluntary Aided Schools', *Educational Management and Administration* No. 23: 176–187, London: Sage, 1995.

Griffiths, M., 'If You Wanted to Change Tomorrow', *Church of England Newspaper*. 1 July, London: Religious Intelligence Ltd, 2005.

Heirich, M., 'Change at Heart', *American Journal of Sociology*, Chicago: Chicago University Press, 1977.

Hodge, C., 'Bushnell on Christian Nurture', *Princeton Review*, October, Princeton: Princeton University Press, 1847.

Hough, A., 'How do You Judge the Success of Church?', *Church Times*, 2004

Kay, W.K., 'Bringing Child Psychology to Religious Curricula: the cautionary tale of Goldman and Piaget', *Educational Review*, Vol. 48. No. 3: 205, London: Taylor and Francis, 1996.

Maslov, A.H., 'A Theory of Human Motivation', *Psychological Review* 50: 370–96, Washington: APA Journals, 1943.

McCoy, M. 'Do Children Need to Be converted?' Southwell and Oxford papers in *Contemporary Society*, 1989.

Mbiti, J., 'Christianity and Traditional Religions in Africa', *International Review of Mission*, Geneva: WCC Publications, 1970.

Mirvis, P.H., and Seashore, S.E., 'Creating Ethical Relationships in Organizational Research', *The Ethics of Social Research: Surveys and Experiments*, New York: Springer, 1982.

Osthathios, M., 'Worship, Mission, Unit', *International Review of Mission* 65, Geneva: WCC Publications, 1976.

Rahner, K., (trans. Bourke, D.), 'Ideas for a Theology of Childhood', *Theological Investigations* 8, New York: Herder, 1971

Rahner, K., 'Original Sin', *Encyclopaedia of Theology*, New York: Seabury Press, 1975.

Rahner, K., 'Baptism and the Renewal of Faith', *Theological Investigations* 23, London: Darton, Longman and Todd, 1992.

Rushkoff, D., 'Open Source Reality', *Disinformation – The Interviews*, New York: The Disinformation Company, 2002.

Rouse, R., 'Missionary Vocation', *International Review of Missions* April: 244–257, Geneva: WCC Publications, 1917.

Sobel, J., 'The Interplay of Religion, Ethnicity and Community in a Galilee Village', *Tradition, Innovation*, New York: New York Press, 1991.

Spiro, M.E., 'Religion: Problems of Definition', *Anthropological Approaches to the Study of Religion*, Monographs No. 3, London: Tavistock Publications, 1966.

Voas, D., 'Three Misconceptions about Religious Decline', *Quadrant*, November, Worthing: Christian Research Organisation, 2005.

Wilson, B., 'Entering a Child's World', *Renewal Magazine*, London: Christian Communication Partnership, 2000.

Worsley, H., 'The Well Church: How the Church Measures Success', *Crucible*, London: Board for Social Responsibility Church House, 2004.

Worsley, H., 'Beyond Dearing', International *Journal of Children's Spirituality* 10, London: Routledge, 2005.

WEBSITES

Archbishop Rowan Williams, 2007. www.archbishopofcanterbury.org

The Columbia Electronic Encyclopaedia, 2005. www.encyclopedia.com

Hutchin's Encyclopaedia Software, 2002. www.en.wikipedia.org

Jewish Families, 2004. www.mishpacha.com/parentintro. shtml

Islamic Education, 2006. www.islamiceducationtrust.org.uk

National Society, 2008. www.natsoc.org.uk

Office for Standards of Education, 2007. www.ofsted.gov.uk

Online Dictionary of Episcopalian Terminology, 2006. www.holycross.net/anonline.htm

Robert Raikes: The Sunday School Movement, 2004. www.uk.geocites/oldglos/raikes. html

Scripture Union, 2008. www.scriptureunion.org.uk

Spring Harvest, 2008. www.springharvest.org

The Welfare Parish in the 18th Century, 2006. www.hjsmith.clara.co.uk/5263.htm